Lighthouse
Spotter's Guide

Michael J. Rhein

Photography by Rudi Holnsteiner

Saraband

Saraband

Published by Saraband (Scotland) Limited
The Arthouse, 752–756 Argyle Street
Glasgow G3 8UJ, Scotland
hermes@saraband.net

EDITOR: *Sara Hunt*
ART DIRECTOR: *Deborah Hayes*
CARTOGRAPHER: *Phoebe Wong*
CONTRIBUTING EDITORS: *Clare Haworth-Maden,
Karen Fitzpatrick, Lone Nerup Sorensen, Lindsie Court*

ISBN 1-887354-43-3

Printed in China

1 2 3 4 5   09 08 07 06 05

PAGE 2: *Mendota (Bete Grise) Light, Bete Grise, Michigan.*

For information on how to become a member of the American Lighthouse
Foundation (*see* page 284), or to make a donation,
please visit www.LighthouseFoundation.org

Important safety warnings and notes on access are given on page 8: readers are
strongly advised to consult these before visiting any lighthouse.

Contents

FOREWORD

Ever since lighthouses were first built, people have been fascinated with them, and the popularity of lighthouses continues to grow at an amazing pace. Even in today's fast-paced modern society, people are planning their vacations around visiting lighthouses. They fall in love at lighthouse sites and some even get married there. Lighthouse settings also provide solace to many people who go there to meditate or make life-altering decisions.

Businesses around the world use a lighthouse in their logo as a symbol of strength. Many churches use a lighthouse as a symbol of hope in troubled times. Lighthouses have appeared on postage stamps, money, and license plates, and lighthouses provide enormous tourism revenue for many communities.

When lighthouses come up in conversation most people immediately imagine what it would have been like to have grown up at a lighthouse or lived the life of a lighthouse keeper. Others dream of retiring to the idyllic life they imagine a remote lighthouse could offer.

Why are so many people so fascinated by lighthouses? The answers are many and varied, yet very simple. If you were to take a piece of paper and start writing down all the words that you associate with lighthouses you'd probably come up with strength, beauty, heroism, romance, ghosts, architecture, and solitude, among other words.

Lighthouses were built for the sole purpose of saving lives. Lighthouses are non-political. Lighthouses stand for everything that is good. Like people, lighthouses come in many different sizes, shapes, and colors. Lighthouses are among the oldest standing buildings on our continent. As you will discover from the pages of this book, one can learn a great deal about early American history by studying lighthouses.

When lighthouses became obsolete and began to be abandoned, many soon fell into disrepair and suffered from neglect and vandalism. However, as lighthouse spotting started to grow, local and national groups sprang up to try to save these historic structures. While it's true that many have been saved, many more are in imminent danger of being lost forever. Fortunately, as their popularity continues to grow, more and more people are becoming dedicated to saving these beacons of yesteryear as well as to preserving the history associated with them.

Whether you are young or old, whether you are an established lighthouse spotter, novice, or just developing an interest in lighthouses, this book is for you.

As a lighthouse spotter you will find that some lighthouses are easy to spot, others will be more challenging, but all will take you and your family on an adventure that you will never forget!

Tim Harrison, President
American Lighthouse Foundation
www.LighthouseFoundation.org
Wells, ME 04090

OPPOSITE: *Holland Harbor ("Big Red") Light, Holland, Michigan.*

ADVICE TO SPOTTERS

It is impossible to be absolutely comprehensive in covering every light station on the continent, but we think this guide comes closer than most: more than 1,100 lighthouses (active, inactive, and replica) are included, along with reference to lightships, ruins, and some other aids to navigation in the "Spotter's Notes." We have been most comprehensive in areas that receive the most visitors or are heavily populated (omitting some of the post- and skeleton-mounted signals in more remote locations), but would welcome the input of readers who may feel that there are any significant omissions.

We have tried to provide identifying information on each lighthouse, so that readers can use this book either as a guide for planning a trip, or to identify a lighthouse by its location and characteristics while in a given coastal area. Readers can also use this book as a spotter's journal, to record the dates of their visits to individual lights and to make notes on them. While space doesn't permit much in the way of history at individual sites or details of sound signals and outbuildings, we hope the book's comprehensive scope and portable format will prove useful.

Locations of the beacons in this book are shown on the locator maps and listed alongside each lighthouse name, generally given as the nearest town or harbor. Where this is not suitable, we have used other identifying features, for example shipping channels (for some offshore lights), islands, and rivers. For precise locations or for driving directions, we advise readers to consult the website of the particular light station they wish to visit. In the absence of such a website, we suggest checking www.lighthousefriends.com or www.lhdepot.com/database/searchdatabase.cfm for travel advice.

Every effort has been made to provide up-to-date information on each light station, but please keep in mind that this is subject to change without notice: change of ownership, weather conditions, storm damage, serious vandalism, and occasional security issues will affect access. When planning a visit to a specific lighthouse, it is a good idea to check online or call beforehand to avoid disappointment. In addition, we apologize in advance for any errors that might have occurred in the compiling and editing of this guide, and again, we welcome readers' input to help us correct these for future editions.

Spotters must respect private property: do not trespass. We have indicated which lights we know to be closed or inaccessible to the public, but this information is subject to change and is not always accurate, and no right of access should be presumed.

And finally a note about safety: please take the utmost care at lights that are situated on clifftops, piers, and breakwaters, and make sure that you are fully aware of any tide tables that might apply. Remember also that not all lighthouses are structurally sound. Where we have indicated vantage points on roadsides or bridges, it should not be presumed that it is safe to stop: please act responsibly and in accordance with road safety at all times. For lighthouses or their grounds that are listed as open to visitors, no assumption should be made that these sites are safe to explore.

INTRODUCTION

When Britain's North American colonies were reborn as a nation in 1789, the fledgling United States found itself in possession of little more than a handful of lighthouses on its East Coast. Yet by 1939, when the U.S. Coast Guard assumed responsibility for America's lights, not only did its charges number nearly a thousand, but they lit up the East, West, and Gulf coasts, the shores of Hawaii and Alaska, the Great Lakes and other inland bodies of water, as well as numerous isolated, wave-swept, offshore sites. And while some have since fallen victim to erosion, neglect, and sadly even vandalism, today's lighthouse enthusiasts are legion and have collectively saved and lovingly restored many of these venerable old beacons to their former glory.

Whether you chance upon a lighthouse or deliberately seek one out, knowing something about the history of these important structures will open your eyes to the number of lives that they have saved, as well as to the tenacity and achievements of those who planned, constructed, and tended to them over the centuries.

THE AGE OF ENLIGHTENMENT

The United States' founding fathers were an enlightened bunch, certainly as far as lighthouses were concerned. "Lighthouses are more helpful than churches," commented Benjamin Franklin in his *Poor Richard* of 1758, at a time when the East Coast colonies were lit by only three lights: the Boston Lighthouse (1716), the Brant Point Light (1746), and the Beavertail Light (1749). It was a view with which George Washington, who was sworn in as the first president of the United States in 1789, must have sympathized, for he lost little time in pressing Congress to set a lighthouse-building program in motion. After all, the growth and prosperity of this infant nation depended to a large extent on favorable trading conditions, and while America's guardians were unable to control the weather, they could at least ensure that as few ships as possible were lost to the storms that battered their shores with violent frequency, or to the jagged reefs that threatened mariners.

BELOW: *Boston Harbor Light (the second at this site) dates from 1783.*

9

Thus it was that the "Lighthouse Bill" was passed, which placed the existing beacons under federal control and brought the "Lighthouse Establishment" into being as part of the Treasury Department. Although President Washington was initially closely involved in the lighthouse-construction program, practical responsibility for America's lights became concentrated in the hands of the Commissioner of Revenue or the Secretary of the Treasury until 1820, when the Fifth Auditor of the Treasury took over. Between 1820 and 1852, this position was held by Stephen Pleasanton, a man who appeared convinced that it was his patriotic duty not spend a cent more on his country's lighthouses than was absolutely necessary, with predictable consequences in terms of technical innovation and effectiveness, particularly when it came to illuminants. That said, Pleasanton made the limited funds that Congress allocated to lighthouse building go far: in 1820, there were fifty-five U.S. lighthouses, while in 1852, there were 331.

The lighthouses that were established during this period were almost exclusively onshore structures that fell into one of two categories, the first being "stand-alone" towers, and the second, integral towers and keepers' dwellings. Yet because Pleasanton's priority was keeping construction costs to a minimum, many of these lighthouses proved unequal to their task, either because they were structurally deficient and thus unable to withstand the prevailing weather or geographical conditions or because their beacons were somehow unsatisfactory.

During the colonial era, a lighthouse's light had been generated by burning candles held steady by candelabra. During the 1790s, spider lamps were introduced into lantern rooms: these comprised at least four wicks whose flame was fueled by a pan full of whale oil. In the meantime, in Europe, the Swiss scientist Aimé Argand had invented a revolutionary lamp that was later named for him: also fueled by oil, the Argand lamp consisted of a glass chimney containing a hollow, circular wick that burned brightly and steadily, while a copper, parabolic reflector behind it focused and

RIGHT: *An 1863 photograph of the ruins of Charleston Lighthouse, South Carolina.*
BELOW: *The historic Morris Island Light was first lit in 1876.*

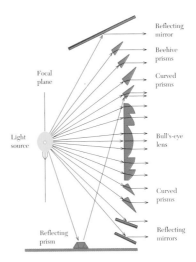

RIGHT: *Light-ray diagram of a Fresnel lens.*
BELOW: *Old Presque Isle Light's third-order Fresnel lens.*

Reflecting mirror

Beehive prisms

Curved prisms

Focal plane

Bull's-eye lens

Light source

Curved prisms

Reflecting prism

Reflecting mirrors

magnified the light's intensity. Inspired by Argand's invention, Winslow Lewis, a former ship's captain, patented a similar system in the United States, and from 1812 until the 1850s his lamps and reflectors lit up America's shores. In 1838, an inquiry into the performance of the United States' lighthouses found that many lamps and reflectors were out of alignment, however, and that a worrying number of reflectors had been bent or dulled. Replacements were urgently required, and thus it was that the United States at last began to follow Europe's lead in ditching Lewis's catoptric system and adopting a catadioptric alternative by purchasing and installing Fresnel lenses in its lighthouses. This process was initiated in 1840, accelerated after 1852, and had virtually been completed by the outbreak of the Civil War in 1861.

The basic components of the Fresnel lenses that had been invented by the French engineer Augustin-Jean Fresnel in 1822 were thin glass lenses that radiated outward, in ever-widening concentric circles, around a central lens, the whole brass-framed panel being surrounded by prisms that refracted any escaping rays of light back into the main beam. Positioned at the center of a group of these panels was an oil, and later a gas- or kerosene-fed, lamp, and then, before electrification and light bulbs took over during the 1920s, an incandescent oil-vapor lamp. Thanks to the focusing action of the hivelike, multiple lenses that encased it, the light that the lamp generated was beamed out horizontally, at an intensity at least four times that of an Argand lamp. Fresnel lenses, which also had the advantage of being relatively lightweight, were manufactured in seven sizes, or "orders," first-order lenses being the largest at around 10 to 12 feet tall, the sizes then dwindling as the orders progressed through the second-, third-, three-and-a-half-, fourth-, and fifth- to the sixth-order Fresnel lens, the smallest. If the central lens was smooth or a cylindrical drum, it produced a fixed light, whereas if it was shaped like a bull's eye, it beamed out a flashing light with the help of a revolving apparatus that rotated the entire lens by clockwork.

In 1851, a board of investigation examined the state of America's lights, found them wanting, and concluded: "The board have not sought so much to discover defects and point them out, as to show the necessity for a better system. Commerce and navigation…claim it; the weather-beaten sailor asks it, and humanity demands it." As a result, in 1852, the discredited Pleasanton was replaced by the Lighthouse Board, which was made up of nine men with military, maritime, and engineering experience, all of whom were resolved to improve the United States' existing lights and to add more to their number. The nation was divided into twelve lighthouse districts (these would eventually number eighteen as the United States' family of states grew), each initially under the control of a naval inspector, but subsequently under an army engineer.

This was the era in which such military engineers as Captain Danville Leadbetter and Lieutenant George Meade entered the hall of American lighthouse fame, Leadbetter on account of the sturdy towers that he erected along the Gulf Coast, and Meade for his role in constructing life-saving lighthouses in Florida's reef-bedeviled waters. Indeed, the development of certain ground-breaking construction techniques during the second half of the nineteenth century further resulted in the Lighthouse Board authorizing the establishment of light stations at previously unthinkable offshore sites. This was therefore also the period during which wave-swept, pile-foundation, screwpile, exposed-screwpile, and caisson lighthouses were first established in American waters.

BELOW: *George Meade—who had become a major general—and his staff in the early 1860s.*

RIGHT: *Cape Henry Light in Virginia received the United States' first automated radio-beacon in 1928.*

THE AGE OF AUTOMATION

Although the nation had much to thank the Lighthouse Board for as it approached its sixtieth birthday—not least around 1,200 efficiently functioning lights—Congress felt that it should be retired and replaced with a less military-dominated administrative body. The Bureau of Lighthouses, or the Lighthouse Service, as it was better known, was founded in 1910, under the umbrella of the Department of Commerce. As the new Lighthouse Commissioner, George R. Putnam now presided over civilian superintendents of the lighthouse districts, and did so until 1935, his watch coinciding with a period during which a number of innovations changed the way that American lighthouses operated forever. The first radio-beacon direction-finders were introduced during the 1920s, for example (these have now been decommissioned), but it was the increasing electrification of light stations from the 1920s that would make keepers' jobs easier, but ultimately, through automation, redundant.

In 1939, responsibility for America's lights was transferred from the Lighthouse Service to the U.S. Coast Guard, and the long-anticipated age of automation became a reality. Electrification, the introduction of a new generation of light, tough, plastic aerobeacons—often solar-powered—and automated sound signals, as well as the use of near-indestructible construction materials like aluminum and fiberglass, have enabled America's lights to operate almost self-sufficiently, requiring only periodic maintenance by the U.S. Coast Guard's aids to navigation teams (ANTs). As a result, many lighthouses have joined their erstwhile keepers in a life of inactivity. Yet lighthouses occupy a special place in American citizens' hearts, and many of these abandoned structures—some of them among the oldest buildings in the United States—have been rescued from neglect by the determination and energy of local lighthouse societies, and, more pertinently, by the funds that they have raised. The chances are, therefore, that any lighthouse you spot on your travels today either continues to serve as an active aid to navigation or has embarked upon a new career as an educator teaching Americans more about their proud heritage as a nation of sailors, traders, explorers, engineers, and altruists.

LIGHTHOUSES IN CANADA

Canada's lighthouse-building history is a complex and interesting subject, partly reflecting the fact that her shores were lit by beacons of the colonial era before Canadian unity, which came relatively late in lighthouse-construction terms.

When sailing from northern Europe, Newfoundland (which did not become part of Canada until 1949) is the first landfall on the North American continent, but this island's coastlines are among the most hazardous anywhere in the world: not only are they precipitous, jagged, and reef-strewn, but they are also frequently fog-bound and plagued by icebergs. The St. Lawrence River and its approach, too, are ice-prone and treacherous, while the waters off Canada's Pacific shores are notorious for their unpredictable, powerful currents and high waves.

Canada's maritime heritage is remarkably rich, and not surprisingly so, considering these factors and the vital role of water-borne freight in the nation's development. In particular, the fishing and lumber industries relied heavily upon the waterways of the Great Lakes, the St. Lawrence, and the Maritime Provinces.

BELOW: *The 1858 Imperial Tower of Griffith Island Light, Lake Huron, Canada.*

ABOVE: *An oval insert on a 1781 chart of Halifax Harbor, Nova Scotia, showing the lighthouse.*

The first lighthouse in Canada went into service in 1743, making it the continent's second-oldest light (after Boston Harbor Light), at the French fortress of Louisbourg on Cape Breton Island. At the entrance to Halifax Harbor, the second was built on Sambro Island, and this has the distinction of being the oldest continuously operating light in North America. Other firsts include Gibraltar Point Light, dating from 1808: this is the oldest light still standing on the shores of the Great Lakes.

The British were responsible for construction of many lights in Lower Canada (now Quebec), the Maritime Provinces, Newfoundland, and British Columbia. The maritime organization Trinity House established a Canadian base in 1805, which often shipped in lenses and other components and construction materials from Scotland, then at the forefront of pioneering lighthouse technology. The most notable lighthouse-building period overseen by the British was 1857–60, when the so-called Imperial Towers were built. These were tall, conical towers of heavy masonry, some of which were erected with granite blocks shipped as ballast from Scotland. The Imperial Towers were expensive and often beset by delays, but have proved enduring. Examples include Race Rocks and Fisgard in British Columbia, as well as six towers on Lake Huron, and four on the approaches to the St. Lawrence River.

In the 1870s following Confederation, responsibility for Canada's navigational aids was assumed by the Department of Marine and Fisheries. The department's Lighthouse Board appointed Colonel William Patrick Anderson as its head in 1900. A flurry of lighthouse building ensued under his energetic tenure, while components that had previously been sourced overseas were increasingly produced in Canada. New designs were introduced, including concrete towers supported by flying buttresses, as well as a new generation of harbor lights and smaller wooden towers that still grace the shores of the Maritime Provinces in such large numbers.

Today, many of Canada's historic lighthouses remain in an excellent state of repair and attract tourists in large numbers, despite their often remote locations. While technology has, in a sense, left these historic structures behind, they remain as compelling as ever in the public imagination, and the dedicated efforts that have contributed to their preservation have helped draw new life into maritime communities.

LIGHTHOUSE TYPES

ONSHORE LIGHTHOUSES

"Stand-alone" Towers

The light towers that were constructed during the eighteenth century and first half of the nineteenth century were generally raised from timber, stone, or brick (and sometimes from a combination of these materials), usually on bedrock, but occasionally on piles or timber grilles. The first cast-iron tower was constructed in 1844, heralding the use of this relatively light and durable material in lighthouse construction, often as a cladding of cast-iron plates over a brick lining. These lighthouses were ideal when it was necessary to elevate the light to give it as high a focal-plane height above sea level as possible, in order to achieve the greatest range.

Integral Towers and Keepers' Dwellings

From the 1820s, many lighthouses took the form of integral towers and keepers' dwellings. These usually consisted of a short tower rising from the roof of the keeper's quarters. The advantages of this configuration were: firstly, that the keeper lived in close proximity to the beacon; secondly, that the lighthouse took up relatively little space at locations where this was at a premium; and thirdly, and perhaps most importantly for Pleasonton, that it was relatively cheap to construct. These lighthouses were suitable for sites where a light with a low focal-plane height was sufficient, such as at the entrance to rivers, harbors, and bays, or at high-elevation sites.

Skeletal, or Skeleton, Towers

Initially made of cast iron and later, steel, skeleton towers can be described as "deconstructed" lighthouses, whose superstructure is pared down to its bare bones. A central cylinder containing a stairway typically supported the lantern, this in turn being held steady by slanting pillars, themselves strengthened by diagonal bracing and standing on pile foundations. Skeletal lighthouses offered minimal wind resistance in storm-prone locations. They also suited muddy or sandy sites, because they were relatively light and had their weight widely distributed.

Reinforced-concrete Towers

Because it has been reinforced with steel, the concrete from which reinforced-concrete lighthouses are constructed is able to withstand earthquakes, which is why these lighthouses are so prevalent in areas that frequently suffer from seismic activity.

OFFSHORE LIGHTHOUSES

Wave-swept, or Rock-foundation, Lighthouses

Englishman John Smeaton's pioneering, during the late eighteenth century, of dovetailed, or interlocking, masonry (each piece having been cut to a custom shape), and of a type of mortar that set under water, facilitated the erection of wave-swept lighthouses on rocky, offshore sites. The keeper's quarters were situated within these towers.

Pile-foundation Lighthouses

As their name suggests, pile- or straightpile-foundation lighthouses were raised on a platform supported by a grouping of timber, iron, or steel piles driven into the rocks, river-, or seabed beneath. The superstructure could consist of timber, iron, or steel components and was usually hexagonal or octagonal in shape. If it took the form of a skeletal tower, the integral keeper's dwelling was enclosed.

Screwpile Lighthouses

Alexander Mitchell, an Irish engineer, developed the screwpile lighthouse during the first half of the eighteenth century. The crucial innovation was that the piles culminated in screws, enabling them to be screwed securely into a relatively soft foundation like compacted sand or mud. Many such lights had low spider-style superstructures.

Exposed-screwpile, or Reef, Lighthouses

The main difference between exposed-screwpile and screwpile lighthouses is that stability was added to the former by the inclusion of footplates above the threaded tips of the piles. This method of distributing their weight made them more suitable for soft, uneven foundations, such as reefs, shoals, and sandbars.

Caisson, Cofferdam, and Crib Lighthouses

In order to erect a caisson lighthouse, an open-ended iron or steel cylinder or rectangular "box" was towed offshore, sunk, pumped full of air or weighted down to displace the water within, and filled with stone or concrete. Lighthouses erected on this type of foundation were typically either conical towers or rectangular buildings incorporating the keeper's accommodation.

Cofferdam and crib lighthouses (as the lighthouses raised on wooden cribs in the Great Lakes are called) were both variations on the caisson-lighthouse theme. All were suitable for offshore locations that were plagued by ice floes.

GLOSSARY

ABOVE: *The Ashlar foundation of Seul Choix Point Light, Michigan.*
BELOW: *Selkirk's birdcage lantern, New York.*

ABOVE: *Rockland Breakwater Light, Maine.*
BELOW: *The Cape Cod-style light at Point Loma, California.*

Acrylic optics: modern, lightweight, solar-powered optics, including 350 mm, 350 mm, and Vega VRB.

Aerobeacon: a cylinder containing a parabolic reflector and an illuminant that emits flashes.

Alternating ("Al"): a light characteristic in which two colored lights are alternately exposed for an equal duration, or one color alternates with an equal period of darkness (isophase).

Argand lamp: a type of oil lamp (obsolete).

Ashlar: prefinished hewn or dressed stone with which walls are either constructed or faced.

Astragal: the framework that holds the individual pieces of glass of a lantern.

Aton: acronym for "Aids to navigation."

Automation: the replacement of manual systems with automatic ones.

Beacon: (a) a lighthouse, or (b) the signal emitted by a lighthouse, usually in the form of a light, but often also by means of radio or radar.

Birdcage lantern: a historic style of lantern that resembles a birdcage.

Bivalve lens: a lens consisting of two bull's-eye component lenses.

Breakwater light: a lighthouse that stands on a harbor's breakwater.

Bull's-eye lens: a convex lens, shaped like a bull's eye.

Caisson: *see* page 17.

Cape Cod style: a style of lighthouse construction, in which a short light tower emerges from the roof of a low keeper's cottage resembling Cape Cod homes.

Catadioptric: methods of light magnification that use both reflection and refraction.

Catoptric: methods of light magnification that use reflection.

Characteristic (or character): the color, type (alternating, fixed, flashing, or occulting, for example), number or group of exposures within a cycle, and the length of the cycle, that together make up the light signal by which a specific beacon can be identified.

Clamshell lens: *see* Bivalve lens.

Coffee-pot lighthouse: a cast-iron lighthouse that resembles a coffee pot, commonly seen in New England.

Cofferdam: *see* page 17.

Crib: an alternative name for a cofferdam.

Daymark: an object, such as a lighthouse or buoy, that can be identified by day and thus acts as an aid to navigation. Many lighthouses are painted in distinctive colors or patterns to cause them to stand out from their surroundings for this purpose. "Daymark" sometimes refers to a separate board attached to a light or buoy with a particular pattern and/or number, often used in range lights where two daymark lines are aligned when seen from the angle of approach. (*See also* page 253).

DCB: a type of rotating aerobeacon that was frequently used to replace Fresnel lenses in the twentieth century (*see* Aerobeacon).

Diaphone: a piston-operated sound signal.

Dioptric: methods of light magnification that use refraction (ie, redirecting light rays through lenses or prisms).

Dovetailed-stone contruction: the use of custom-shaped masonry blocks that interlock to provide extra stability to an exposed tower (for example, as used at Halfway Rock Light, Maine).

Drum lens: a drum- or barrel-shaped lens.

Eclipse: the dimming or extinguishment of a light.

Elevation: the height of a structure above sea level.

Fixed ("F"): a light that shines steadily and does not flash or revolve.

Fixed and flashing: a light whose beam is regularly punctuated with a flash.

Flashing ("Fl"): a light that regularly flashes on and off, whose eclipse exceeds the period when the light is visible. This can be achieved by switching the light on and off, or by rotating the beam of light to give the impression of a flash.

ABOVE: *Long Island's Orient Point Light, also known as "The Coffee-pot."*

BELOW: *Cape Hatteras Light's painted stripes make it a striking daymark.*

ABOVE: *Minnesota's Split Rock Light's diaphone foghorns.*

BELOW: *The dovetailed-stone tower of Halfway Rock Light.*

ABOVE: *Flying buttresses.*
BELOW: *A Fresnel lens.*

ABOVE: *The gallery and lantern of Old Presque Isle.*
BELOW: *A pepper-shaker light in Canada.*

Flying buttress: a supportive buttress that appears to soar upward or downward from the main body of a building at a pronounced angle.

Focal plane: the perpendicular plane bisecting a lens' focal point; the height of the signal above mean water level.

Focal point: the point at which rays of light converge when directed through a lens.

Fog signal: a sound signal (a blast produced by a horn, for example) that aids navigation in foggy conditions.

Fresnel lens: a type of lens that consists of concentrically ridged glass panels, with prisms positioned above and below them that refract the light of an illuminant (*see* page 11).

Gallery: a railed walkway that surrounds a lantern.

Isophase ("Iso"): *see* Alternating.

Lantern: the glazed "cage" at the top of a lighthouse that shelters the illuminant.

Light list: an annual register of aids to navigation and their characteristics.

Light station: a lighthouse and its supporting instruments (like sound signals and radio beacons) and structures (such as a keeper's dwelling, an oil house, a fog-signal building, a generator building, storehouses, and boathouses).

Making light: a lighthouse with a long range, whose primary function is to be seen from a distance, to help mariners find a port from open water, for example (as opposed to navigational aids that highlight specific local hazards or indicate harbor channels).

Occulting ("Oc"): a light that flashes on and off at regular intervals, with the period of light exceeding the period of darkness.

Pepper-shaker light: a style of harbor lighthouse common in Canada's Maritime Provinces, square-pyramidal in shape and usually made of wood.

Pierhead light: a lighthouse that stands on a harbor's pierhead.

Pile or piling: *see* page 17.

Radio beacon: a structure that transmits a distinctive radio signal, usually in Morse code.

Range: the distance from which a signal is visible under normal conditions.

Range lights: a pair of lighthouses that indicate a safe passage when aligned.

Reinforced concrete: concrete whose tensile strength is enhanced by the incorporation of steel mesh or rods.

Screwpile: *see* page 17.

Sector: a radial portion of a light that is seen from a particular angle; a lighthouse may emit a light with one or more sectors having a different color than the rest, to identify a channel, for example.

Skeletal/skeleton tower: *see* page 16.

Spark-plug light: a style of lighthouse that resembles a spark plug, usually made of brick-lined cast iron, particularly common in New England.

Straightpile: *see* page 17.

Texas tower: a steel, offshore lighthouse constructed on piles during the 1960s that resembles an oilrig.

Vega VLB: an optic using light-emitting diodes (LEDs) in an acrylic lens.

Vega VRB: a lightweight, efficient type of electronic, solar-powered lighthouse optic with a high-intensity light bulb enclosed in acrylic panels.

ABOVE: *The pierhead light at Manistee.*

BELOW: *Sea Girt Light's radio beacon was one of the first to be installed in the United States (1921).*

BELOW: *The spark-plug light at Plum Beach.*

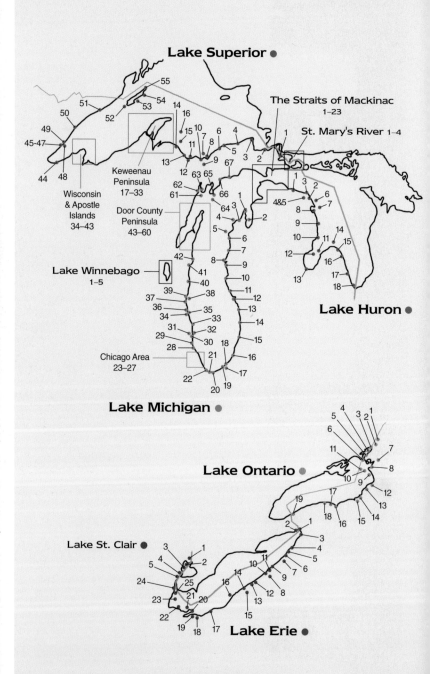

Lake Superior ●

55
51
50
54
53
52
49
45–47
44
48
14
16
15
10
7
8
9
6
4
5
11
13
67

The Straits of Mackinac
1–23

St. Mary's River 1–4

Wisconsin & Apostle Islands
34–43

Keweenau Peninsula
17–33

Door County Peninsula
43–60

62
63
65
61
66
64

1
3
4
5
2
6
7
8
9
10
11
12
13
14
15
16
17
18

1
3
2
6
7
4&5
8
9
10
11
14
16
17
18
13
12
15

Lake Huron ●

42
41
40
39
38
37
36
35
34
33
32
31
30
29
28
22

Lake Winnebago
1–5

Chicago Area
23–27

18
21
20
19
17
16
15
14
13
12
11
10
9
8
7
6
5
4
3
2
1

Lake Michigan ●

4
3
2
1
5
6
11
7
8
10
9
12
13
14
15
16
17
18
19

Lake Ontario ●

2
1
3
4
5
6
7

Lake St. Clair ●

3
1
4
2
5
24
25
23
22
21
20
19
18
17
15
13
12
8
9
7
6
5
4
3
10
11
14
16

Lake Erie ●

THE
GREAT
LAKES

LAKE ONTARIO

The U.S. side of Lake Ontario lies within the state of New York. Most of these lights were built in the nineteenth century, and spotters can access some of them via the Seaway Trail.

1. Ogdensburg Harbor Light
Ogdensburg
Established in 1834 on the bank of the St. Lawrence River, this 65-foot stone tower is gray at the bottom with its upper part white, crowned by a red lantern. The light is now a private residence and not open to the public. It can be seen from Ogdensburg Harbor and from the nearby bridge.

ABOVE: *Crossover Island Light.*
BELOW: *Sunken Rock Light.*

2. Crossover Island Light   *Crossover Island*
Located in the St. Lawrence River, this light is only accessible by boat but can be viewed from Riverledge Road northeast of Chippewa Bay. The 30-foot white, conical cast-iron tower (built 1882, deactivated 1942) is not open to the public. Its red lantern contains a sixth-order Fresnel lens.

3. Sisters Island Light   *Sisters Island*
Located in the Thousand Islands, this lighthouse can only be viewed from the water and is not open to the public. Its 60-foot, square limestone tower is attached to the keeper's dwelling. The light was built in 1870 and deactivated in the 1950s.

4. Sunken Rock Light   *Alexandria Bay*
This light (built 1884) stands on an artificial island. The white, conical cast iron tower, with a sixth-order Fresnel lens in its green lantern, is not open to the public, but can be seen from the shore at Alexandria Bay.

5. Rock Island Light *Orleans*

This light is preserved by the Rock Island Lighthouse Historical & Memorial Association. The present 60-foot structure dates from 1882 (moved in 1894). The white, conical cast-iron tower is built on a limestone base and has a sixth-order Fresnel lens. The light was deactivated in 1958 and now serves as an attraction in the Thousand Islands State Park.

6. Tibbetts Point Light *Cape Vincent*

The present white, conical brick-and-stucco tower with its black cast-iron lantern was built in 1854, replacing the original stone tower of 1827. The 58-foot beacon has a fourth-order Fresnel lens (focal plane 69 feet), which is still in use. Not only is this light operational, it is also open to the public and functions as a hostel and a museum.

7. Cape Vincent Breakwater Light *Cape Vincent*

This 15-foot beacon originally stood on the breakwater at Cape Vincent, but after its deactivation in 1934 it was moved onshore, where it welcomes visitors to the town. Built in 1900, the square concrete tower with aluminum siding was originally one of a pair.

ABOVE: *Rock Island Light.*
BELOW: *Tibbetts Point Light.*
BOTTOM: *Cape Vincent Breakwater Light.*

SPOTTER'S NOTE
The first light at Sacket's Harbor, an important military post during the War of 1812, was built in 1831.

BELOW: *Stony Point Light.*

8. Horse Island Light *Sacket's Harbor*

This white, square tower with black lantern is attached to a Queen Anne Italianate keeper's house built of brick on a limestone foundation. The historic 50-foot tower, with its fifth-order Fresnel lens, dates from 1870. A steel skeletal tower, erected in 1957, has now replaced it. The light is not open to the public but can be viewed from the shore across from Horse Island.

9. Stony Point (Henderson) Light *Henderson Harbor*

This square, white wooden tower is attached to the keeper's dwelling, now a private residence. The 73-foot tower (built 1869, deactivated 1945) has a black lantern with a fourth-order Fresnel lens. A new steel skeletal tower has replaced the old lighthouse, which is not open to the public. It can be viewed from the road, along with the foundations of an even older structure (1830).

10. Galloo Island Light *Galloo Island*

The island of Galloo (or Galoo) lies near Sacket's Harbor. Its first lighthouse was built in 1820, but the present structure dates from 1867. Its 55-foot, conical limestone tower with attached keeper's residence has a fourth-order Fresnel lens with a 58-foot focal plane. The light is no longer operational and not open to the public.

11. East Charity Shoal Light *Cape Vincent*

This light was moved from Vermilion, Ohio (*see* page 36), and was eventually reassembled at its current location near the entrance to the St. Lawrence River. The white, octagonal cast-iron structure is still operational. The 16-foot tower had a sixth-order Fresnel lens dating from 1935 until a modern optic was installed in 1992 (focal plane 52 feet). It can be seen with binoculars from Tibbett's Point.

ABOVE: *Selkirk's birdcage lantern.*
LEFT: *Oswego West Pierhead Light is said to be haunted.*
BELOW: *Sodus Outer Light.*

12. Selkirk Light *Pulaski*

Also known as Salmon River Light, the 1838 structure is open to visitors as a bed-and-breakfast inn. Inactive from 1859 to 1989, it now uses a 190-mm modern optic, but its rare birdcage-style lantern remains in place. The integral stone keeper's house has an octagonal, red wooden tower topped with the silver lantern.

13. Oswego West Pierhead Light
Oswego

Built in 1934 to replace the Outer Harbor Light, this lighthouse emits alternating red and white light. The 57-foot, white square tower and attached keeper's house are not open to the public but can be seen from Oswego town.

14. Sodus Outer Light *Sodus Point*

This light replaced Sodus Point Light (now a museum) when it was built in 1938. Its 50-foot square-pyramidal cast-iron tower stands at the entrance to Sodus Bay. Its white lantern (focal plane 51 feet) has a red roof. It is not open to the public, but there is access to the tower via the pier.

ABOVE: *Old Sodus Point Light.*
BELOW: *Charlotte-Genessee Light.*
BOTTOM: *Braddock Point Light.*

15. **Sodus Point Light** *Sodus Point*

Built in 1871 to replace the 1824 original, this light was itself replaced by a nearby pier light and now functions as a museum. Its square, 45-foot limestone tower is attached to the keeper's house and has a black cast-iron lantern. The optic is a three-and-a-half-order Fresnel lens with a 70-foot focal plane. The foundations of the original lighthouse, which stood on the same spot, can still be seen.

16. **Charlotte-Genessee Light**
Rochester

Also known as Port of Genessee Light, this beautiful 40-foot octagonal-pyramidal rubble-stone tower is located on a bluff on the western side of Genessee River about a half mile from Lake Ontario. Built in 1822, the light was abandoned in 1884. When there was talk of tearing it down in 1965, high-school students helped save it with a letter-writing campaign. A new black lantern was fitted, and in 1984 a fourth-order Fresnel was loaned from Ohio, and the light was reactivated (focal plane 45 feet). It is now a museum, and visitors can climb the tower.

17. **Braddock Point Light** *Hilton*

This 40-foot, truncated, octagonal red-brick tower was originally built in 1896 to a height of 97 feet and topped with the lantern and lens from Ohio's Cleveland Light (demolished 1895), but it was deactivated in 1954 when a steel skeletal tower was erected nearby, and its upper two thirds were removed because of structural damage. It was then sold privately, restored, and a new faux lantern was added some time later. The original Victorian brick keeper's quarters (1896) and a carriage house still stand adjacent to the tower. The site is privately owned and closed to the public. Reactivated as a private navigational aid in 1999, its alternating white signal has a focal-plane height of 55 feet.

LEFT: *Thirty Mile Point Light.*
BELOW: *Fort Niagara Light.*

18. Thirty Mile Point Light *Somerset*

This 61-foot square limestone tower with red-and-white lantern is attached to a two-story limestone keeper's house. It was built in 1876 and was deactivated between 1959 and 1998, since when it has been used as a private navigational aid. The original third-order Fresnel lens has now been removed, but its signal could once be seen for up to 16 miles. Situated within Golden Hill State Park, 30 miles east of the mouth of Niagara River (hence its name), the 1935 fog-signal building is now a recreation hall for campers in the park. The lighthouse itself is open for tours.

19. Fort Niagara Light *Youngstown*

Replacing a beacon on top of Fort Niagara, the present structure was built in 1872 just outside the fort. This octagonal-pyramidal, gray stone tower attached to its Queen Anne keeper's quarters was originally 50 feet high, but in 1900 it was increased by 11 feet above the protruding ring of arches on the tower. The fourth-order Fresnel lens could consequently be seen for 25 miles (91-foot focal plane). The light was deactivated in 1993 as it was increasingly obscured by trees and now serves as a museum.

LAKE ERIE

Four states share the U.S. shoreline of Lake Erie, which is graced by more than two dozen historic beacons of diverse styles, ages, and construction materials.

NEW YORK

ABOVE: *Buffalo Main Light.*
BELOW: *"Old Bottle" Light.*

1. Buffalo Main Light *Buffalo*

Also known as Chinaman's Light as it welcomed immigrants to the U.S. heartland, a great deal has gone into the restoration of this lighthouse. The tower has been carefully preserved, a shoreline promenade added, and a new fourth-order Fresnel (focal plane 76 feet) fitted. The 61-foot octagonal-pyramidal tower is built of limestone and has a black cast-iron lantern. It dates from 1833 and was deactivated in 1914. It is opened to the public on special occasions.

2. Buffalo North Breakwater ("Old Bottle") Light *Buffalo*

Located next to the Buffalo Main Light, this was one of two lighthouses of this shape to stand in Buffalo Harbor, where it was originally erected. Built in 1903, the 29-foot cast-iron bottle had a sixth-order Fresnel lens, but is now inactive.

3. Buffalo Harbor South Entrance Light *South Buffalo*

This operational tower was first lit in 1903. The 27-foot, conical steel structure with white markings rests on a foundation of dressed stone and timber. It is believed that the original optic was the fourth-order Fresnel that is now in the 1833 Buffalo Main Light. A new 300-mm optic has replaced it (focal plane 40 feet). A utilitarian concrete sound-signal building stands adjacent to the tower. The lighthouse, which is located on Stony Point Breakwater, is not open to the public.

4. South Buffalo North Side Light
Dunkirk

This is one of two bottle-shaped lights (*see also* Buffalo North Breakwater Light, previous page) that originally stood at the entrance to Buffalo Harbor. Built in 1903, the 29-foot light was deactivated in 1988 and relocated to the grounds of the Dunkirk Historical Lighthouse and Veterans Park Museum (*see below*).

5. Dunkirk (Point Gratiot) Light
Dunkirk

This operational lighthouse was built in 1875. The square rubblestone-and-brick tower is unpainted at the base, painted white above, and has a red cast-iron lantern, which houses the third-order Fresnel lens from the previous tower. The Victorian Gothic brick keeper's house is now used as a museum.

ABOVE: *Dunkirk (Point Gratiot) Light, whose grounds also feature a skeleton tower from Grand Island and the bottle light listed at left.*

SPOTTER'S NOTE
Buffalo Harbor has had as many as nine lighthouses and a lightship marking its entrance. Buffalo Intake Crib Light (1920) is an active optic (flashing white) atop a circular stone water-intake crib. The original Buffalo Breakwater Light of 1872 was rammed several times by ships; it became known as the "leaning lighthouse" (demolished).

6. Dunkirk Pierhead Light *Dunkirk*

This is the fourth light to mark the entrance to Dunkirk Harbor. It is a cylindrical tower, white with a red horizontal band in the middle. Built in 1992, it uses an 1857 sixth-order Fresnel lens that flashes red every 6 seconds (focal plane 36 feet). The grounds are open to the public.

7. Barcelona Light *Barcelona*

Also known as Portland Harbor Light, this 40-foot, conical fieldstone tower was built in 1829 and is the oldest tower still standing on the U.S. shores of the Great Lakes. It was also the first lighthouse in the United States to be fueled by gas (1831); a pipeline was fitted to a nearby pocket of natural gas. Modern gas lamps are still used by its private owner. The lighthouse is closed to the public but can be seen from the nearby marina's parking lot.

PENNSYLVANIA

8. Erie Yacht Club Breakwater Light *Erie*

A privately maintained lighthouse, this 36-foot, white, conical steel tower has a black lantern and flashes a white signal (focal plane 32 feet) during the summer months.

9. Presque Isle North Pier Light *Erie*

Also known as Erie North Pierhead Light, this lighthouse has been moved twice, latterly in 1940, and now marks the mouth of Presque Isle Bay. The light replaced an earlier tower (1828) that was toppled by a schooner in a gale in 1857. The tapering, square cast-iron tower is painted white with a central black band and black lantern; it is still operational (automated 1940) and can be viewed from the pier; visitors can walk along the wide, concrete breakwater.

BELOW: *Presque Isle North Pier Light.*

SPOTTER'S NOTE
Presque Isle is actually a sandspit peninsula. The first keeper here described it as the loneliest place on earth until a road was built in 1927 to connect it to the mainland.

LEFT: *Presque Isle Light.*
BELOW: *Erie Land Light. Its replica lantern was destroyed in a 2003 storm and subsequently replaced.*

10. Presque Isle Light *Erie*

Built in 1873 to replace Erie Land Light, Presque Isle Light's 40-foot tower was constructed of brick "five courses thick" to withstand Lake Erie's dramatic storms, and raised to a height of 68 feet in 1896. Its alternating red and white electric light of 1920 gave rise to the nickname "Flashlight." In 1962 a new optic was installed, which still emits its white signal. The light stands in Presque Isle State Park, whose manager resides in the attached keeper's house.

11. Erie Land Light *Erie*

The 1818, 20-foot stone tower, originally known as Presque Isle Light, was one of the first two lights on Lake Erie. Structural instability due to quicksand twice led to the construction of a new tower. This 49-foot sandstone tower was completed with a massive foundation in 1869. Its third-order Fresnel lens was removed in 1901, two years after the light was permanently closed. The tower was restored in 1989 and fitted with a replica lantern to form a tourist attraction in the city's Land Lighthouse Park.

OHIO

12. Conneaut Harbor West Breakwater Light *Conneaut*

This 60-foot, white, square-pyramidal steel tower with a black band was built in 1936 and now has no lantern. Its 375-mm optic produces alternating red and white flashes with a 5-second period (range 17 miles). It is located on a breakwater at the entrance to Conneaut Harbor, and can be viewed from Conneaut Township Park.

13. Ashtabula Harbor Light *Ashtabula*

Built in 1905, this light was moved to its current location on a concrete caisson and enlarged in 1916. The white cylindrical tower sits on top of the square, red-roofed keeper's building. The modern optic beams out an amber light (focal plane 51 feet). An onshore museum in the earlier keeper's house is open to the public.

14. Fairport Harbor West Breakwater Light *Fairport*

Built in 1925, this white, square tower is attached to the keeper's house. The light is still operational, with an automated solar-powered optic (focal plane 56 feet), which replaced the original fourth-order Fresnel lens. While not open to the public, the lighthouse can be viewed from Headlands Beach State Park.

BELOW: *Fairport Harbor West Breakwater Light.*

15. Fairport Harbor Light *Fairport*

Also known as the Grand River Light, this beacon was deactivated in 1925, replaced by the new breakwater light. It was restored after an appeal by locals and is now a listed building; the adjacent keeper's quarters function as a marine museum at 129 Second Street, Fairport Harbor. The 60-foot, conical sandstone tower was built in 1871 and has sixty-nine steps leading to an observation platform. Its octagonal iron lantern still holds the original third-order Fresnel lens (focal plane 102 feet).

16. Cleveland Harbor West and East Pierhead Lights *Cleveland*

These white, conical cast-iron towers with black lanterns frame the entrance to the harbor. Both established here in 1911, the 25-foot East tower is believed to have been built around 1880. Its modern lens has a focal plane of 31 feet. The West light has a focal plane of 63 feet and an attached keeper's dwelling and fog-signal building. Both lights are still operational and neither is open to the public.

17. Lorain Light *Lorain*

Emitting a red flash every 4 seconds, 58 feet above the lake, this integrated lantern and keeper's quarters remains an active navigational aid. It was erected in 1917, the fourth light in Lorain. The shuttered windows and pitched roof adorn concrete-and-steel walls more than 10 inches thick, designed to withstand the harsh conditions.

ABOVE: *Lorain Light.*
BELOW: *Fairport Harbor Light.*

SPOTTER'S NOTE
Cleveland East Entrance Light consists of a 31-foot, white steel cylinder, with a red band, supporting the modern optic. Several small aids to navigation have been used in this harbor.

ABOVE: *Vermilion Light (see Spotter's Note, below).*

SPOTTER'S NOTE
Vermilion Light was raised in 1991 as a replica of the 1877 lighthouse that once stood in the harbor. The original tower was dismantled in 1929 and later re-erected on Lake Ontario at the entrance to the St. Lawrence Seaway, renamed East Charity Shoals Light (*see* page 26).

SPOTTER'S NOTE
The 352-foot Perry Memorial (1915) on South Bass Island commemorates the Battle of Lake Erie in the War of 1812. The tower is a pink granite column topped with a bronze urn, from which shines an alternating light.

18. Huron Harbor Light *Huron*

Located at the end of a breakwater in the harbor, this white, cylindrical steel tower on a square fog building was erected in 1936 on concrete foundations. The 72-foot Art Deco tower is still active (focal plane 80 feet, range 12 miles), emitting an alternating red signal.

19. Cedar Point Light *Sandusky*

The integral limestone keeper's house and square tower rising from the roof was completed in 1867, replacing an earlier building. Deactivated in 1904, the tower was removed. The restored lighthouse and rebuilt tower is now part of the Cedar Point Amusement Park.

20. Marblehead Light *Marblehead* (*opposite*)

21. South Bass Island Light *Put-In-Bay*

This 80-foot lighthouse (1897) is a square brick tower with a red-and-white lantern, attached to a Queen Anne house. Deactivated in 1962, it is now part of Ohio State University, which offers a public tour every year in late August.

Marblehead Light

Sandusky Sentinel

Also known as Sandusky Bay Light, this is the oldest continuously operated lighthouse on the Great Lakes. Marblehead Light was featured on a U.S. postage stamp and depicted on Ohio state license plates. Built in 1921, it is a 65-foot, conical limestone tower with red trim and a red lantern. The signal is a green flash every 6 seconds, visible for 12 miles. The keeper's house is a separate Victorian, two-story wood-framed building dating from 1880, now used as a museum by the Ottawa County Historical Society.

Description: conical limestone tower
Markings: white; red trim and lantern
Lens: plastic beacon
Height: 65 feet (tower); 67 feet (focal plane)

BELOW: *This venerable Lake Erie landmark is the main attraction at Marblehead Lighthouse State Park.*

22. West Sister Island Light

West Sister Island

This 55-foot, conical, white limestone-and-brick tower (1848) is one of the oldest surviving lights on the Great Lakes, now emitting a solar-powered signal (focal plane 57 feet, lantern removed). There is no access to the site.

23. Toledo Harbor Light   *Toledo*

This unique 69-foot, three-story, ochre-yellow Romanesque integrated lighthouse (1904), with its black lantern rising from the roof of the keeper's quarters, is located on an artificially created island. Attached to the house is a single-story fog-signal building. The light is still active; it is closed to the public and can only be viewed by boat.

MICHIGAN

24. Grosse Ile North Channel Range Front Light   *Grosse Ile*

A white, octagonal wooden tower standing 50 feet tall, the present structure was built in 1906. The wooden Victorian keeper's house is located off site and now privately owned. The tower is on private property but tours can be arranged by contacting the Grosse Ile Historical Society.

25. Detroit River (Bar Point Shoal) Light   *South Rockwood*

Also known as "The Rock" because of its isolated location, this spark-plug light stands on a concrete crib near the entrance of the Detroit River. The 49-foot tower, built in 1885, is constructed of cast iron with a brick lining; it is white with a black upper and lantern and has an attached fog-signal building and integral keeper's quarters. Other structures include a storage building and a radio beacon. An active aid to navigation, it is closed to the public.

BELOW: *An aerial view of Detroit River (Bar Point Shoal) Light, which replaced a Canadian lightship that had served since 1875.*

LAKE ST. CLAIR

This heart-shaped lake, which divides Michigan from Canada, also connects Lakes Huron and Erie. More properly a delta known as St. Clair Flats, it was dredged extensively to form a vital shipping canal, which was opened in 1871.

1. Peche (Peach) Island Range Rear Light *Marine City*

This 1908 light was originally built on Peche (Peach) Island, Ontario. It is a white, conical cast-iron tower standing 60 feet tall. Moved in 1983, the inactive light is now an exhibit in a park on Marine City's waterfront.

2. St. Clair Flats South Channel Range Lights *near Harsen's Island*

The front range light is an offshore, 17-foot conical brick tower (1859) that leans over at a noticeable angle, built on a wooden crib. Despite its leaning problem, it is still active. The former rear range light was deactivated in 1970 and is now very run down. There are plans to restore both towers.

3. Lake St. Clair Light *off Detroit*

This active light replaced a lightship in 1941. The cylindrical steel pillar on a caisson (lower and upper parts painted white, and the middle and lantern, green) can only be seen by boat.

ABOVE: *Peche Island Light.*
BELOW: *St. Clair Flats South Channel Range Lights.*

4. Windmill Point Light *Detroit*

This 40-foot white, conical steel tower (1933) on a red base is an active aid to navigation; it stands in Detroit Mariners Park and can be viewed up close.

5. William Livingstone Memorial *Belle Isle Park, Detroit*

First lit in 1930 as a memorial to the 1902–25 president of the Lake Carriers' Association, this 58-foot, white, fluted Art Deco marble tower is an active aid to navigation. Its occulting light can be seen for up to 16 miles.

LAKE HURON

Lake Huron was named *La Mer Douce* (the sweet, or freshwater, sea) by the first French explorers in the area, but there is nothing sweet about the navigational hazards along its shores (now Michigan).

ABOVE: *Forty Mile Point Light.*
BELOW: *Old Presque Isle Light.*
BOTTOM: *Presque Isle Harbor Rear Range Light.*

1. Forty Mile Point Light *Rogers City*

Attached to an unpainted brick keeper's house, this lighthouse is a white, square brick tower, with black-roofed lantern room, standing 52 feet high. The structure dates back to 1897 and still uses its 1935 fourth-order Fresnel lens to produce a flashing white signal. Additional buildings include a brick fog-signal house. The light station is located in Lighthouse Park, which is open to the public.

2. Old Presque Isle Light *Presque Isle*

This 38-foot white, conical stone-and-brick tower (1840) has been inactive since 1871, when it was replaced by New Presque Isle Light, located one mile away. It now functions as a museum.

3. Presque Isle Light *Presque Isle*

This active lighthouse is a 109-foot, white, conical brick tower, attached to a white-painted brick keeper's residence. The house is now used as a museum, which is open during the summer, and visitors can climb the tower.

4. Presque Isle Harbor Front Range Light *Presque Isle*

This 25-foot white, octagonal wooden tower (1870) is inactive and now forms the entrance to the museum at Old Presque Isle Light.

5. Presque Isle Harbor Rear Range Light *Presque Isle*

Once used in tandem with its front range counterpart, the wooden structure resembles an old schoolhouse. The building (1870) is now used as a private residence and not open to the public.

6. **Middle Island Light** *Alpena*

Built in 1905 and standing 71 feet tall, this is a conical brick-and-stucco tower, painted white with a red band in the middle, attached to a service room. It is an active aid to navigation in the waters near Thunder Bay and is under restoration; guest accommodation will be offered in the former keeper's house.

7. **Thunder Bay Island Light** *Alpena*

Standing 50 feet tall, with a signal of alternate green and white flashes at a focal-plane height of 69 feet, this white, conical brick tower with red lantern was built in 1832. The tower is attached to a two-story brick keeper's house constructed in 1868. The light station is under restoration and is closed to the public; it can only be seen by boat.

> **SPOTTER'S NOTE**
> The Thunder Bay Island Light was raised by 10 feet in 1857. It is conical in the lower portion, but the top slopes at a smaller angle, giving the building a tapered profile.

8. **Alpena Light** *Alpena*

Also known locally as "Sputnik," this red lantern on a square-pyramidal, skeletal, red steel tower (1914) stands 38 feet tall at the end of a breakwater. Built in 1914, it is still active and is said to be "short on beauty, long on duty."

9. **Sturgeon Point Light** *Harrisville*
(overleaf)

10. **Tawas Point (Ottawa Point) Light** *East Tawas*

This active light is located in Tawas Point State Park and is open to the public. It is a 67-foot, white, conical brick tower (1876) with red trim, attached by a passageway to a red-painted brick keeper's house.

BELOW: *Tawas Point Light.*

11. **Charity Island Light** *Au Gres*

The conical brick tower is white with a cast-iron lantern. The tower was built and first lit in 1857 but deactivated in 1939 when it was replaced by the new light at Gravelly Shoal. The original keeper's house had severely decayed and was finally torn down in 2003; a replica has since been built by the private owners and is available for vacation rentals.

> **SPOTTER'S NOTE**
> The Tawas Point Light was among the first on the continent to be fitted with an innovative clockwork mechanism that created an occulting signal by regularly dropping and raising a brass cylinder over the light.

Sturgeon Point Light

ABOVE: *Sturgeon Point Light and the museum seen from the southeast.*

Description: conical brick tower; attached keeper's dwelling
Markings: white with red trim
Lens: third-and-a-half-order Fresnel
Height: 71 feet (tower); 69 feet (focal plane)

A Finer Point

Located on a narrow, sandy point near Alcona, Michigan, north of Harrisville, this light marks a gravel reef that runs out into Lake Huron and endangers vessels navigating the coast. The reef can be seen from the top of the tower. Still operational and using an 1889 Fresnel lens that was previously installed in the lighthouse at Oswego, New York, this 71-foot tower (1869) is white with red trim, conical, and made of brick. It is attached to a white limestone-and-brick keeper's house, currently used as a maritime museum that is open to visitors during the summer; the grounds are open year-round.

12. Gravelly Shoal Light *off Point Lookout, near Charity Island, Au Gres*

Located in Saginaw Bay near Charity Island, this offshore, 65-foot Art Deco tower (1939), concrete with a skeletal steel upper portion, stands on a concrete crib foundation. It is an active aid to navigation and can only be viewed by boat.

SPOTTER'S NOTE

The Saginaw River Range Lights are believed to be the first range lights ever established. The idea of placing two lights in a row for mariners to line up and follow as they made their way down the river came from the keeper's fifteen-year-old son.

---

13. Saginaw River (Range Rear) Light *Bay City*

A square, white, 55-foot brick tower (1876) with black trim, integral with the white, two-story brick keeper's dwelling, this light was deactivated in 1960. The light is in private ownership and under restoration, with plans to open it as a museum; at present there is no public access, and the light must be viewed by boat. The front range light has been demolished.

14. Port Austin Reef Light

Port Austin

Built in 1878, with an attached fog-signal building added in 1899, the 60-foot tower is square, of tan brick, topped with a black lantern, and built on an offshore octagonal concrete foundation. Once scheduled for demolition, the tower was saved and is still active. There is no public access to the site, and it can only be viewed by air or water.

15. Pointe Aux Barques Light

Port Hope

Standing 89 feet tall, this brick tower is conical in shape, white with black trim and a red-roofed lantern, and attached via a passage to the keeper's house. A friendly female ghost is said to inhabit the lighthouse, which is still active and also serves as a museum. The light is located in Lighthouse County Park.

BELOW: *Pointe Aux Barques Light.*

16. Harbor Beach Light *Harbor Beach*

Built of cast iron and lined with brick, this white, conical tower (1885) with black lantern and trim is located at the end of a detached breakwater. The lighthouse stands 45 feet tall, and its keepers were housed within the tower itself. The light is still active and can be seen in the distance from a fishing pier at Harbor Beach.

RIGHT: *Port Sanilac Light and keeper's house, with its step-gabled roof.*
BELOW: *The* Huron *lightship (see Spotter's Note).*

SPOTTER'S NOTE
Commissioned in 1921, the *Huron* served as a relief vessel for other Great Lakes lightships. On clear nights the beacon from the *Huron* could be seen for 14 miles. After 1940 this was the only lightship on the Great Lakes and the only lightship to keep its post during World War II. Retired from service in 1970, the *Huron* now stands in Pine Grove Park in Port Huron. In 1989 it was designated a National Historic Landmark.

17. **Port Sanilac Light** *Port Sanilac*

This 59-foot, octagonal-pyramidal brick tower (1886), painted white with red trim, is attached to a two-story brick keeper's house. It is still an active lighthouse, but the keeper's house is now a private residence, and there is no access to the site.

18. **Fort Gratiot (Port Huron) Light** *Port Huron* *(opposite)*

Fort Gratiot (Port Huron) Light

Green Light

This is the oldest surviving lighthouse in Michigan, and it still emits its flashing green signal, which is visible for up to 18 miles. Now standing 82 feet tall, this white, conical brick tower with red-roofed lantern was built in 1829 and was extended in 1861 from its original height of 65 feet. It is attached to a workroom, and the brick keeper's dwelling (1875, now a residence for Coast Guard personnel) stands nearby. The tower is open to the public (reservations required) during the summer.

Description: conical brick tower; attached workroom
Markings: white; red-roofed lantern
Lens: DCB-24
Height: 82 feet (tower); 86 feet (focal plane)

BELOW: *Fort Gratiot Light was built by Winslow Lewis.*

ST. MARY'S RIVER

The narrow passage of St. Mary's River, which connects Lakes Huron and Superior, is a navigator's nightmare, with tight curves, severe weather conditions, and several locks. These lights are all in Michigan (St. Mary's River is the international border).

SPOTTER'S NOTE
Mariners navigating St. Mary's River have always used street lights and lights mounted on houses and yards as well as official aids to find their way through the passage.

RIGHT: *Round Island (St. Mary's River) Light.*

1. Round Island (St. Mary's River) Light *DeTour*
Now a private residence, this lighthouse was established in 1892 but was deactivated in 1929 when a skeletal tower replaced its function. A white, square wooden keeper's dwelling with a tower rising from one side, topped with an empty black lantern room, it stands 35 feet tall. This light can only be viewed from the water.

2. Pipe Island Light *DeTour*
Still an active light, this is a white, octagonal brick tower (1888) whose lantern was removed when a skeletal steel tower (1937), orange in color, was added to the top of the lighthouse. The island is privately owned and the light can only be seen from the water.

3. Frying Pan Island Light *Sault Sainte Marie*
This inactive tower was moved from Frying Pan Island (offshore from DeTour) in 1988 after being replaced by a modern beacon. A white, conical cast-iron tower with black trim, dating from 1887, it is now on display outside a Coast Guard base.

4. DeTour Reef Light *DeTour*
Built in 1931, made of reinforced concrete and steel, this offshore square, Art Deco light is white with a red roof and stands above its keeper's quarters on a caisson. The tower is 63 feet tall and is located at the entrance to the St. Mary's River on Lake Huron. This light replaced the onshore DeTour Point Light of 1847. It is not open to the public and can only be viewed by water.

THE STRAITS OF MACKINAC

The busy Mackinac Straits, connecting Lakes Huron and Michigan, are kept open by icebreakers to allow for year-round shipping. All the lighthouses listed here are in Michigan.

1. Spectacle Reef Light *Cheboygan*

Standing 93 feet tall, this 1874 offshore, conical limestone tower, with red trim, stands on a square limestone crib. The light is an early example of an exposed crib: more than 200 men worked on its construction for four years. It is not open to the public and can only be viewed by air or water.

2. Martin Reef Light *Cedarville*

A 1927 white, octagonal reinforced-concrete tower with red-roofed lantern stands on the integral, square three-story keeper's quarters. The 52-foot-tall lighthouse is located on a dangerous reef and is not open to the public.

ABOVE: *Round Island Passage.*
BELOW: *Round Island Light.*

3. Round Island Passage Light
Mackinac Island

A 60-foot white, hexagonal concrete obelisk built on a red storage area over a white base, this offshore crib-foundation lighthouse was established in 1947. There is no public access, but the light can be seen from the south shore of Mackinac Island.

4. Round Island Light *Mackinac Island*

This is a 53-foot, square brick tower, red with a black lantern, attached to the red-and-white painted keeper's quarters (constructed in 1895). The lighthouse stands on a small island near Mackinac Island and can be seen from the ferries. Inactive and abandoned for a period, this much-loved light station is now restored and functions as a private aid to navigation. The grounds are open to the public.

SPOTTER'S NOTE
Bois Blanc Island Light on Mackinac Island is a 37-foot integrated lighthouse/keeper's house, now privately owned. Constructed in 1867 of Cream City brick, with a white lantern, it was replaced by a skeletal tower.

5. Mackinac Point Light *Mackinaw City*

Built of Cream City brick in 1892, this handsome cylindrical tower, topped with a red-and-white lantern, adjoins the brick keeper's dwelling, which resembles a small castle. Deactivated in 1957, the light is now a museum, and visitors may climb the tower.

6. St. Helena Island Light
St. Helena Island

Standing 71 feet tall, this conical, white brick tower with red lantern was built in 1873; it is attached via a walkway to a brick keeper's cottage. The lighthouse has undergone a recent program of restoration, and the grounds are open to the public. The island can be reached by boat from Mackinaw City.

7. McGulpins Point Light
Mackinaw City

An octagonal tower and attached keeper's house of Cream City brick, this 1869 light only served as an active navigation aid for thirty-seven years. Now a private residence, its lantern long since removed, this light cannot be viewed.

ABOVE: *Cheboygan Crib Light.*
BELOW: *Cheboygan River Range Front Light.*

8. Cheboygan Crib Light *Cheboygan*

Located in Gordon Turner City Park at Cheboygan Harbor, this lighthouse (1884) was originally located offshore. Standing 25 feet tall, it is an octagonal-pyramidal cast-iron tower, white with red lantern and trim. The light is inactive.

9. Cheboygan River Range Front Light *Cheboygan*

Established in 1880, still an active navigation aid as well as being used as offices, this white tower no longer has a light in its lantern but possesses a locomotive-style light on the gallery. The lighthouse consists of an integrated white wooden keeper's house with tower rising from the gable end, located on a public street. The rear range light was replaced with a skeletal tower.

10. Fourteen Foot Shoal Light
Cheboygan

This offshore light (1930) is a white, cylindrical steel tower with red trim rising from the center of the roof of a white, rectangular house. With a focal plane of 55 feet, the lighthouse sends its signal from an artificially created island near the entrance to Cheboygan Harbor. This tower is best viewed from a boat and is closed to the public.

ABOVE: *Fourteen Foot Shoal Light.*

11. Poe Reef Light   *Cheboygan*

Featuring a white band against black paintwork, with a red roof, this 1929 lighthouse replaced a lightship that had been stationed near the offshore reef from 1893. The square concrete tower stands 60 feet high and rises from the three-story keeper's quarters. The light is not open to the public but can be seen from Cheboygan State Park.

12. White Shoal Light   *Mackinaw City*

Painted in red-and-white spiral bands, this "barber pole" lighthouse is unique in the United States for its markings. The offshore tower was constructed in 1910 of terra cotta and steel with a brick lining. It is conical in shape and stands 121 feet high, with integral keeper's quarters at the base. Recently repainted, the light can only be viewed by boat and is not open to the public.

13. Waugoshance Light
Waugoshance Shoal

Built in 1851, this offshore light has been abandoned since 1912, having been replaced by White Shoal Light. Standing 76 feet tall, it is a conical, buff brick tower encased with black iron plating near the base, and it features a birdcage-style lantern. The light is not open to the public and only distant views by boat are possible, as the waters around the light are treacherous; directly in the path of vessels passing through the Straits of Mackinac, the shoals have claimed many lives.

> **SPOTTER'S NOTE**
> The Cheboygan ruins, located in Cheboygan East State Park, are all that remains of an old lighthouse that was abandoned in 1920. Poe Reef Light and Fourteen Foot Shoal Light can be seen from the beach next to these ruins. Several well-marked trails in the park allow hikers to see expansive vistas of the Lake Huron shore and inland natural areas.

> **SPOTTER'S NOTE**
> Waugoshance Light is said to be haunted by past keeper John Herman, who either jumped or fell to his death from the light in 1894. From that day forth, many a light keeper reported unusual events, and things got so bad that keepers eventually refused to serve there.

49

ABOVE: *Gray's Reef Light.*
BELOW: *A historical photograph of Skillagalee (Ile Aux Galets) Light.*
BOTTOM: *Lansing Shoal Light.*

SPOTTER'S NOTE
Skillagalee Light is identical to Port Sanilac Light on Lake Huron (*see* page 44)

14. Grays Reef Light *St. Ignace*

Built in 1936, this white Art Deco tower, with a black lantern, stands 65 feet tall. The offshore tower is octagonal and stands on a square base on an artificially created island. Constructed of concrete and steel, with integral keeper's quarters, it replaced lightships that had been stationed in the area since 1891. It is not open to the public.

15. Skillagalee (Ile Aux Galets) Light *Cross Village*

This 58-foot brick lighthouse is octagonal-pyramidal in shape, painted white with a black lantern. The former keeper's residence and sound-signal buildings were demolished in 1969 when the light was automated. The tower is not open to the public and can only be seen by boat, from a distance, as the waters around the island are dangerous.

16. Little Traverse (Harbor Point) Light *Harbor Springs*

Also known as Harbor Point Light, this two-story keeper's house with an integral, 40-foot, square tower (topped with a red-roofed lantern) is made of red brick. Built in 1884, the light's fourth-order Fresnel lens was deactivated in 1963. The light is now part of a gated community and can only be seen by boat

17. Petoskey Pierhead Light *Petoskey*

This white steel cylinder on a square, red base sends its red signal from the end of the west pierhead in Petoskey.

18. Charlevoix South Pierhead Light *Charlevoix*

This steel, partially skeletal tower was built in 1948 to replace an older wooden structure. The active lighthouse is white and square-pyramidal, with a black lantern, and stands on a concrete-and-steel pier.

19. Lansing Shoal Light *Naubinway*

Built in 1928 on a remote concrete crib in northern Lake Michigan, this square reinforced-concrete tower stands 59 feet high above square integral keeper's quarters. The off-white building is not accessible and can only be seen by boat or by air.

20. Squaw Island Light *Gladstone*

Built in 1892, this light is an octagonal red-brick tower with black lantern, attached to the two-story red-brick keeper's quarters. Deactivated in 1928, it is privately owned and can only be seen by air.

21. St. James (Beaver Harbor) Light *St. James*

Also known as Whiskey Point Light, this 41-foot, cylindrical brick tower (1870) was originally painted yellow and attached to the keeper's house (demolished). It is now white and has a black lantern. An active aid to navigation, the lighthouse stands near the ferry dock and is easily viewed.

22. Beaver Head (Beaver Island) Light *Beaver Island*

This light station, deactivated in 1962, is now run as Beaver Island Lighthouse School, an environmental education facility. The 46-foot yellow-brick tower (1858), which is attached to the keeper's dwelling, had a focal plane height of 103 feet. The site is open to the public.

23. South Fox Island Light *South Fox Island*

Originally built in 1905 at Sapelo Island, Georgia, this 60-foot skeletal steel tower with black lantern was moved in 1934 to replace the old South Fox Island Light of 1868. Badly deteriorating, the former lighthouse, a square brick tower, white with red trim and attached to a keeper's dwelling, still stands near the new tower. This site is not open to the public and is best seen by air.

ABOVE: *Charlevoix South Pierhead Light.*
BELOW: *Beaver Island Light when it was an active beacon.*

LAKE MICHIGAN

Some 12 million people live in the cities along Lake Michigan's beautiful shores: the area owes its economic development to successful navigation on the lake, and, in turn, to the efficacy of these historic lighthouses.

MICHIGAN, EASTERN SHORE

ABOVE: *Grand Traverse Light.*
RIGHT: *(Old) Mission Point Light.*

SPOTTER'S NOTE
The white, cylindrical Manning Memorial Light was built in Empire in 1991 to commemorate a local fisherman.

1. Grand Traverse Light *Northport*

Built in 1858, and deactivated in 1972, this light is also known as Cat's Head or Northport Light. Constructed of brick, wood, and iron, the square tower with its red lantern rises to 47 feet above the keeper's dwelling. It is now open to visitors as the Grand Traverse Lighthouse Museum.

2. (Old) Mission Point Light *Traverse City*

A white, wooden tower, built in 1870 and deactivated in 1933, rises to 30 feet atop the keeper's dwelling. Located in a city park, the station is on the 45th parallel, halfway between the equator and the North Pole. The tower itself is not open to the public.

3. North Manitou Shoal Light *offshore, near Glen Arbor*

Constructed on a concrete crib in 1935, this square, white steel tower stands on top of a square flat-roofed keeper's dwelling (focal plane 79 feet). It marks the dangerous Manitou Passage and replaced a lightship that had been here since 1910. It can be viewed from the Leland–Manitou Islands ferry.

4. South Manitou Island Light

South Manitou Island

This 54-foot, white, conical brick tower with black lantern was built in 1872 (deactivated 1958). A covered walkway attaches it to the brick keeper's dwelling, which was retained from the 1858 light station. A fog-signal building also survives at this site, which is located within the Sleeping Bear Dunes National Lakeshore.

BELOW: *Point Betsie Light.*

5. Point Betsie Light *Frankfort*

This 37-foot, white, cylindrical brick tower with red roof was built in 1858, and is attached to keeper's quarters that were built in 1894. There are several other structures at the light station, which is an active aid to navigation. The Friends of Point Betsie Lighthouse are working with the county to provide visitation opportunities for the public, who can otherwise spot the tower from the end of the Point Betsie Road.

6. Frankfort (North) Breakwater Light *Frankfort*

Relocated from Frankfort's north pier and moved to the end of the northern breakwater in 1932, this white, square-pyramidal tower with black lantern (focal plane 72 feet) stands 67 feet tall atop a two-story metal base. It is not open to the public, but can easily be viewed from the lakeside in Frankfort.

BELOW: *Frankfort North Breakwater Light, seen from the beach.*

Above, right: *Big Sable Point Light.*

Above: *Manistee (North Pierhead) Light.*

Bottom: *Ludington North Breakwater Light.*

7. Manistee (North Pierhead) Light *Manistee*

This 39-foot, white, conical cast-iron tower is attached to its lakeside keeper's quarters by a long, elevated catwalk. Built in 1927 to mark the entrance to Manistee River, it still serves as an active aid to navigation.

8. Big Sable Point Light *Ludington*

Also known as Grand Point Au Sable Light, this tower was constructed of brick in 1867 but was encased in steel in the early 1900s. Standing 112 feet high, it is conical in shape, white with a black band around its middle third, and is attached to a large brick keeper's dwelling. Although it is still an active navigational aid, visitors may climb the tower and can reach the light (open May through October) via the Lighthouse Trail in Ludington State Park.

9. Ludington North Breakwater Light *Ludington*

Also known as Ludington North Pierhead Light, this 57-foot, white, square-pyramidal steel tower with black lantern was built in 1924. An active navigational aid (with a modern optic), the lighthouse developed a slight lean when work was being carried out on it in 1994. The grounds are open to the public.

10. Little Sable Point Light *Mears*

Built in 1874, this 107-foot conical tower is the oldest brick lighthouse on the Great Lakes. The attached keeper's dwelling was razed in 1955 on automation of the light. In 1977 the paint was sandblasted from the tower, exposing its natural color. The grounds, situated in Silver Lake State Park, are open to the public.

11. White River Light *Fruitland*

This 38-foot, unpainted octagonal limestone tower (1875), with a black lantern and attached keeper's dwelling, is no longer active but operates as a museum (open in summer). Guided tours are available by arrangement. Other buildings on site include an oil house, garage, and storage building.

ABOVE: *White River Light.*
BELOW: *Little Sable Point Light.*

ABOVE, RIGHT: *Muskegon South Pierhead Light.*
BELOW: *South Haven South Pierhead Light.*

12. Muskegon South Pierhead and Breakwater Lights *Muskegon*

The South Pierhead light is a 48-foot, red, conical cast-iron tower with a fourth-order Fresnel lens in its red lantern. Standing 53 feet tall, the red, square-pyramidal South Breakwater tower has a focal-plane height above sea level of 70 feet. They were both built in 1903 and are still active aids to mariners negotiating the channel that connects lakes Michigan and Muskegon. Visitors may view the lights from Pere Maquette Park; the former keeper's residence is onshore.

13. Grand Haven South Pierhead Lights *Grand Haven* (opposite)

14. Holland Harbor (South Pierhead) Light *Holland* (page 58)

15. South Haven South Pierhead Light *South Haven*

Also known as South Haven Light, the 35-foot cast-iron tower that stands at the end of the pier is cylindrical in shape and red with a black lantern. The keeper's house is located near the foot of the pier, where there is a good view of the light. There is a raised catwalk to the tower, which was built in 1903. The grounds are open to the public.

Grand Haven South Pierhead Lights

Grand Haven Siblings

This is a pair of range lights connected on one pier by an elevated catwalk. Grand Haven Inner Light, a 51-foot, red, conical cast-iron tower (1907) has a red light that occults every 4 seconds. Grand Haven Outer Light (c. 1905) is a lantern set on the roof of a square, red fog-signal building that stands 36 feet tall, its light flashing red every 10 seconds. Visitors can reach the pier and the lighthouses via South Harbor Drive; they can be viewed from the beach or pier.

ABOVE: The water side of the outer tower's base is V-shaped, to deflect the force of incoming waves and ice.

BELOW, LEFT: The lights at sunset.

Description: Inner: conical cast-iron tower; Outer: square cast-iron-clad fog-signal building

Markings: Inner: red with red lantern; Outer: red with red lantern

Lens: Inner: 250 mm; Outer: 190 mm

Height: Inner: 51 feet (tower), 52 feet (focal plane); Outer: 36 feet (tower), 42 feet (focal plane)

Holland Harbor Light

Big Red

Also known as Big Red, this red, square wooden tower reaches to 32 feet above an integral red, brick, two-story, twin-gabled keeper's dwelling. The main building, which also housed the fog signal, dates from 1907, but the tower was only added in 1936, replacing a free-standing light. The lighthouse is not open to the public, but visitors can walk to the pier via a boardwalk in Holland State Park. Security guards from the Macatawa Cottagers Association, posted at the end of South Shore Drive, will also provide a day-entry card to visitors who wish to get close to the lighthouse, but visits are limited to one hour.

ABOVE, RIGHT, AND BELOW:
Three different views of the famous lighthouse.

Description: square wooden tower; integral rectangular, twin-gabled, brick keeper's dwelling
Markings: red; red lantern
Lens: 250 mm
Height: 32 feet (tower); 52 feet (focal plane)

ABOVE: *St. Joseph North Pierhead Lights.*

16. St. Joseph North Pierhead Lights/St. Joseph Inner and Outer Pier Lights *St. Joseph*

Connected by a catwalk, these two lights form a pair of range lights. The 35-foot outer light (1906) is a white, cylindrical cast-iron tower, its black lantern housing the original fifth-order Fresnel (still active). The 57-foot inner tower (1907) is a cast-iron octagonal tower (white with black lantern) on top of a square fog-signal building (white with red roof). The original fourth-order Fresnel lens is still in use today. Visitors can walk to the pier from Tiscornia City Park, Benton Harbor.

INDIANA

17. Old Michigan City Light *Michigan City*

Built in 1858, Old Michigan City Light was deactivated in 1904. Its white wooden tower rises to 34 feet on top of a brick keeper's dwelling. Today, it functions as a maritime museum in Washington Park.

18. Michigan City Breakwater Light *Michigan City Harbor*

Built in 1911, this is a white square-pyramidal tower with a red horizontal band. With a focal-plane height of 36 feet, the light emits a red flash every 4 seconds. It is closed to the public, but can be seen from the Michigan City East Pierhead Light.

ABOVE: *Michigan City (East) Pierhead Light, with catwalk in the foreground.*

19. Michigan City (East) Pierhead Light *Michigan City*

This light replaced the Old Michigan City Light in 1904, but the keeper here continued to use the old light's quarters. Standing 49 feet tall, this white, octagonal steel tower (with black lantern) is situated on top of a square, white, brick fog signal building (with red roof), and is still an active aid to navigation. It can be seen from the marina on Lakeshore Drive, Michigan City, near the Old Michigan City Lighthouse.

20. Gary (West) Breakwater Light *Gary Harbor, Gary*

This red, tapered steel tower was constructed at the end of a very long breakwater (West Pier) in 1911. An active aid to navigation, its optic emits three red flashes every 40 seconds, but views from shore are blocked by a number of steel plants. The grounds are open to the public, but it is best viewed by boat.

21. Buffington (Harbor) Breakwater Light *Buffington*

At the end of a long, private industrial breakwall, this light, built in 1926, is best seen by boat. The red, conical steel tower sits on a round concrete foundation and has a focal-plane height of 48 feet (its light flashing red every 4 seconds). An active private aid to navigation, it is not open to the public.

SPOTTER'S NOTE

The Indiana Harbor East Breakwater Light is almost identical to Port Washington Breakwater Light in Wisconsin (*see* page 66).

22. Indiana Harbor East Breakwater Light

Indiana Harbor, East Chicago

Constructed in 1935, this 75-foot, white, square, Art Deco steel tower is still an active aid to navigation with an isophase green light. Not open to the public, it is best seen by boat.

ILLINOIS

23. 68th Street (Dunne) Crib Light   *Chicago*
Located on a crib built for South Chicago's water intake, this 50-foot skeletal tower, with a gray lantern, was built in 1909. The operational light flashes red every 3 seconds and can be seen distantly from Jackson Park.

24. Four Mile Crib Light   *Chicago*
Seen distantly from the Navy Pier, this light is a red, hexagonal skeleton tower atop a water-intake crib. The light is operational with a focal-plane height of 66 feet.

25. (William E.) Dever Crib Light   *Chicago Harbor*
Also known as Harrison–Dever Crib, this light is a square skeletal tower on a large, cylindrical water-intake structure that can be seen from the Chicago waterfront. It is an active aid to navigation (flashing white light, focal plane 72 feet) and is not open to the public.

26. Chicago Harbor Southeast Guidewall Light   *Chicago Harbor*
Marking a breakwall near Chicago's Navy Pier, this 30-foot, steel, square-pyramidal tower (1938) is an active aid to navigation. Its upper half supports a black lantern and is enclosed (painted white at the top and green below), while the lower half is open (skeletal). It is not open to the public, but can be seen from Navy Pier or, for a closer view, by boat.

27. Chicago Harbor Light   *Chicago*
(overleaf)

28. Grosse Point Light   *Evanston*
(page 63)

29. Waukegan Harbor (Little Fort) Light   *Waukegan*
Built in 1889 at the end of Government Pier in Waukegan's harbor, this light is a cylindrical cast-iron tower with no lantern. Its upper part is painted green, and the lower, white. An attached fog-signal building and the lantern room were removed after a fire in 1967. It is an active aid to navigation and not open to the public, but visitors may walk along the pier.

BELOW: *Little Fort Light, the 1849 predecessor to Waukegan Harbor Light.*

Chicago Harbor Light

Description: conical cast-iron tower; integral fog-signal building and boathouse
Markings: white; black trim and lantern roof
Lens: third-order Fresnel
Height: 48 feet (tower); 82 feet (focal plane)

BELOW: *Towers old and new.*

Safe Harbor

Originally built in 1893, this 48-foot tower was moved in 1919 to its present location at the end of the north breakwater in Chicago Harbor. The brick-lined, white, conical cast-iron tower, with its integral, red-roofed keeper's quarters, is an active aid to navigation (focal plane 82 feet) and is not open to the public. While fully automated in 1979, the black-roofed lantern still houses its original third-order Fresnel lens. It is visible from several locations along Chicago's lakeshore, and from some harbor cruises.

Grosse Point Light

LEFT AND BELOW: *This tall making
light has a range of up to 21 miles.*

Chicago Approach

Built on Sheridan Road in 1873 to mark the
approach to Chicago Harbor, this 113-foot, conical
Cream City brick tower (*see* page 64) encased in
concrete is painted cream with red trim and is
attached to a storage building. Other structures
include a three-story brick keeper's house in the
Italianate style, an oil house, storage building, and
a covered walkway that connects the tower with
the dwelling. Now a private navigational aid, the
tower and keeper's house also serve as a museum
(open weekends, June–September, except holi-
days), and visitors may climb the tower.

WISCONSIN

ABOVE, RIGHT: *Kenosha Light.*
BELOW: *Racine Breakwater Light.*
BOTTOM: *Wind Point Light.*

30. Kenosha (Southport) Light
Simmons Island, Kenosha

First lit in 1866, this 55-foot conical tower made of Milwaukee's Cream City brick was deactivated in 1906 but relit in 1996 as a private aid to navigation. The grounds are open to the public.

31. Kenosha Pierhead/North Breakwater Lights *Kenosha*

A 1906 red, conical cast-iron tower replaced Kenosha Light and is still active (focal plane 50 feet). A white cylinder with green band stands on the opposite pier.

32. Racine Breakwater Light *Racine*

Built in 1901 and deactivated in 1987, this 46-foot, red, square steel tower's upper part is enclosed and lower part, open (skeletal). It served as the North Pier Light until 1916 when it was moved to its current breakwater location. It can be seen from a park near Racine's South Pier.

33. Wind Point Light *Racine*

This 108-foot, white, conical brick tower (black trim, red roof) has been operational since its construction in 1880. Automated with a modern optic in 1964, it has a focal-plane height of 111 feet. The tower is attached to a white, brick keeper's house (1880) via a covered walkway and is open to the public for occasional tours.

34. Milwaukee Pierhead Light
Milwaukee

Built in 1906 to replace an 1857 light, this conical, red steel tower with black lantern stands 41
feet tall (focal plane 45 feet). It is an active aid
to navigation, whose fifth-order Fresnel lens
emits a red flash every 4 seconds with a range of
12 miles. It is located at the end of a pier in
Milwaukee Harbor to mark the Milwaukee and
Kinnickinnic river entrances. The light can be
viewed from Milwaukee's Festival Park.

ABOVE: *Milwaukee Pierhead Light.*
BELOW: *Milwaukee Breakwater.*
BOTTOM: *North Point Light.*

35. Milwaukee Breakwater Light
Milwaukee

Built in 1926, at the end of Milwaukee's outer
breakwater, this light tower rises from the
square, white, Art Deco two-story keeper's
quarters. An active aid to navigation, its black
lantern houses a modern optic (focal plane 61
feet, red flash every 10 seconds). It can be
viewed from a pier near Festival Park in
Milwaukee.

36. North Point Light   *Milwaukee*

This octagonal-pyramidal tower was built in
1888 and later raised 35 feet (1913) to a height
of 74 feet. The white lighthouse, with red
lantern (focal plane 154 feet), was deactivated in
1994 but is now a major tourist attraction. It is
located in Lake Park, which was designed by
Frederick Law Olmsted, and the light will be
open for tours from Fall 2005.

37. Kevich Light   *Port Ulao, Grafton*

A 40-foot white stucco-clad tower with black
lantern and attached residence, this light was
built by the Bennett family in 1981 atop a 120-
foot bluff and is a certified navigational aid. Its
alternating white light has a focal-plane height
of 160 feet above sea level. The light is privately
maintained and is not open to the public.

38. Port Washington Breakwater Light *Port Washington*

Located at the end of a breakwater, this 58-foot, square, white Art Deco steel tower curves into a wider base. Built in 1935, its open-arched concrete foundation allows visitors to pass beneath it, though walking on the breakwater can be dangerous. Its lantern room has been removed and a modern beacon emits the signal (focal plane 78 feet).

39. (Old) Port Washington Breakwater Light
Port Washington

This light was built in 1860 (deactivated 1903). Its reconstructed square white tower and black lantern sit atop the original, two-story, unpainted, red-roofed brick keeper's dwelling. Currently a museum, this light station is open to the public in summer.

ABOVE: *Port Washington Breakwater Light.*
BELOW: *Manitowoc Breakwater (Pierhead) Light.*

40. Sheboygan Breakwater Light
Sheboygan

Built in 1915, this active aid to navigation is a red, conical cast-iron tower. Its lantern has been removed and replaced with a modern optic. Visitors can walk along the breakwater from Deland Park, but the tower is closed to the public.

41. Manitowoc Breakwater Light
Manitowoc

Also known as Manitowoc Pierhead Light, this 40-foot, white, cylindrical steel tower (black lantern) and integral square steel keeper's dwelling is located at the end of the northern breakwater in the harbor. Constructed in 1918 and automated in 1971, its fifth-order Fresnel lens has an alternating white signal (focal plane 52 feet). Visitors may walk the breakwater or view the light from the south breakwater, but cannot gain access to the tower.

42. Rawley Point Light   *Two Rivers*

Situated within Point Beach State Forest, this 111-foot, skeletal, white, octagonal-pyramidal cast-iron tower with a two-story watch room and red lantern has been active since 1894 (automated 1979, modern optic, focal plane 113 feet, range 25 miles). Also referred to as Two Rivers Point Light, this tower replaced an earlier brick tower (c. 1873), the bottom part of which is still standing nearby, attached to its two-story, red-roofed, white-painted brick keeper's quarters. Though not open to the public, vacation accommodations in the keeper's dwelling are available to U.S. Coast Guard personnel. Visitors can view the light station from the beach in the state park.

43. Kewaunee Pierhead Light
Kewaunee

This white, steel, rectangular fog-signal building was built in 1909 beside a front range light (1891) at the end of a breakwater on the north side of the Kewaunee River entrance. In 1931, the range light was removed and its red-roofed lantern and fifth-order Fresnel lens were moved onto a 43-foot, white, square steel tower that had been newly constructed on the roof of the fog-signal building. Today, the original lens still shines its fixed white light (focal plane 45 feet). It is closed to the public but can be seen from the shore.

ABOVE: *Rawley Point Light.*
BELOW: *Kewaunee Pierhead Light.*

SPOTTER'S NOTE
Rawley Point Light was originally erected in Chicago and displayed at the 1893 Columbian Exposition before being moved to its present site in 1894.

ABOVE: *Sturgeon Bay Canal Light.*
BELOW: *Sturgeon Bay Ship Canal North Pierhead Light.*
BOTTOM: *Cana Island Light.*

44. Algoma Pierhead (Front) Light
Algoma

Originally built in 1908, this red, conical steel tower was raised in 1932 to its present height of 48 feet by adding a red, cylindrical steel base. Located at the end of a breakwater on the north side of the Ahnapee River entrance, it is still operational; it is best viewed from the southern breakwater.

45. Sturgeon Bay Canal Light
Sturgeon Bay

First lit in 1899, this is a steel cylinder supported by eight latticed buttresses, topped with a watch room and black cast-iron lantern. It was painted white in 1900, and in 1903 steel legs were added to give the pyramidal skeletal form as it is today. Still active, the 98-foot lighthouse is open to the public during the annual Door County Lighthouse Walk, held in late May.

46. Sturgeon Bay Ship Canal North Pierhead Light
Sturgeon Bay

This red, cylindrical cast-iron tower (1903) rises to 39 feet above a red, square steel fog-signal building at the canal's entrance. A raised catwalk leads to the light, which is an active aid to navigation. The light can be viewed from the south pierhead or from Portage Park.

47. Bailey's Harbor Range Lights
Bailey's Harbor (opposite)

48. Cana Island Light
Cana Island, eastern Door Peninsula

Built of Cream City brick c. 1870, this 81-foot, white conical tower was encased in steel in 1902. The light is still active, and the attached brick keeper's quarters and oil house serve as a museum. A rock causeway (sometimes flooded) for pedestrians connects the island to the mainland.

Bailey's Harbor Range Lights

Old Baileys

Established in 1870, the Bailey's Harbor Range Front Light is no longer operational. Its white-painted, octagonal wooden lantern atop a square wooden tower once housed a fifth-order Fresnel lens (focal plane 22 feet). Bailey's Harbor Range Rear Light (1870) is a 35-foot clapboard keeper's dwelling; its original fifth-order Fresnel lens (deactivated 1969 but still in place) once shone from the cupola. The lights are located in the Ridges Wildlife Sanctuary, which is open to visitors.

ABOVE: *The front light.*

ABOVE, LEFT: *The rear light.*

Description: Front: octagonal wooden lantern on square wooden tower; Rear: clapboard keeper's dwelling with cupola

Markings: Front: white with green roof; Rear: white with red roof

Lens: Front: fifth-order Fresnel; Rear: fifth-order Fresnel

Height: Front: 21 feet (tower), 22 feet (focal plane); Rear: 35 feet (tower), 39 feet (focal plane)

LEFT: *Old Bailey's Harbor Light was replaced by the range lights after only seventeen years of service.*

49. Pilot Island Light *Pilot Island, off the tip of Door Peninsula*
Previously known as Port des Morts Light, this square tower with black lantern rises to 41 feet above the red roof of the Cream City brick keeper's dwelling (1873). An active navigational aid (modern optic, focal plane 48 feet), it is not open to the public, but can be seen from the Northport–Washington Island ferry.

50. Boyer Bluff Light *Washington Island, off the tip of Door Peninsula*
Located on the northwest corner of the island, this 80-foot, square-pyramidal steel skeletal tower has a focal-plane height of 220 feet and is an active aid to navigation (white flash every 6 seconds).

51. Plum Island Range Lights *Plum Island, off tip of Door Peninsula*
The front range light is a white, square-pyramidal steel skeletal tower with a red-and-white daymark. Constructed in 1964, it is an active aid to navigation (alternating red signal, focal plane 41 feet). The rear light is a 65-foot, white, square-pyramidal, iron skeletal tower with a red-roofed lantern. Built in 1897, its original fourth-order Fresnel lens (focal plane 80 feet) is still in use. The lights can be seen from the Northport–Washington Island ferry.

52. Pottawatomie Light *Rock Island*
This was Wisconsin's first federal lighthouse station on Lake Michigan. Situated in Rock Island State Park, its square limestone tower with black lantern rises to 41 feet atop a red-roofed limestone keeper's dwelling. Built in 1858 and deactivated in 1988, the light station is currently under restoration and open for public tours. Rock Island is accessible via passenger ferry from Washington Island.

53. Chamber's Island Light *Chamber's Island*
This lighthouse (1868) is an octagonal Cream City brick tower (lantern removed) integrated with the brick keeper's house. Deactivated in 1961, it is occasionally open for public tours in the summer and fall.

Below: *Eagle Bluff Light.*

54. Eagle Bluff Light *Peninsula State Park, between Fish Creek and Ephraim*
Built in 1868, this square Cream City brick tower with a red-roofed black lantern stands 43 feet tall and is attached to a Cream City brick keeper's dwelling. A modern solar-powered optic mounted on the gallery produces a white flash every 6 seconds. The keeper's dwelling now functions as a maritime museum, and public tours are offered.

55. Sherwood Point Light
Sherwood Point, near Idlewild

Built in 1883, this 37-foot, square, white brick tower with a red roof is attached to a keeper's dwelling. Its modern optic emits an alternating white light. The light station is sometimes open to visitors during the Door County Lighthouse Walk, which takes place in May.

56. Grassy Island Range Lights
Green Bay

Originally located at the entrance to Green Bay Harbor, these lights were moved to Green Bay Yacht Club when they were deactivated in 1966. Both are white square-pyramidal towers with black lanterns, built in 1872. The lights can be seen from the Coast Guard building at the end of Bay Beach Road.

57. Green Bay (Harbor) Entrance Light   *offshore, Green Bay*

Located in the middle of the bay, this white, cylindrical, Art Deco steel tower with a black lantern was built on a concrete caisson in 1935. An active navigational aid (focal plane 72 feet), it can be seen by boat.

58. Peshtigo Reef Light   *offshore, Green Bay*

A conical steel tower (painted white with a red central band) on a concrete crib, this light was built in 1934. An active aid to navigation, it is best seen from the water or air.

59. Green Island Light   *Green Island*

Located in Green Bay, off Marinette, this 1863 lighthouse is now in ruins. A short wooden tower stands on the roof of a two-story brick keeper's dwelling to a height of 48 feet. The light is not open to the public, and must be viewed from the water or air.

ABOVE: *Sherwood Point Light.*

SPOTTER'S NOTE
Automated in 1983, Sherwood Point was the last staffed lighthouse on the Great Lakes.

BELOW: *Green Bay Entrance Light.*

SPOTTER'S NOTE
Long Tail Point Light in Green Bay was a 65-foot, conical stone tower (built 1849, deactivated 1849). Abandoned and decaying, with no lantern, the remains can be seen by boat or air.

MICHIGAN, WESTERN SHORE

60. Menominee (North Pier) Light
Menominee

Also known as Marinette North Pierhead Light, this rises to 34 feet on a white base. Built in 1927, the red, octagonal cast-iron tower with black lantern is still operational, using a modern optic. Visitors may view the light from the pier.

61. Minneapolis Shoal Light
offshore, entrance to Little Bay de Noc

Located south of Peninsula Point on a concrete crib, this octagonal, Art Deco concrete tower built above the keeper's quarters rises to 70 feet. Built in 1935, it is painted white with a red central band and black lantern. Still active, it can be seen distantly from the tip of Peninsula Point.

ABOVE: *Menominee Light.*

62. Sand Point (Escanaba) Light   *Ludington Park, Escanaba*

Attached to a keeper's dwelling, this square white tower, with red-roofed black lantern, stands 41 feet tall. Built in 1868, it was deactivated in 1939 but relit in 1989; it is now also a museum (open daily).

63. Peninsula Point Light   *Stonington Peninsula*

This square, unpainted brick tower (1866) stands 40 feet high and has a black lantern. Deactivated in 1936, it is open to the public and can be found in Hiawatha National Forest.

RIGHT: *Sand Point Light.*
BELOW: *Peninsula Point Light.*

64. St. Martin Island Light

St. Martin Island

Built in 1905, this is a white, hexagonal iron tower, supported by six exterior steel posts and latticed buttresses, and topped with a black lantern; it is unlike any other Great Lakes light. Standing 75 feet tall, its modern optic flashes an alternating white and red light (focal plane 84 feet). The light must be viewed from the water as the island is privately owned.

65. Poverty Island Light

Poverty Island

This lighthouse is a 60-foot white, conical brick tower without a lantern. Deactivated 1976–82, a small modern optic now sits on a pole atop the tower (focal plane 80 feet). The light is in poor condition and is closed to the public.

ABOVE: *Manistique (East Breakwater) Light.*
BELOW: *Seul Choix Pointe Light.*

66. Manistique (East Breakwater) Light *Manistique*

This 35-foot, red, square-pyramidal steel tower with a black lantern was first lit in 1917. Automated in 1969, its modern optic shines at a focal-plane height of 50 feet above sea level. Visitors can view the light from the end of the breakwater (near the entrance to the Manistique River); there is no public access to the tower.

67. Seul Choix Pointe Light

southeast of Gulliver

"Seul Choix" translates as "only choice," reflecting the fact that this is the only harbor of refuge in this area. The light station consists of a 78-foot, white, conical brick tower with an attached brick keeper's house (1892) and various outbuildings. Built in 1895, this lighthouse is still an active aid to navigation: its red-roofed lantern holds a modern optic (focal plane 80 feet). The keeper's dwelling is now a museum and gift shop, and visitors may climb the tower.

LAKE WINNEBAGO

Lake Winnebago, Wisconsin, lies upriver from (southwest of) Green Bay.

1. Calumet Harbor Light
Columbia Park, near Pipe

This 70-foot, square-pyramidal, steel skeletal tower was originally used as a water tower at the Fond du Lac table factory. It was moved to its present location in 1936 and is now a private navigational aid and observation tower. A smaller, hourglass-shaped tower once stood nearby, but was removed in 2003. The park is open to the public.

2. Fond du Lac Light   *Fond du Lac*

Located in Lakeside Park, this 56-foot, white, octagonal wooden tower was built in 1933 atop a masonry foundation and now operates as a private aid to navigation (flashing red light). It is open to the public in summer.

ABOVE: *Fond du Lac Light.*
BELOW: *Neenah Lighthouse.*

3. Brays Point (Rockwell) Light
Oshkosh

This 42-foot, octagonal brick tower (1909) has white trim and is topped with an ornate iron lantern. It is a private aid to navigation on the north side of the Fox River entrance. Closed to the public, it can be seen from the street nearby.

4. Asylum Point Lighthouse   *Oshkosh*

This 31-foot, conical stone tower, built in 1940, is no longer operational. Visitors can access Asylum Point County Park, where the light is situated.

5. Neenah (Kimberly Point) Lighthouse   *Neenah*

Located in Kimberly Point Park, on the south side of the Fox River entrance, this white, octagonal-pyramidal brick tower was privately built in 1945; it has black-roofed porches on either side. Visitors cannot climb the tower.

LAKE SUPERIOR

Some of the loneliest light stations in the United States are those that light up the largest freshwater lake on the planet. With more than fifty historic beacons, every lighthouse type is represented here.

MICHIGAN

1. Middle Neebish Front Range Light *Neebish Island*

Also known as Lower Nicolet West Range Front Light, this tower was relocated from Windmill Point, Detroit, to its current location in 1931. The red, cylindrical steel tower reaches a height of 55 feet and dates from 1907. Standing next to a skeletal tower, it is no longer in use, not open to the public, and best viewed from the water.

ABOVE: *Point Iroquois Light.*
BELOW: *Whitefish Point Light.*

2. Point Iroquois Light *near Bay Mills*

Beautifully restored, with a museum in the keeper's house, this station stands within Hiawatha National Forest. The 65-foot white, conical brick tower is attached to the keeper's dwelling (1902) and is crowned by a black lantern (focal plane 68 feet). Built in 1871, and deactivated a century later, its original fourth-order Fresnel lens is now held at the Smithsonian Institution, Washington, D.C. Visitors may climb the tower.

3. Whitefish Point Light *Whitefish Bay, near Paradise*

Situated in the so-called "Graveyard of the Great Lakes," this is the oldest active light-house on Lake Superior. The current white, square-pyramidal cast-iron skeletal tower replaced an older stone structure in 1861. At a height of 76 feet, the tower has a focal plane of 80 feet and its red-roofed, black lantern holds a DCB-24 lens (flashing white light). The station also houses the Great Lakes Shipwreck Museum and a bird observatory. Visitors can tour the beautifully restored 1861 keeper's house that is attached to the tower, or even stay overnight in one of the restored U.S. Coast Guard crew's lodgings.

4. Crisp Point Light *Paradise*

This 58-foot, white, conical brick tower overlooks a beautiful stretch of coastline, 18 miles off the main road. Built in 1904, the tower was deactivated and restored in the 1990s. The red-roofed black lantern no longer holds an optic. The grounds of the light are open to the public.

5. Grand Marais Harbor Range Lights *Grand Marais*

Also known as Grand Marais Harbor of Refuge Inner and Outer Lights, these two white, square-pyramidal steel skeletal towers (upper sections enclosed) are still active aids to navigation. They were built in 1898 and 1895, to heights of 55 and 34 feet respectively. The inner range light still holds its original fifth-order Fresnel lens, while the outer now holds a modern optic. The grounds are open to the public, and the 1908 keeper's dwelling now houses a museum (open summer, hours vary).

6. Au Sable (Point) Light *near Grand Marais*

This lighthouse is within the Pictured Rocks National Lakeshore, overlooking Lake Superior's most dangerous coastline. Its 86-foot, white, conical brick tower has been restored to its 1910 appearance, though it and the attached, two-story, unpainted brick keeper's dwelling date from 1874. Automated in 1958, its black cast-iron lantern now holds a 300-mm solar-powered lens (focal plane 107 feet). Still operational, this light is open to the public, with guided tours available in summer.

7. Grand Island North (Old North) Light *Grand Island, off Munising*

Standing 40 feet high, this schoolhouse-style light had an impressive range due to its elevation on a dramatic 175-foot cliff. Its white, square brick tower with black lantern and trim is attached to a brick keeper's house that is painted yellow. Built in 1867, and deactivated in 1961 when its signal was transferred to a post-mounted optic, it is now a private residence, closed to the public, and can only be viewed from the air. Grand Island is a National Recreation Area served by passenger ferries.

BELOW: *Au Sable Light.*

8. Grand Island East Channel Light *Grand Island, off Munising*

Also known as South Light, this square, unpainted wooden tower with a cast-iron lantern and attached keeper's house was built on brick foundations in 1870. Replaced in 1908 by a pair of range lights at Munising, and abandoned in 1913, it subsequently fell into severe disrepair. It is still not in use and not open to the public, but there has been some recent preservation work at the site. Various boat tours offering views of the lighthouse depart from Munising.

9. Munising Range Lights *Munising*

Operational since 1908 (see Grand Island East Channel Light), the front range light is a red-roofed, 58-foot, white, conical steel tower (modern optic, fixed red light, focal plane 79 feet). A two-story brick keeper's house stands nearby. The rear range light (also 1908) is similar in structure and signal to the front range light, but shorter, at only 33 feet. Situated within Pictured Rocks National Lakeshore, the grounds of these lights are open to the public.

ABOVE: *The old Grand Island East Channel Light.*

10. Christmas Light *Christmas*

Also known as Grand Island Harbor Rear Range Light, this 64-foot, conical steel tower was built in 1914, its upper 32 feet consisting of a tower from Vidal Shoals, on the Upper St. Mary's River, that had been decommissioned and transported here. The lower section is painted black, the top, white, and the light that shone from its black lantern had a focal plane height of 72 feet. The lighthouse grounds are open to the public, and the tower can also be seen from the shore at Christmas or from the water.

11. Marquette Breakwater *Marquette*

This square-pyramidal skeletal tower, whose upper part is enclosed, is located at the end of the breakwater in Marquette Harbor. For a while it held Marquette Harbor Light's original fourth-order Fresnel lens, which is now on display at Marquette Maritime Museum.

12. Marquette Harbor Light *Marquette* *(overleaf)*

Marquette Harbor Light

Description: square brick tower; attached keeper's house
Markings: red; white lantern
Lens: DCB-24 aerobeacon
Height: 40 feet (tower); 77 feet (focal plane)

BELOW: *Marquette Harbor Light.*

Harbor View

Built in 1866, this square, red-painted brick tower, with white lantern, rises to a height of 40 feet and is attached to a two-story brick keeper's house (also painted red). An active aid to navigation, its modern optic, which replaced a fourth-order Fresnel lens, emits a white flash every 10 seconds (focal plane 77 feet). This lighthouse is leased to the Marquette Maritime Museum, and tours are offered seasonally (although the grounds are open year-round). The museum is located at the corner of Lakeshore Road and Ridge Street in Marquette.

13. Presque Isle Breakwater Light
near Marquette
Built in 1941 at the end of a 2,600-foot breakwater in Presque Isle Park, this is a cylindrical steel-and-concrete tower, painted white with a central red band. An active aid to navigation, its grounds are open to the public.

14. Big Bay Point Light *Big Bay*
This square red-brick tower with a red-roofed white lantern stands 65 feet tall and is attached to a brick duplex keeper's dwelling. Built in 1896, automated in 1941, and deactivated from 1961 to 1990, this light is an active aid to navigation once more. It is also a bed-and-breakfast inn (open year-round). The grounds are open daily, and guided tours of the light are available three days a week from May to September.

ABOVE: *Big Bay Point Light, with its castlelike tower.*

15. Granite Island Light *Granite Island, off Marquette*
Built in 1869, this schoolhouse-style light consists of a 40-foot, square granite tower with a black cast-iron lantern attached to a two-story granite-and-limestone keeper's dwelling. Abandoned in 1939, it fell into severe disrepair until rescued by a private buyer in 1999. One of the oldest surviving lighthouses on Lake Superior, it has been fully restored in recent years, but is closed to the public and not operational. It is best viewed from the water.

16. Stannard Rock Light *offshore,*
24 miles southeast of Manitou Island
Standing an impressive 110 feet tall, this lighthouse was built in 1882 on a submerged offshore reef in an exposed location; it is therefore considered an important achievement in engineering. The conical stone tower stands on a cylindrical concrete crib, and its black lantern now holds a modern optic (focal plane 102 feet, range 18 miles). The keeper's quarters are integral to the tower, the interior of which was badly damaged by a fire in 1961. It is not open to the public, but Keweenaw Excursions offers cruises that pass the lighthouse.

SPOTTER'S NOTE
Stannard Rock, lying about 23 miles southeast of Manitou Island, was for years the most serious hazard to navigation in Lake Superior. The rock was first marked by a day beacon in 1868, but by 1871 the rapid increase in commerce between Duluth and the lower lakes demanded the construction of a lighthouse on the rock.

17. Huron Island Light   *Lighthouse Island*

Constructed from granite in 1877, this 39-foot, unpainted square tower with a white lantern is attached to a two-story granite keeper's dwelling. An active aid to navigation, its modern oscillator light has a focal-plane height of 197 feet. The lighthouse is closed to the public, but Lighthouse Island can be visited during daylight hours by private boat. Keweenaw Excursions also offers cruises that pass by.

18. Sand Point (Baraga) Light   *Baraga*

Built in 1878, this lighthouse was moved 200 feet inland twenty years later, and an automated light on a skeletal tower was erected in its original place. The square brick tower is topped by a white lantern and attached to a brick keeper's dwelling. Deactivated in the 1920s or '30s, it is now privately owned and closed to the public.

19. Portage River (Jacobsville) Light   *Jacobsville*

Also known as Jacobsville Light, this 1870 lighthouse has stood inactive since 1900. Currently privately owned, it is not open to the public and is best viewed by boat. The white, conical brick tower stands 45 feet tall and is crowned with a red lantern. It is attached to a red-brick keeper's house via a covered walkway.

BELOW: *Mendota Light.*

20. Mendota (Bete Grise) Light   *Bete Grise*

Built in 1895, this 44-foot, square yellow-brick tower is topped with a black lantern and attached to a T–shaped brick keeper's house. Deactivated in 1960, its original fourth order Fresnel lens was restored and returned to the lantern in 1998, and the beacon has been relighted as a private aid to navigation. The light station is open to the public by appointment only, but can be viewed from the water.

21. Gull Rock Light   *off the tip of Keeweenaw Peninsula*

This 46-foot square, white-painted Cream City brick tower and attached 2-story yellow brick keeper's dwelling was built in 1867 and is of the schoolhouse style. An active navigational aid, its modern optic shines from the black lantern at a focal plane height of 50 feet. It is not open to the public, but Keweenaw Excursions offers occasional cruises that pass by.

ABOVE: *The schoolhouse-style Copper Harbor Light replaced an 1848 stone tower.*

22. Manitou Island Light

Manitou Island

This square-pyramidal, iron skeletal tower with a central column was built in 1861 and is attached to a two-story keeper's dwelling via an enclosed passageway. The tower stands 80 feet tall and is still an active aid to navigation: its red-roofed white lantern holds a modern optic (focal plane 81 feet). It is not open to the public, but boat tours are occasionally available.

SPOTTER'S NOTE

Manitou Island Light is the oldest skeletal tower on the Great Lakes, along with the one at Whitefish Point. After the opening of the Soo Locks in 1855, it played an important role in growth of the Michigan copper industry.

23. Copper Harbor Light   *Copper Harbor*

Now part of Fort Wilkins State Historic Park, this schoolhouse-style light was built in 1866 and is a 62-foot, unpainted, square brick tower with a red-roofed, black lantern, attached to a keeper's dwelling. It was deactivated in 1933 when an automated light on a skeletal tower was erected nearby. The keeper's dwelling now houses a museum (open in summer), and access is by boats that depart from Copper Harbor Marina during the summer.

24. **Copper Harbor Rear Range Light** *Copper Harbor*

The red-roofed, wood-frame keeper's dwelling was built in 1869, and its light shone from a square cupola. It was deactivated in 1964, when a steel skeletal tower was erected nearby. A smaller tower replaced the front light in 1927. Located in Fort Williams State Park, the building is privately owned, but visitors have access to the grounds.

25. **Eagle Harbor Light** *Eagle Harbor*

This 44-foot, octagonal, white-painted brick tower attached to a red-roofed brick keeper's dwelling was built in 1871. An active aid to navigation, its red-roofed black lantern holds an automated modern optic (focal plane 60 feet). The keeper's house is now a museum, open seven days from mid-June through early October.

26. **Eagle Harbor Rear Range Light** *Eagle Harbor*

The original 1877 range lights were deactivated in 1911 when their optics were transferred to metal towers. The front range light was subsequently destroyed. The rear range light, also known as Cedar Creek Range Rear Light, was sold at auction to a private bidder who moved the structure from its original location in 1932. When operational, the light shone from the window of a cupola on the roof of the dwelling that is now a private home. It is not open to the public.

27. **Eagle River Light** *Eagle River*

Built in 1857, this is a white, square brick tower, topped with a white lantern, and integral red-roofed, white keeper's house. Deactivated in 1908, it is now a private residence and not open to the public. The light can, however, be seen from the main road that runs through Eagle River.

28. **Sand Hills Light** *Eagle River* *(opposite)*

BELOW: *Keepers at Eagle Harbor Light were sometimes able to see the Northern Lights.*

Sand Hills Light

Old Soldier

Also known as Five Mile Point Light, this is a square brick tower with a black lantern, built in 1919, rising to 91 feet above a large brick keeper's dwelling. The lighthouse was commissioned when the shoreline at nearby Eagle Point became filled in, so that the light there was no longer effective. Automated in 1939, the station was used as a barracks during World War II, and was deactivated in 1954. Fully restored in the 1990s, it is now open as a bed-and-breakfast inn, which is decorated with lighthouse artifacts and paintings. Visitors can tour the tower at certain times during the summer

ABOVE: *This historic structure was the last manned lighthouse built on the Great Lakes.*

Description: square brick tower; integral keeper's dwelling
Markings: yellow; black lantern
Lens: fourth-order Fresnel
Height: 91 feet (tower); 91 feet (focal plane)

ABOVE: *Keweenau Waterway Upper Entrance Light.*

29. Keweenau Waterway Upper Entrance Light *near Houghton*

Also known as Portage Lake Ship Canal Light, this light was built in 1950 at the end of a breakwater at the western end of the Keweenaw Waterway, which bisects the Keweenaw Penninsula. Rising to a height of 82 feet, it is a white, steel, tapering square tower built above a white concrete fog signal building that sits on a red caisson foundation. An active aid to navigation, which exhibits a white flash every 15 seconds, it is not open to the public. It is best viewed from across the waterway near the end of Houghton Canal Road.

30. Keweenau Waterway Lower Entrance Light *Jacobsville*

Located on a crib at the end of a breakwater on the east pier at the entrance to the Portage River near Jacobsville, this 31-foot, white, octagonal brick tower was built in 1920. It is also known as Portage River Lower Entrance Light or Portage Lake Lower Entrance Light. An active aid to navigation, the original fourth-order Fresnel lens shines from its red lantern at a focal-plane height of 68 feet. The light can be seen from the parking lot next to the pier, and Keweenaw Excursions offers cruises that pass this lighthouse.

31. Fourteen Mile Point Light *east of Ontonagon*

This lighthouse, which was built in 1894 and deactivated 1934, was gutted by fire in 1984, and the present owners are working to restore the buildings. The castlelike, square brick tower stands 55 feet tall and is integral to the large brick keeper's dwelling. A circular watch room supported the lantern. The light station is not open to the public and is best viewed by boat.

32. Ontonagon West Pierhead Light *Ontonagon*

Built in 1897 at the end of Ontonagon's west pier, this is a white, square-pyramidal, partly skeletal steel tower with a black lantern that stands 20 feet tall (focal plane 31 feet). An active navigational aid, it is not open to the public, but can be viewed from the Ontonagon Light.

33. Ontonagon Light *Ontonagon*

First lit in 1866 and deactivated in 1964, this schoolhouse-style light is made of yellow brick. Its square tower, with black lantern, stands 34 feet high and is attached to a one-and-a-half story brick keeper's house. Other structures on the premises include an oil house and a privy. It is not open to the public, but can be viewed by appointment.

BELOW: *Ontonagon Light.*

WISCONSIN

ABOVE: *Ashland Breakwater Light.*

34. Ashland (Harbor) Breakwater Light *Ashland*

Built in 1915, this light is located at the end of a detached breakwater that extends from near Ashland far out into Chequamegon Bay. The structure is made of reinforced concrete and steel; it is white with a black lantern and stands 58 feet high. The upper part of the tower is cylindrical, the main section, hexagonal. A keeper's dwelling and a boathouse were built onshore in 1916. There are also living quarters located on the second and third stories of the tower. It is an active aid to navigation but not open to the public.

35. Chequamegon Point Light *Bayfield*

Built in 1896, this light was moved away from the shore by 150 feet in 1987 and replaced by a cylindrical tower nearby. Standing 42 feet tall, this tower is made of iron, is white, square-pyramidal in shape, and has an enclosed workroom on the lower level. It is not operational and now abandoned. The light is within park boundaries and the grounds are accessible to the public.

36. LaPointe (Long Island) Light *Bayfield*

This light was built in 1896 to replace an old wooden tower (1858) on this site. The ruins of the old light and its keeper's dwelling still remain near the new tower. The present light is a white skeletal tower with central column that stands 65 feet tall. This is one of the oldest skeletal lights on the Great Lakes. The grounds are open to the public.

37. Michigan Island New Light *Bayfield*

This tower was moved from its original location in Pennsylvania in 1919 and was reassembled ten years later on Michigan Island to replace the earlier light. The white steel skeletal tower stands 118 feet high and has a focal-plane height of 170 feet. The grounds are open to the public.

38. Michigan Island Old Light *Bayfield*

This 1857 light is a 64-foot, whitewashed, conical masonry tower with black lantern, connected to a keeper's house. Originally built in the wrong location, this tower was not used until twelve years after construction. Deactivated in 1929, the light is open to the public in summer.

39. Gull Island Light   *St. James*

This skeletal tower stands 73 feet tall on an islet off Michigan Island. It is an active aid to navigation, flashing white every 6 seconds, and best seen by boat.

40. Outer Island Light   *Bayfield*

This 90-foot, white, conical brick tower (1874), with black trim and lantern (focal plane 129 feet), is attached to a wood-frame keeper's house via a covered passageway. The lighthouse and its outbuildings are endangered by the erosion of the bluff on which they stand. It is an active navigational aid, and its grounds are open to visitors.

41. Devils Island Light   *Bayfield*

This square-pyramidal cast-iron tower, standing 71 feet tall, was built in 1898. There is an 1891 Queen Anne–style keeper's house nearby. An active aid to navigation, and an attraction in a national park, the tower is open to the public in summer.

42. Raspberry Island Light   *Bayfield*

Located in The Apostle Islands National Lakeshore, Raspberry Island Light (1863) is under restoration and endangered due to bluff erosion. Made of wood, with a square, white tower and black lantern, the tower rises to 35 feet above the integral two-story, red-roofed keeper's house. It is open to the public.

43. Sand Island Light   *Bayfield*

A Gothic, octagonal, 40-foot tower of red-brown sandstone, this light was built in 1881. The attached keeper's quarters are Norman Gothic in style. This is an active aid to navigation that also serves as a national park attraction. Volunteer keepers offer guided tours in the summer.

> **SPOTTER'S NOTE**
> The Apostle Islands National Lakeshore has more lighthouses than any other national park.

RIGHT: *A period photograph of Sand Island Light. The island can be visited by private boat, or on a lighthouse cruise offered during September each year.*

44. Wisconsin Point/Superior Harbor Entry Light *Superior*

Also known as Superior South Light, this is a white, concrete, cylindrical tower, with a red-roofed lantern, attached to a cylindrical fog-signal building. Built in 1913, the tower rises to 56 feet. The light is an active aid to navigation and is located at the end of a breakwater that marks the entrance to Superior Bay. It is closed to visitors, but can be seen from near the breakwater.

ABOVE: *Wisconsin Point Light.*

MINNESOTA

45 to 47. Duluth Breakwater Lights *Duluth* *(opposite)*

48. Two Harbors East Breakwater Light *Two Harbors*

Also known as Two Harbors Breakwater Light, this is a short (25 feet), square-pyramidal, steel skeletal light with its upper part enclosed, painted white with black trim. Built in 1897, it is still active and can be seen from the breakwater.

SPOTTER'S NOTE
Located in Duluth, only aproximately half of the abandoned conical brick tower of Minnesota Point Light still exists today. Built in 1856 and deactivated in 1913, visitors can hike to this ruined tower.

LEFT: *Two Harbors East Breakwater Light flashes red every 6 seconds and has a range of 11 miles.*

Duluth Breakwater Lights

Description: South, inner: square-pyramidal skeletal steel tower; South, outer: cylindrical brick tower and integral fog-signal building; North: conical steel tower

Markings: South, inner: black with white lantern; South, outer: white with red roofs; North: white with black base and lantern

Lens: South (both): fourth-order Fresnel; North: fifth-order Fresnel

Height: South, inner: 67 feet (tower); South, outer: 35 feet (tower); North: 37 feet (tower)

Duluth South Breakwater Inner Light

Located near the southern end of the lift bridge in Duluth, this light was important in the development of the port. A square-pyramidal skeletal steel structure with a central cylinder, the tower was built in 1901. It stands 67 feet high and is black with a white lantern. It is still an active aid to navigation.

Duluth South Breakwater Outer Light

A 35-foot, white, cylindrical brick tower with a red roof, located on top of a fog-signal building, this light was built in 1901 and is an active aid to navigation. There is a keeper's house located onshore.

Duluth Harbor North Breakwater Light

This 37-foot tower marks the entrance to the canal in Duluth. Built in 1910, the tower has a black base and lantern, its body painted white. It is still an active navigational aid.

ABOVE, LEFT: The south breakwater inner light.
BELOW: The south breakwater outer light.
BOTTOM: The north breakwater light.

ABOVE: *The flashing signal of Two Harbors Light is today generated by a DCB-224 aerobeacon.*

49. Two Harbors Light *Two Harbors*

A red-brick structure with white trim, this is a handsome light located between Agate and Burlington Bays. The 1892 tower stands 50 feet high and is integral with the keeper's house. Other buildings include a storage building, fog-signal building, an assistant keeper's house (1892), an oil house, and a garage (1936). It is an active aid to navigation (focal plane 78 feet), a museum, and a bed-and-breakfast inn.

50. Split Rock Light *Two Harbors*
(*opposite*)

51. Grand Marais Light *Grand Marais*

A steel, white skeletal tower standing 34 feet high, this 1922 light is an active navigational aid situated on a concrete pier. The grounds are open to the public, and there is a keeper's house onshore (1885) that is now used as a museum.

Split Rock Light

Description: octagonal masonry tower
Markings: buff with white trim; black lantern
Lens: third-order bivalve Fresnel
Height: 54 feet (tower); 168 feet (focal plane)

ABOVE: *The diaphone foghorns.*
LEFT: *The famous landmark sits 130 feet above the lake.*
BELOW: *The bivalve lens and view.*

Split Personality

Located in Split Rock Park, this magnificently sited light has been restored to its 1920s appearance. The octagonal-pyramidal tower is made of Cream City brick and reinforced concrete, with white trim. It stands 54 feet high and had a focal plane of 168 feet. A keeper's dwelling remains on the site, as well as three additional keeper's houses (1909), two storage barns (1909), a tram house (1915), and a pumphouse. Deactivated in 1969, it is now a museum and one of the nation's most spectacular tourist attractions.

MICHIGAN, ISLE ROYALE

52. Rock of Ages Light *west of Isle Royale* (*opposite*)

53. Isle Royale Light *Isle Royale*

An octagonal-pyramidal, whitewashed red-sandstone tower, this active aid to navigation is located in Isle Royale National Park. Also known as Menagerie Island Light, the 1875 tower stands 61 feet tall. The attached keeper's house has been boarded up for a number of years. Lighthouse spotters visiting Isle Royale can see the lighthouse from the Grand Portage ferry.

54. Rock Harbor Light *northeastern Isle Royale*

White with a black lantern, this brick-and-stone cylindrical tower stands 50 feet high. It is attached to a rubblestone keeper's house. The 1855 light is no longer operational, replaced by the light on nearby Menagerie Island. The restored tower is located in Isle Royale National Park and is open in the summer: the keeper's house is now a museum, and the tower is open for self-guided tours.

55. Passage Island Light *off Isle Royale*

Constructed of fieldstone, this tower, standing 44 feet high, is unpainted and has a white-and-red lantern. An active aid to navigation in Isle Royale National Park, the tower, built in 1882, is attached to a Gothic-style, red-roofed stone keeper's dwelling. This light is identical to Sand Island Light (see page 87). Ranger-guided tours take visitors to the light station by boat (with a hike).

RIGHT: *Rock Harbor Light, pictured when partially restored.*

SPOTTER'S NOTE
Isle Royale National Park is open to visitors in the summer. Cars are not permitted on the island (or anywhere on the archipelago), and lighthouse spotters must be prepared to hike and use water taxis or rental boats.

Rock of Ages Light

Rock Steady

A white, bottle-shaped steel tower with black trim, this lighthouse was built on a circular caisson in 1908. The integral keeper's quarters were used until the 117-foot light was automated in 1978. The isolated location not only made construction an enormous challenge, but also means that viewing this light requires a seaplane or charter boat. A current navigational aid, it is within the Isle Royale National Park.

ABOVE AND BELOW, LEFT: *The light from above, and the south elevation.*

SPOTTER'S NOTE

The *George M. Cox* was shipwrecked in fog near the Rock of Ages Light in 1933. The light keepers rescued the 125 crew and passengers and housed them in the tower for the night. The wreck makes this a popular location for divers.

Description: cylindrical, bottle-shaped steel tower on a circular caisson
Markings: white with black trim; black-roofed lantern
Lens: 190 mm
Height: 117 feet (tower), 130 feet (focal plane)

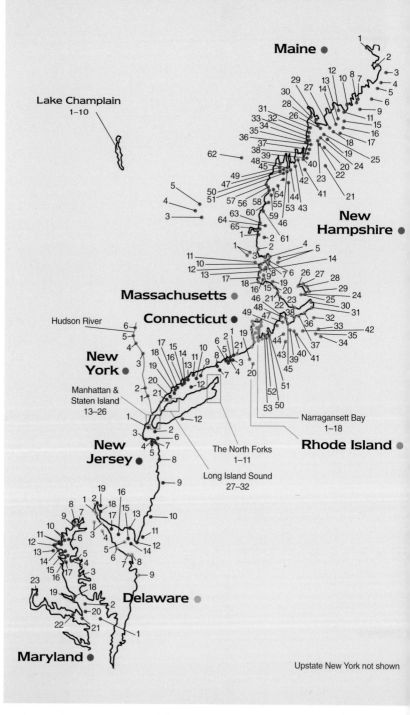

Maine ●

Lake Champlain
1–10

New
Hampshire ●

Massachusetts ●

Connecticut ●

Hudson River

New
York ●

Manhattan &
Staten Island
13–26

New
Jersey ●

The North Forks
1–11

Long Island Sound
27–32

Narragansett Bay
1–18

Rhode Island ●

Delaware ●

Maryland ●

Upstate New York not shown

THE NORTHEAST

MAINE

Perhaps more than any other state, Maine is famous for the picturesque lighthouses that are found on its coastal cliffs, rocky headlands, and offshore reefs and islands. Its citizens preserve their heritage proudly and share it with tourists by offering boat cruises from many local harbors. Often shrouded in impenetrable fog, the sound signals are as important as the lights to mariners in these waters.

ABOVE: *West Quoddy Head Light and keeper's dwelling.*
BELOW: *Little River Light.*

1. Whitlock's Mill Light *Calais*

This 25-foot, cylindrical, white brick tower (1909), with a black lantern, stands on the south bank of the St. Croix River. It can be viewed from nearby on U.S. Highway 1. The present optic has a flashing green signal (focal plane 32 feet); it was installed in 1969.

2. Lubec Channel Light *Lubec*

An offshore spark-plug lighthouse (one of just three that survive in Maine), this beacon marks the channel that separates Canada's Campobello Island from Quoddy Head. The 40-foot, brick-lined cast-iron tower (1890) is painted white, and its caisson and lantern (focal plane 53 feet), black. It is closed to the public, but can be seen from the mainland.

3. West Quoddy Head Light *Lubec*

This red-and-white-banded, 49-foot, conical brick tower stands in West Quoddy State Park, marking the easternmost extremity of the United States. First lit in 1858, its original third-order Fresnel lens still beams a flashing white signal (focal plane 83 feet).

4. Little River Light *Cutler Harbor*

This 41-foot, white, brick-lined cast-iron beacon built in a coffee-pot style (1876) on Little River Island aided navigation until it was superseded by a skeletal tower in 1975. A Victorian cottage-style keeper's dwelling (1888) stands adjacent to the tower. Recently restored, it is best viewed by boat.

ABOVE: *Nash Island Light before the keeper's house and outbuildings were demolished.*

5. Libby Island Light *Machiasport*

Built in 1822 of local granite, and topped with a black lantern room, this 42-foot conical beacon emits a flashing white signal (focal plane 91 feet) from its solar-powered VRB-25 optic (automated 1974). The site is part of a wildlife sanctuary and is not open to the public, but can be viewed by boat.

6. Moose Peak Light *Mistake Island*

Also known by the name of the rocky island on which it stands, this lighthouse is fitted with a flashing white solar-powered optic (focal plane 72 feet). The 57-foot, white-painted brick lighthouse was built in 1851 and automated in 1972. It is not accessible to the public and is best viewed by boat.

7. Nash Island Light *Nash Island*

This recently restored lighthouse (deactivated 1982) stands 29 feet tall (focal plane 57 feet). Its square brick tower, painted white, was built in 1874 and fitted with a fourth-order Fresnel lens. The keeper's dwelling was dismantled in 1947 along with the other outbuildings. Located near Mount Pleasant Bay, the light can be viewed by boat.

8. Narraguagas (Pond Island) Light *Pond Island*

In 1875, this 31-foot, white-painted, granite-block cylindrical tower (focal plane 54 feet) replaced an 1853 beacon, and in 1887 a workroom was built between the tower and keeper's dwelling, connecting the two. Deactivated in 1934, the keeper's house was subsequently razed. Privately owned, it can be viewed by boat.

9. Petit Manan Light *Petit Manan Island*

This 119-foot, conical, granite-block tower near Milbridge is the second tallest in the state. Automated in 1972, it currently holds a VRB-25 (white, range 25 miles; the original lens was removed to Rockland's Maine Lighthouse Museum). It can be seen from Petit Manan Point.

LEFT: *Egg Rock Light.*

10. Prospect Harbor Point Light *Prospect Harbor*

Rumored to be haunted, this beacon is a 38-foot, conical wooden tower that replaced an 1850 structure in 1891 and was fitted with a fifth-order Fresnel lens (focal plane 43 feet). Automated in 1934, its modern optic emits a signal of red and white flashes. Painted white and topped with a black lantern, the tower stands near a keeper's cottage on a naval station. It is not open to the public, but can be viewed from the entrance to the naval station or from across the harbor.

11. Winter Harbor Light *Winter Harbor*

This diminutive 1856 light (19 feet, focal plane 37 feet) on Mark Island was deactivated in 1934, when it was replaced by a lighted buoy. The white, cylindrical brick-and-asphalt tower is attached to a keeper's dwelling, which is privately owned and maintained. The light can be seen from Schoodic Point in Acadia National Park.

12. Egg Rock Light *Bar Harbor*

Mounted at the apex of the red roof of a white, square keeper's dwelling, this 40-foot beacon stands on a small island in Frenchman's Bay. Built in 1875 and automated in 1976, when it was fitted with a 250-mm optic, the light emits a flashing red signal (focal plane 64 feet). The best view is from Cadillac Mountain, Acadia National Park.

13. Bear Island Light *Bear Island*

This 31-foot, white, cylindrical brick tower with black lantern (and attached workroom) was first lit in 1889 and remained active until 1981. Its private owners restored and relit it in 1989 with a flashing white signal (focal plane 100 feet). It can be seen from Cranberry Isles ferries.

14. Bass Harbor Head Light *Bass Harbor* (*opposite*)

15. Baker Island Light *Baker Island*

This 43-foot, white-painted, cylindrical brick tower, with black lantern, was built in 1855 and served until 2002. Located in Acadia National Park, the grounds are open to the public during the summer.

Bass Harbor Head Light

Acadian Jewel

Perched on a narrow ledge on a rugged cliffside at the southwestern edge of scenic Mount Desert Island (pronounced "dessert"), the lighthouse at Bass Harbor Head, Tremont, is one of the premier attractions of Acadia National Park—indeed, it is regarded by many as the most photogenic beacon on the Atlantic Coast. The light station was established in 1858 with construction of a cylindrical brick tower, painted white and with a black lantern, attached to a wood-framed keeper's dwelling. The tower rises to a height of 32 feet, and its red signal, which has a focal-plane height of 56 feet, can be seen from a distance of 15 miles. A fifth-order Fresnel lens was installed originally, but this was replaced in 1902 by a fourth-order lens that is still in operation, having been automated in 1974. The grounds are open to the public, and a trail leads around the light and down a stairway to an excellent vantage point for photographers, but there is no public access inside the buildings. A pyramidal fog-signal building still stands, though the bell has been removed, and an oil house and barn also remain at the site.

Description: cylindrical brick tower; attached keeper's dwelling
Markings: white; black lantern
Lens: fourth-order Fresnel
Height: 32 feet (tower); 56 feet (focal plane)

ABOVE AND BELOW: *The lighthouse serves the lobster boats active in the area.*

16. Great Duck Island Light *Great Duck Island*

Built in 1890 and automated in 1986, the 42-foot, white, cylindrical brick-and-granite tower emits flashes of red light (focal plane 67 feet) from its black lantern. Located at the southern end of this remote island, it is not accessible to the public.

17. Mount Desert Rock Light *Mount Desert Rock*

Situated on a ledge more than 20 miles south of Mount Desert Island, this lighthouse was designed by the noted architect and engineer Alexander Parris (*see* Spotter's Note, left), and replaced an 1830 beacon. The 58-foot, unpainted, conical granite-block tower (focal plane 75 feet) was first lit in 1847. Its lantern was replaced in 1985 and has a white flashing signal. There is no public access to this site.

18. Burnt Coat Harbor Light *Swans Island*

This 32-foot, square brick tower (1872) at Hockamock Head was automated in 1975. The white beacon supports a black lantern that houses a 250-mm optic (focal plane 75 feet) with an occulting white signal. The grounds (but not the light itself) are open to the public, with access from a ferry from Bass Harbor.

19. Isle Au Haut (Robinson Point) Light *Isle Au Haut*

First lit in 1907, this 40-foot granite-and-brick light's upper part is white, with a black lantern (focal plane 48 feet). Automated in 1934, its solar-powered lens flashes red and white. The Victorian keeper's house is today a bed-and-breakfast inn, which allows visitors to see this beacon at close range, though the lighthouse itself is not open to the public. Access to the island is by mailboat/ferry.

BELOW: *Saddleback Ledge Light soon after its automation.*

20. Saddleback Ledge Light *Vinalhaven*

Located on a remote islet, this lighthouse was designed by Alexander Parris (*see* Spotter's Note, above). Built in 1839, the 42-foot, unpainted, conical granite tower (focal plane 52 feet) was automated in 1954. Its 300-mm optic has a flashing white signal. There are no other structures on the island, which is not accessible to the public; viewing can be arranged by boat from Penobscot Bay, conditions permitting.

ABOVE: *Matinicus Rock's twin lights with their former keepers.*

21. Matinicus Rock Light (Twin Towers)   *Matinicus Rock*

A prominent hazard threatening mariners approaching Penobscot Bay, Matinicus Rock lies 18 miles offshore. A light station was first established here in 1827, but in 1857 two taller, cylindrical granite-block structures were built to a design by Alexander Parris. The northern tower was deactivated in 1923, but the 48-foot southern tower remains operational, using a white flashing solar-powered VRB-25 optic (automated in 1983, focal plane 90 feet). Matinicus Rock Light is steeped in history and legend and has become one of the best-known beacons in Maine. Open to the public during the summer months, it is accessed by boat trips that can be arranged from Rockland.

> **SPOTTER'S NOTE**
>
> Visitors to Matinicus Rock can still see the remains of the two granite towers dating from 1848 that were attached to the second keeper's dwelling (1846). The tops were removed when their signals were superseded by those fitted in the present towers. The lantern has also been removed from the northern tower; the remaining lantern room on the south tower is painted red and surmounts a tower whose lower part is unpainted granite and upper section, white.

22. Heron Neck Light   *Green's Island*

Situated just off Vinalhaven Island and marking safe passage to Carver Harbor, this restored beacon is a 30-foot, cylindrical masonry tower that is painted white, with red and black trim (focal plane 92 feet), on a granite foundation. First lit in 1854 and automated in 1982, it emits a red signal with a white sector. The attached white keeper's dwelling (1895) has a red roof. The lighthouse can only be viewed by boat or by air.

23. Browns Head Light   *Vinalhaven*

Now the residence of Vinalhaven's Town Manager, this light station has a 20-foot, cylindrical brick tower (white, with a black lantern) that uses a fourth-order Fresnel lens to project its white signal, with red sectors (focal plane 39 feet). Constructed in 1857 to replace an earlier tower, it was automated in 1987. The original fog bell is on display in the Vinalhaven Historical Society Museum. The grounds are open to the public year-round; access to the island is provided by the regular ferry service from Rockland.

24. Goose Rocks Light   *Fox Islands Thorofare*

This 51-foot spark-plug tower off the northeast of Vinalhaven Island is painted white with a black base and trim and stands on a caisson. It emits a red signal with white sectors, and can be seen from Calderwood Point.

> **SPOTTER'S NOTE**
> Just three spark-plug lights remain in the state of Maine: Goose Rocks Light, Lubec Channel Light, and Spring Point Ledge Light.

BELOW: *Deer Island Thorofare (Mark Island) Light.*

25. Deer Island Thorofare (Mark Island) Light   *Mark Island*

This 25-foot, square brick lighthouse (1858) is painted white with a black lantern, and the tower is attached to a small, red-roofed workroom. Its solar-powered lens flashes white (focal plane 52 feet). Other structures were demolished in the 1970s, the original keeper's quarters having been destroyed by fire in 1959. The lighthouse can be seen from nearby Stonington or by water.

26. Eagle Island Light   *Eagle Island*

This 30-foot, white-painted conical tower (1838) is built of granite rubblestone, and its black lantern room is fitted with a solar-powered lens (automated 1963), which flashes white (focal plane 106 feet). The pyramidal sound-signal building was built in 1939; all other structures have been razed. The site is closed to the public.

27. Blue Hill Bay Light   *Green Island*

Operational from 1857 until 1933, this light was replaced by an automated skeleton-tower signal (1935), and it is now a private summer home, with no public access. The 22-foot, cylindrical masonry tower is painted white, with a black lantern, and is attached to the keeper's dwelling. It used a fifth-order Fresnel lens (focal plane 26 feet).

28. Pumpkin Island Light

Eggemoggin Reach

This 1854 lighthouse was in use until 1933; it resembles Blue Hill Bay Light and is also now a private residence. The 28-foot, cylindrical, white brick tower has a black lantern room that was fitted with a fifth-order Fresnel lens (focal plane 43 feet). There is no access to the island, but it can be seen from Eggemoggin Road on Little Deer Isle.

ABOVE: *Fort Point Light.*
BELOW: *Curtis Island Light.*

29. Dice (Dyce) Head Light   *Castine*

Located at the mouth of the Penobscot River, this 1829 lighthouse was deactivated in 1937. The 51-foot, conical, brick-lined, granite rubblestone tower, painted white with a black lantern, originally had a lamp-and-reflector apparatus (focal plane 130 feet). The keeper's cottage burned down in 1999 but was restored within a year. The lighthouse is now a private residence, but can be seen from nearby.

30. Fort Point Light   *Fort Point*

Open from Memorial Day through Labor Day, Fort Point State Historic Site, near the town of Stockton Springs, commemorates the 1759 Fort Pownall as well as the important light station that was established here in 1836 to guide vessels into Bangor. This 31-foot, square brick tower (painted cream with black trim) replaced a granite beacon in 1857. It retains its original, fourth-order Fresnel lens, which still has a fixed white signal (focal plane 88 feet, automated 1988). The tower is attached to the keeper's quarters, an L-shaped colonial-style dwelling.

31. Grindel (Grindle) Point Light   *Islesboro*

This 39-foot, square masonry tower (1874) is painted white, with black lantern and trim. Deactivated in 1934, the Coast Guard restored the flashing green signal in 1987 (focal plane 39 feet). The original keeper's quarters are attached to the tower, and the light is open to the public.

32. Curtis Island Light   *Curtis Island*

Known for many years as Negro Island Light, this beacon is open to the public, though the island is accessible only by boat. The 25-foot cylindrical masonry tower (1896) is painted white, with a black lantern (focal plane 52 feet); a storage room is attached. In 1994, it received a solar-powered optic with a fixed green signal. The white clapboard keeper's dwelling (1889) stands nearby.

33. Indian Island Light *Rockport*

Visible from Rockport's Marine Park, this square, white-painted brick tower (1874) has an attached storage room and black lantern; the white keeper's dwelling of 1850 stands nearby. Deactivated in 1934, the light is privately owned and is not open to the public.

34. Rockland Harbor Breakwater Light *Rockland*

Built in 1902 on a platform at the end of a mile-long breakwater, this 25-foot lighthouse (flashing white, focal plane 39 feet) consists of a brick fog-signal building with a stone-and-brick tower, topped with a black lantern, rising from one corner. A gambrel-roofed keeper's dwelling is attached. It is open to the public during the summer.

35. Rockland Harbor Southwest Light *Rockland*

Privately built in the 1980s (completed 1987), this beacon consists of a shingled, salt-box cottage with a short, square wooden tower, painted white, rising from the roof. The fifth-order Fresnel lens, which emits a yellow flashing signal, was originally installed at the Doubling Point Range Lights. The grounds are open to visitors.

36. Owls Head Light *Rockland*

Perched on a headland at the mouth of the harbor, this 30-foot, cylindrical brick tower (1854), painted white with a black lantern, is open to visitors at Owls Head State Park. The light is approached via a wooden walkway and staircase. The original fourth-order Fresnel lens is still active, with a fixed white signal (focal plane 100 feet).

BELOW: *Rockland Harbor Breakwater Light at sunset.*

37. Whitehead Light *Sprucehead*

One of the oldest light stations in Maine (1807, present tower 1852), this 41-foot, conical granite tower (focal plane 75 feet) is unpainted and has an attached storage room with nearby keeper's quarters. The light was automated in 1982 and generates an occulting green signal.

38. Two Bush Island Light *Sprucehead*

One of the last lighthouses built in Maine (1897), this 42-foot, square, white-painted brick tower, with attached sound-signal building and black lantern room, stands on a small island on the approach to Penobscot Bay. Automated in 1964, it emits its flashing white signal, with red sectors, from a DCB-224 (focal plane 65 feet). This station is not open to the public and can be viewed only by boat.

LEFT: *Marshall Point Light.*

39. Tenants Harbor Light   *Southern Island*

This light (active 1857–1933) is a 27-foot, cylindrical brick tower (painted white, with a black lantern) attached to a Cape Cod–style keeper's cottage. There is no public access to the light, which can be glimpsed from Tenants Harbor.

40. Marshall Point Light   *Port Clyde*

Attached to the mainland by a white wooden catwalk, this 31-foot, white, cylindrical granite-and-brick tower has a black lantern. First lit in 1857, it was automated in 1980 with a 300-mm optic (fixed white signal, focal plane 30 feet). The 1895 keeper's dwelling now houses a museum caretaker. The station is open to the public.

41. Monhegan Island Light   *Monhegan Island*

A 47-foot, conical granite-block tower, with black lantern, this lighthouse was first lit in 1850 and automated in 1959, when it received a VRB-25 optic (flashing white, focal plane 178 feet, range 23 miles). The nearby keeper's house (1874) is a white, red-roofed structure (now a museum that is open July 1 through Labor Day). The island can be reached by ferry from Port Clyde.

42. Franklin Island Light   *Friendship*

This 1855 (automated 1967) 45-foot, cylindrical brick tower (painted white, with gray and red lantern and trim), is located on the third-oldest light-station site in Maine (established 1805) and uses a solar-powered lens (flashing white, focal plane 57 feet). It is closed to the public, but can be viewed by cruise from New Harbor.

40. Pemaquid Point Light   *Damariscotta*

This 38-foot, white-painted, conical rubblestone tower, with black cast-iron lantern, was built on a cliff in 1827. Its 1846 fourth-order Fresnel lens (focal plane 79 feet) is still in use (flashing white every 6 seconds). The light was the first in Maine to be automated, in 1934. The tower and grounds are open to the public during the summer.

ABOVE: *Ram Island Light was reached via a walkway (removed in 1977).*

44. Ram Island Light   *Boothbay Harbor*

This 1833 lighthouse is a brick cylindrical tower (upper portion white) on an unpainted granite base, topped with a black lantern (focal plane 36 feet). Automated in 1965, its 250-mm optic produces an alternating red signal. Occasional summer tours of the light are arranged by the Maine Maritime Museum in Bath.

45. Burnt Island Light   *Southport*

Built in 1821 at the entrance to Boothbay Harbor, this 30-foot, conical rubblestone lighthouse is painted white and has a black lantern. The light is attached via a covered walkway to the 1857 keeper's quarters. Automated in 1989 with a solar-powered optic (focal plane 61 feet), it emits a flashing signal, red with two white sectors, 24 hours a day. It is open to the public; guided tours are offered, and the 1,000-pound 1895 cast-iron fog bell is displayed in its original building.

46. The Cuckolds Light   *Boothbay Harbor*

Originally a fog-signal station dating from 1892, a light tower was placed on its roof in 1907. The 48-foot, octagonal wooden tower, white with red trim, uses a VRB-25 optic (focal plane 59 feet, automated 1975, flashes white twice every 6 seconds). Not open to the public, it can be seen from the pier at Newagen Center's public landing.

47. Hendricks Head Light   *West Southport*

This 39-foot, square brick tower is whitewashed and has a black lantern. First lit in 1875 (deactivated 1935–51), it was automated in 1975 and fitted with a 250-mm optic (fixed white signal, with a red sector, focal plane 43 feet). There is no public access, but the light can be seen from West Southport, or by boat.

48. Doubling Point Light   *Arrowsic Island*

This white, octagonal wooden tower, with black cast-iron lantern, built at the end of a footbridge, was first lit in 1899. Automated in 1988, it now uses a 300-mm lens (focal plane 23 feet, flashing white light). The former keeper's house (1898) is privately owned and there is no access to the site, but the light can be seen from Doubling Point Road.

49. Doubling Point Range Lights   *Arrowsic Island*

These 13-foot, octagonal wooden towers were first lit in 1898. Painted white with red trim, their lights are projected through a small window in each tower. Since automation (1980) a 250-mm optic (focal plane 33 feet) has operated in each tower, the front signal being a rapidly flashing white light, and the rear, an alternating white signal of 6 seconds. There is no public access to the site.

50. Squirrel Point Light   *Arrowsic Island*

This 25-foot, white-painted, octagonal wooden tower and attached fog-signal building was first lit in 1898. The 250-mm optic (automated 1992) in its black lantern generates a red signal, with a white sector, alternating every 6 seconds with darkness (focal plane 33 feet). A Victorian keeper's house still stands nearby. The grounds may be visited, and the light can also be seen from Phippsburg, across the Kennebec River.

51. Perkins Island Light   *Perkins Island*

Visible across the Kennebec River from a vantage point south of Bath, the grounds of this partially restored, active light station are open to the public. First lit in 1898, the 23-foot, white octagonal tower (with black trim) was constructed of wood on a rocky outcrop and is topped with a red lantern. Its 250-mm optic (automated 1959) has a flashing red signal with two white sectors (focal plane 41 feet).

52. Pond Island Light   *Popham Beach*

The 20-foot, cylindrical, white brick tower (with black lantern and trim) dates from 1855. It projects an alternating white signal at a height of focal plane of 52 feet, and can only be viewed by boat.

BELOW: *Pond Island Light.*

53. Seguin Island Light   *Popham Beach*

This lighthouse is sited higher than any other in Maine (tower height, 53 feet; focal plane, 186 feet) and houses the state's only first-order Fresnel lens. The white, cylindrical granite-and-brick tower (1857) was automated in 1985, and emits a fixed white signal. The lighthouse can be seen in the distance from Popham Beach.

54. Halfway Rock Light

South Harpswell

Some 10 miles offshore from Portland, the flashing red signal (focal plane 77 feet) sent from this dovetailed-granite tower can be seen from 20 miles away. The 76-foot, conical, white-painted structure has a black lantern with a VRB-25 solar-powered optic (automated 1975). Hardy keepers once lived inside the tower, which can be seen distantly from the Portland Observatory.

> **SPOTTER'S NOTE**
> The original third-order Fresnel lens of Halfway Rock Light was removed in 1994, almost twenty years after having been superseded by a modern optic, and is now on display at the U.S. Coast Guard Academy in New London, Connecticut.

55. Ram Island Ledge Light   *Casco Bay, entrance to Portland Harbor*

This 72-foot, conical granite-block structure with a black lantern stands on a rocky ledge. Automated in 1959, it now uses a solar-powered lens (focal plane 77 feet) to produce a white signal, flashing twice every 6 seconds. This light is not open to the public, but can be seen by boat, or in the distance from Portland Head.

56. Spring Point Ledge Light

Portland

This 54-foot spark-plug light (1897) on the western side of the harbor is a brick-lined, prefabricated cast-iron structure. In 1950 it was connected to the mainland by a 900-foot granite breakwater. It emits a flashing white signal with two red sectors (focal plane also 54 feet). The tower is white, with a black base, walkway, gallery, and lantern.

ABOVE: *Spring Point Ledge Light.*
BELOW: *Portland Breakwater Light.*

57. Portland Breakwater ("Bug") Light   *South Portland*

This unique 26-foot beacon (first lit 1875, automated 1934, deactivated 1942, relit 2002) stands on a granite-block base. The white, cylindrical, brick-lined cast-iron tower was modeled on the Choragic Monument of Lysicrates. The black lantern houses a 250-mm lens (flashes white, focal plane 30 feet). A private aid to navigation, it is situated in Bug Light Park. Visitors can walk along the breakwater to the tower.

58. Portland Head Light   *Portland*

(opposite)

Portland Head Light

Picture Perfect

The gracefully tapering lighthouse and attached red-roofed keeper's dwelling at Portland Head are familiar to many as a much-photographed, quintessential New England scene. Not just beautiful but also historic, this was Maine's first light station and the first built under the auspices of the U.S. government: the tower, begun in 1787, was eventually lit in 1791. More than two centuries later, the 80-foot fieldstone tower is still standing and fully operational. It is painted white, with a black lantern, and emits a flashing white signal from its DCB-224 optic (focal plane 101 feet, automated in 1989), visible from a distance of 25 miles. A popular tourist attraction, the light station is open to the public during the summer months, and the keeper's dwelling now houses a museum, but visitors cannot enter the tower. For those who cannot visit, a webcam on the Portland Head Light's homepage (www.portlandheadlight.com) shows the view—and the local weather conditions.

ABOVE: *The tower and residence at Portland Head.*
BELOW: *The southeast elevation.*

Description: conical fieldstone tower; attached keeper's dwelling
Markings: white; black lantern
Lens: DCB-224
Height: 80 feet (tower); 101 feet (focal plane)

59. Cape Elizabeth Light *Cape Elizabeth* *(opposite)*

60. Wood Island Light *Biddeford Pool*
Visitors can tour this 1858 light station, with its 47-foot, white, conical rubblestone tower and attached keeper's house (1857), by arrangement. Its black lantern houses a VRB-25 optic (focal plane 71 feet), which emits alternating green and white flashes.

61. Goat Island Light *Cape Porpoise*
This 1859 cylindrical, 25-foot brick tower is white with a black lantern (focal plane 38 feet). Automated in 1990, its 300-mm optic emits a flashing white light. The lighthouse may be visited only by arrangement with the Kennebunkport Conservation Trust.

SPOTTER'S NOTE
Lighthouse spotters visiting Maine should make Wells their first stop: it is home to the American Lighthouse Foundation Museum of Lighthouse History and the neighboring Lighthouse Depot store.

62. Ladies Delight Light
Lake Cobbosseecontee
This 16-foot, white-painted, conical stone tower is Maine's only beacon at a freshwater site. It can be seen from the lake shore near Manchester.

63. Cape Neddick "The Nubble" Light *York*
This inaccessible light can be seen from Sohier Park. The 41-foot, white, brick-lined cast-iron tower has a black lantern housing a fourth-order Fresnel lens (focal plane 88 feet) that sends an alternating red signal visible up to 15 miles away.

64. Boon Island Light *Boon Island*
This 1855 tapered, 133-foot granite tower is among the most remote of all U.S. lighthouses. Automated in 1980, its solar-powered Vega VRB-25 (focal plane 137 feet) has a flashing white signal. It can be seen from Cape Neddick.

ABOVE: *Cape Neddick Light.*
BELOW: *Boon Island Light.*

65. Whaleback Ledge Light
Kittery Point
Visible from Kittery and Portsmouth, this 50-foot, conical granite-block tower with integral keeper's quarters was automated in 1963, and its flashing white light is now generated by a DCB-224 optic (focal plane 59 feet). There is no public access to the lighthouse or grounds.

Cape Elizabeth Light

Description: cast-iron
conical tower
Markings: white; black
lantern and trim
Lens: FA-251
Height: 67 feet (tower);
129 feet (focal plane)

ABOVE: *The 1970 postage stamp.*

SPOTTER'S NOTE
The lighthouse and adjacent
Victorian, gingerbread-trim
keeper's house, dating from
1878, were immortalized in
several paintings by Edward
Hopper, whose 1927
"Lighthouse at Two Lights"
is one of America's best-
loved paintings: it was
featured on a postage stamp
in 1970. The western tower,
decommissioned in 1924,
is now a well-maintained
decorative structure in the
yard of a private home,
300 feet from its more
famous neighbor.

Artist's Model
Built in 1874, the 67-foot cast-iron tower, white
with black lantern and trim, at Cape Elizabeth
marks the entrance to Portland Harbor. Its flashing white signal (focal-plane height 129 feet) is
Maine's most powerful at 4 million candlepower,
with a range of 27 miles. The beacon is located
adjacent to the 41-acre Two Lights State Park, so
named because there were two active light towers on this site from 1828 until 1924—Maine's
first twin lights. Visitors can view the active (eastern) light from the park, but the grounds and
lighthouse itself are not accessible.

Today, the keeper's house no longer resembles
the photograph below: a private home, it was completely remodeled in 1999, despite vigorous efforts
by conservationists to secure its preservation.

RIGHT: *The Victorian keeper's
dwelling before remodeling.*

NEW HAMPSHIRE

New Hampshire's short Atlantic coastline has two lighthouses serving Portsmouth Harbor, but the state also has three further lighthouses on Lake Sunapee.

1. Portsmouth Harbor (Newcastle) Light *Newcastle*

Also known as Fort Point Light and Fort Constitution Light, this 48-foot, conical cast-iron tower (painted white with a black lantern) was constructed in 1877, automated in 1960, and is still in use today. It retains its original fourth-order Fresnel lens (focal plane 52 feet, fixed green light, range 12 miles). It is not open to the public except for tours by appointment and occasional open houses, but can be viewed from the Fort Constitution State Historic Site, or from boat tours (departing from Portsmouth).

2. Isles of Shoals (White Island) Light *Portsmouth (opposite)*

ABOVE: *Portsmouth Harbor Light.*

3. Burkehaven Light *Burkehaven Island, Lake Sunapee*

This 20-foot, white-painted, wooden, hexagonal frame tower (no lantern) is a 1983 replica of an offshore 1893 structure. Solar-panel lights were installed in the mid-1980s and are still active. Although not open to the public, the lighthouse can be seen from scenic cruises offered at Sunapee Harbor.

4. Loon Island Light *Loon Island, Lake Sunapee*

Originally built for $400 in 1893, this 25-foot, white-painted, wooden, hexagonal frame tower was rebuilt in 1960. Still active, with its solar-panel lights (installed mid-1980s), it is not open to the public, but can be seen by boat (cruises from Sunapee Harbor).

SPOTTER'S NOTE
In 2003 the Herrick Cove Light was helicopter-lifted to shore for repairs. It weighed more than expected, and briefly dipped into the lake, giving onlookers quite a scare!

5. Herrick Cove Light *offshore, near Georges Mills, Lake Sunapee*

Originally constructed in 1893 (refurbished in the mid-1960s), this 27-foot, white-painted, wooden, octagonal frame tower (no lantern) is still active (solar-panel lights were installed mid-1980s). Although closed to the public, boat tours run from Sunapee Harbor.

Isles of Shoals (White Island) Light

White Light

Located 9 miles offshore, the Isles of Shoals form a cluster of eighteen granite islets that threaten vessels approaching Portsmouth Harbor. The first lighthouse was built on White Island in 1820, but was too short for its location. Its 1859 replacement (automated 1987) is still operational. The 58-foot, conical, white-painted granite-and-brick tower's black lantern now houses a 190-mm solar powered lens (flashing white every 15 seconds, focal plane 82 feet). Hurricane Bob (1991) ripped away the walkway that connected the tower, keeper's house, and fog-signal building. The site is now on lease to a diving school and there is no public access, but cruises operate from Portsmouth and Rye.

Description: cylindrical granite-and-brick tower
Markings: white; black lantern
Lens: 190 mm
Height: 58 feet (tower); 82 feet (focal plane)

BELOW: *The solar panels can be seen against the tower in this view of the lighthouse.*

LAKE CHAMPLAIN

Lake Champlain is part of the Erie Canal system (1825), built to connect the Great Lakes with the Hudson River, dramatically shortening shipping times between the important lake ports and New York City. Its aids to navigation were therefore vital, and today, some of these historic beacons have been relit.

VERMONT

SPOTTER'S NOTE
Two replica wooden lights were lit on the breakwater at Burlington Harbor in 2003, reconstructing the originals that were first lit there in 1857.

1. Windmill Point Light *Alburg*
First lit in 1858, this 40-foot, unpainted, octagonal limestone tower (with orange lantern) was replaced with a skeletal tower, but was relit in 2002 (300-mm lens, flashing white every 4 seconds, focal plane 52 feet) as a private aid to navigation. A private residence, this light is closed to the public, but can be viewed from Windmill Point Road.

2. Isle La Motte Light (Old) *Isle La Motte*
This 25-foot, conical, cast-iron, faded red tower was active from 1881 until 1933, and was relit as a private aid to navigation in 2002, with a 300-mm optic (flashing white every 6 seconds). The old lighthouse now functions as a private residence and is not open to the public, but it can be glimpsed through the trees from Lighthouse Point (at the end of Shrine Road), from points along the shore in Chazy, New York, or by boat.

3. Juniper Island Light (Old) *Burlington*
This 1846 lighthouse is no longer operational (replaced by a skeleton tower, 1954), and the 25-foot, white-painted, conical cast-iron tower with red lantern (focal plane 93 feet) is now earmarked for restoration. It is attached to a recently reconstructed two-story, brick/stucco keeper's residence (now a privately owned home). It is not open to the public, but can be glimpsed from the water.

4. Colchester Reef Light *Shelburne*
This lighthouse was replaced with a buoy when it was relocated from Lake Champlain to the grounds of the Shelburne Museum in 1952. Operational from 1871 to 1933, it consists of a 35-foot, square wooden tower (painted white, with dark trim) atop an integral, two-story, white, Second Empire dwelling. Its original sixth-order Fresnel lens is still in situ, but it is inactive.

NEW YORK

5. Crown Point (Champlain Memorial) Light   *Crown Point*

This cylindrical tower of cut granite blocks is surrounded by eight Doric-style columns and has an ornate cornice, parapet, and lantern room, as well as a bronze sculpted by Auguste Rodin. Decommissioned in 1926, the lighthouse is now part of the Crown Point State Historic Site; visitors can find it in the the the public campground just south of Highway 17/903, and it can also be seen from the lake.

6. Barber's Point Light (Old)   *Westport*

This 36-foot octagonal tower (painted white with black trim) stands atop a two-story keeper's cottage: it was operational from 1873 until 1935. Spotters can see the lighthouse from Barber Road, but it is now a private home, closed to the public.

7. Split Rock Point Light (Old)   *Whallon Bay*

Constructed in 1867, this 39-foot, octagonal limestone tower (red-and-white lantern), attached to the 1899 keeper's house, originally held a fourth-order Fresnel lens (focal plane 100 feet). Deactivated in 1928, it was relit as a private aid in 2003. It is not open to the public, but can be seen from the opposite side of the lake.

8. Bluff Point (Valcour Island) Light   *Plattsburgh*

This historic light consists of an octagonal, blue-limestone tower (painted red with white lantern), rising to 35 feet on the red roof of the 1874 limestone keeper's house. Deactivated in 1930, it was relit in 2004.

9. Cumberland Head Light   *Plattsburgh*

This 50-foot, unpainted, conical limestone tower and attached two-story granite keeper's dwelling (1868) originally used a fourth-order Fresnel lens (deactivated 1934, relit 2003). Currently a private residence, it can be viewed from the Grand Isle, Vermont, to Plattsburgh, New York, ferry.

10. Point Aux Roches Light
near Plattsburgh

Constructed from blue limestone in 1858, this 50-foot, unpainted octagonal light tower was operational until 1989. The wooden keeper's house stands adjacent to the tower. The tower can be glimpsed from Point Au Roche Road.

BELOW: *Crown Point Light.*

MASSACHUSETTS

Massachusetts, to whose shores the *Mayflower* sailed in 1620, is home to the United States' oldest light station. The rich maritime history of the state is reflected in the diversity of its aids to navigation, which include coffee-pot and spark-plug lights, tall masonry towers, and cottage-style beacons, among other lighthouse types.

ABOVE: *Newburyport Harbor Light (period photograph).*
BELOW: *Annisquam Harbor Light.*

1. Newburyport Harbor Range Lights *Newburyport*

These lights date from 1873 (deactivated 1961). The 15-foot, conical cast-iron front range light is white, with an orange-and-white lantern; the 53-foot rear light is an unpainted, tapered, square brick tower (white cast-iron lantern). The front tower was moved in 1964 from Bayley's Wharf to the nearby Coast Guard station. Neither tower is open to the public, except by special arrangement.

2. Newburyport Harbor (Plum Island) Light *Newburyport*

This 45-foot, white, conical wooden tower, with its black cast-iron lantern room, became operational in 1898 (light station established 1788) and was automated in 1951. The fourth-order Fresnel lens beams out an occulting green light (focal plane 50 feet). The nearby white Victorian keeper's house was built in 1872. The tower also functions as a museum on some summer weekends when it is open to the public.

3. Annisquam Harbor (Squam) Light *Wigwam Point*

Also known as Wigwam Point Light, this 41-foot cylindrical structure (1897) of white brick with a black cast-iron lantern is still fully operational (automated 1974). The 190-mm optic flashes white with a red sector every 7.5 seconds (focal plane 45 feet). The grounds are open to the public. The lighthouse can be viewed from the road or from the nearby rocky beach; good views can also be had from Wingaersheek Beach, Gloucester.

4. Straitsmouth Island Light
Straitsmouth Island

First lit in 1896, this 37-foot, white, cylindrical brick tower's solar-powered optic emits a flashing green light (focal plane 46 feet). The wooden keeper's house was built alongside the original lighthouse in 1835. The light is not open to the public and is best viewed by boat.

5. Cape Ann Light   *Thatcher Island*

The site that houses this tower and its outbuildings—which include the north lighthouse of twin lights (1816) and various outbuildings—is now a National Historic Landmark. The current 124-foot, conical granite tower was built in 1861, and its solar-powered VRB-25 optic's flashing red signal is visible for 19 miles (focal plane 166 feet). The lighthouse is closed to the public, but the island may be visited in summer by appointment.

6. Eastern Point Light   *Gloucester*

This 36-foot, white brick tower (with black lantern and red roof) was completed in 1890. Automated in 1985, its DCB-224 optic has a focal plane of 57 feet. The 1879 keeper's house is a Gothic Revival duplex. The site is open to the public.

ABOVE: *Early depictions of the twin towers on Thatcher Island.*
BELOW: *Eastern Point Light as depicted c. 1907.*

7. Gloucester (Dog Bar) Breakwater Light   *Gloucester*

This 37-foot white building (1905) perches on a brown, square skeletal framework (focal plane 45 feet, range 11 miles). Visitors may walk on the breakwater, but the building is closed.

> **SPOTTER'S NOTE**
> Eastern Point Light's 1857 Fresnel lens is at the Cape Ann Historical Association Museum, Gloucester.

8. Ten Pound Island Light   *Gloucester*

At 30 feet tall, this white, conical cast-iron lighthouse with a black cast-iron lantern has been in operation since 1881. The current tower houses a 250-mm optic that emits an alternating red light. The beacon can be seen from many points along the coast, and the grounds are open to the public.

9. Baker's Island Light *near Salem*

This 59-foot tower is the taller of a pair of light-houses built here in 1820 (the shorter was demol-ished in 1926), replacing a 1798 pair of lights. The surviving white, conical granite tower, with a black cast-iron lantern, still functions, sending out white and red flashes from the solar-powered optic (range 18 miles). The island is closed to the public and the best views of the light station are by boat.

> **SPOTTER'S NOTE**
> The 1798 twin lights at Baker's Island were among the first twin lights in the U.S. New towers were built in 1820. They were known as the "Ma and Pa" or "Mr. and Mrs." lighthouses.

10. Hospital Point Range Front Light *Beverly*

Built in 1872, this 45-foot, white, square-pyramidal brick tower, with a black cast-iron lantern, first became a range light in 1927 in tandem with the steeple light listed below. Still in operation, a fixed white beam shines from the original Fresnel lens (focal plane 70 feet). The light station is opened to the public one day (in early August) each year.

11. Hospital Point Range Rear Light *Beverly*

Discarded lightship equipment was installed in Beverly's First Baptist Church (located 2,050 yards from the front range light) in 1927; the rear-range fixed white light shines from the steeple (focal plane 183 feet). The grounds and the church are open to the public. This is the only functioning harbor light on a church steeple in the United States.

BELOW: *Derby Wharf Light.*

12. Fort Pickering (Winter Island) Light *Salem*

Built in 1871, this white, conical cast-iron tower, with a black cast-iron lantern, stands on a concrete foundation. Deactivated in 1969, relighted in 1983, and refurbished by 1999, its solar-powered optic emits a white flash every 4 seconds (focal plane 28 feet). The grounds are open to the public.

13. Derby Wharf Light *Salem Harbor*

At the end of Derby Wharf stands this 23-foot, white, square brick tower, with its black cast-iron lantern. Built in 1871, the light was deactivated between 1977 and 1983 but is now fully function-ing again, managed by the National Park Service. Its solar-powered optic (replacing the original sixth-order Fresnel lens) emits a flashing red signal (focal plane 25 feet). The wharf is open to the pub-lic year round, but the lighthouse is closed.

14. Marblehead Light *Marblehead*

A striking construction of brown cast iron, this 105-foot skeletal tower, with a black cast-iron lantern, is the only one of its type in New England. Completed in 1895, its 300-mm optic shines a fixed green light at a focal-plane height of 130 feet. The grounds are open to the public.

15. Graves (Ledge) Light *Boston*

Completed in 1905, this lighthouse took almost two years to build, and for many years its light was one of the most powerful in New England. An unpainted, conical granite tower with a black cast-iron lantern, it stands 113 feet tall on an offshore ledge. In 2001, the original first-order Fresnel lens was removed (now stored at the Smithsonian Institution) and a solar-powered optic installed in its place; the signal (two white flashes every 12 seconds) is visible for 17 miles. The best views of the tower are from the water.

16. Boston Harbor Light
Little Brewster Island (overleaf)

17. Deer Island Light *Deer Island*

This brown, flaring cylindrical fiberglass tower was erected in 1983 on the foundations of a cast-iron tower of 1890. Its modern optic emits alternate flashes every 10 seconds (red and white, with red sector) at a focal-plane height of 51 feet.

18. Long Island Head Light
Long Island

This pretty location in Long Island has served as a lighthouse site since 1819, although the current 52-foot, white, conical brick tower, with its black cast-iron lantern, was first lit in 1901. Deactivated from 1982 until 1985, its solar-powered optic emits a white flash every 2.5 seconds (focal plane 120 feet). The lighthouse and grounds are not open to the public and are best viewed by boat.

BELOW: *Graves (Ledge) Light.*

Boston Harbor Light

Description: conical rubblestone tower
Markings: white; black lantern
Lens: second-order Fresnel
Height: 89 feet (tower); 102 feet (focal plane)

SPOTTER'S NOTE
The first lighthouse at this site was destroyed by the British in 1776, at the close of the American Revolution.

BELOW: *The light at sunset.*

The Ancient Mariner

Boston Light, originally a stone tower, became North America's first light station in 1716 and was the last U.S. light to be automated (1998). The current lighthouse, an 89-foot white, conical rubblestone tower with a black cast-iron lantern, was first lit in 1783, and its second-order Fresnel lens of 1859 is still in use today, emitting a white flash every 10 seconds (focal plane 102 feet). The lighthouse is open for public viewing, and a small museum is housed in the entryway, where a small display of artifacts includes the original 1719 fog cannon. Outbuildings consist of a two-story, white wood keeper's house (1884), a brick fog-signal building (1876), a boathouse (1899), a cistern building (1884), and a brick oil house (1889).

LEFT: *Plymouth (Gurnet) Light.*

SPOTTER'S NOTE
Minots Ledge Light is affectionately known as the "I Love You" light because of its 1-4-3 flash cycle.

BELOW: *Minots Ledge Light.*

19. Minots Ledge Light *Cohasset*

Built on a submerged shoal in extremely difficult conditions, this 114-foot, conical granite tower, topped with a green cast-iron lantern, has stood the test of time since it was first lit in 1860. The 300-mm, solar-powered optic flashes white (focal plane 85 feet). Although visible from Cohasset, the best views of the tower are by boat.

20. Scituate Light *Scituate (overleaf)*

21. Plymouth (Gurnet) Light *Duxbury*

This 34-foot, white, octagonal-pyramidal wooden tower, with a black-and-red cast-iron lantern, was built in 1843 alongside a twin light. In 1924, the northeast light was discontinued, and the remaining tower now stands alone, sending out three white flashes (with a red sector) every 30 seconds (focal plane 102 feet). Closed to the public, the best views are by boat.

22. Duxbury Pier ("Bug") Light *Duxbury*

This white, conical cast-iron tower on a red-and-white base was the first offshore caisson lighthouse in the United States (1871). Its modern optic flashes red, twice every 5 seconds (focal plane 35 feet). The lighthouse is best seen by boat.

Scituate Light

Description: tapering, octagonal masonry tower; attached keeper's quarters
Markings: white; green lantern
Lens: FA-250
Height: 50 feet (tower); 49 feet (focal plane)

RIGHT: *A distinctive landmark.*
BELOW: *The light in 1934.*

Let There Be Light

Marking Cedar Point, this 1811 lighthouse was inactive from 1850 to 1852, and then from 1860, but it was relit in 1994 as a private beacon. The white, octagonal granite-and-brick tower stands at 50 feet and is topped with a green lantern. The tower is attached to the keeper's quarters (an 1811 Cape Cod house) by a covered walkway. It has a height of focal plane of 49 feet and uses a FA-250 optic. The lighthouse is occasionally opened to the public during the summer.

BELOW: *Architect's diagram of the north elevation.*

23. Sandy Neck Light *Barnstable*
This cylindrical brick tower was built in 1857 and painted white. The distinctive black bands were not added until 1887—to reinforce cracks that had emerged. The nearby Victorian keeper's house (1880) now has the same private owner as the lighthouse, which was deactivated in 1931. The tower is best seen by boat.

> **SPOTTER'S NOTE**
> All that's left of Mayo's Beach Light (established 1838), Wellfleet, is the privately owned keeper's house; the cast-iron tower was torn down in 1939.

24. Long Point Light *Provincetown*
The 300-mm solar-powered optic of this 38-foot, white, square-pyramidal brick tower, with a black cast-iron lantern, first shone its fixed beam of green light in 1875, and still continues to do so (focal plane 36 feet). The grounds are open to the public.

25. Wood End Light *Provincetown*
Built in 1872, this 39-foot, white, square brick tower is still in operation, flashing a red signal every 10 seconds. A solar-powered Vega VRB-25 lens is now in use (focal plane 45 feet). The lighthouse is being restored by the American Lighthouse Foundation.

26. Race Point Light *near Provincetown*
Built in 1876 alongside the keeper's house, this 45-foot, white cast-iron lighthouse, with a black lantern, emits a flashing white signal every 10 seconds (focal plane 67 feet) from a Vega VRB-25 optic. It is open to the public in summer: the keeper's house offers accommodation (though a long hike is required to reach the lighthouse).

27. Cape Cod (Highland) Light *North Truro (overleaf)*

28. Three Sisters Lights (Three Towers) *Eastham*
Two of these three white, conical wooden towers were active from 1892 until 1911, while the third remained in use until 1923. After several moves, they have been returned to the original site near Nauset Light, arranged in their original configuration, and serve as an interpretive museum. Rangers offer tours during the summer.

> **SPOTTER'S NOTE**
> Before restoration, the Three Sisters Lights formed part of a private cottage that was used as a dance studio.

RIGHT: *Three Sisters Lights.*

Cape Cod (Highland) Light

Description: conical brick
tower; attached
keeper's dwelling
Markings: white; black
lantern
Lens: VRB-25
Height: 66 feet (tower);
183 feet (focal plane)

RIGHT: *The tower is attached
to the keeper's dwelling by a
red-roofed walkway.*

BELOW: *A photograph taken from
the southeast in 1959.*

High and Mighty

Standing 66 feet tall on the Cape Cod National
Seashore, this light was built in 1857. Made
from brick, the conical tower is white, with a
black cast-iron lantern. Because of severe erosion, the tower was moved back 450 feet in
1996. Every 5 seconds a white light flashes from
the VRB-25 lens (focal plane 183 feet). The
keeper's house has a small gift store, and the
Highland House Museum of the Truro
Historical Society is nearby. The lighthouse
itself is also open to the public.

29. Nauset (Beach) Light *Eastham*

This 48-foot, conical cast-iron tower, with a concrete foundation, has a white bottom half and red upper half, with a black cast-iron lantern. The lighthouse was constructed in Chatham in 1877, where it operated as one of a pair, but was moved to Eastham (the site of the original Three Sisters light station) in 1923. Currently a private aid to navigation, it flashes every 5 seconds (alternate red and white, focal plane 102 feet).

30. Chatham Light *Chatham (overleaf)*

31. Stage Harbor Light *West Chatham*

A 36-foot, white, conical cast-iron tower with its lantern removed, this lighthouse was built in 1880 and is attached to a wood-framed keeper's house. It was deactivated in 1933, and the buildings are now privately owned. The light can be seen from across Stage Harbor.

32. Monomoy Island (Monomoy Point) Light *Monomoy Island*

Located within the Monomoy National Wildlife Refuge, this lighthouse has not been in use since 1923. Built in 1849, the red, cylindrical cast-iron tower with a black lantern is 40 feet tall. A Cape Cod-style keeper's house stands nearby. The grounds are open to the public.

TOP: *Nauset (Beach) Light.*
ABOVE: *Monomoy Island Light.*
BELOW: *Great Point Light.*

33. Great Point (Nantucket) Light *Nantucket*

This 60-foot, white conical tower stands at the northeastern point of the island, within the Coskata-Coatue Wildlife Refuge. Built in 1986, it is a concrete-and-plastic replica of an 1818 lighthouse that was destroyed in a severe storm in 1984. The solar-powered optic sends out a white flash every 5 seconds (focal plane 71 feet). The lighthouse grounds are open to the public, and the tower is opened occasionally during the summer.

Chatham Light

ABOVE: *The remaining tower.*
BELOW: *When there were two.*

Description: conical cast-
iron tower
Markings: white; black
lantern
Lens: DCB-224
Height: 48 feet (tower);
80 feet (focal plane)

Two Become One

Built in 1877 as a twin to what is now Nauset (Beach) Light (which moved from Chatham to Eastham in 1923, *see* previous page), the current Chatham light is a white, conical cast-iron tower, with a black lantern, that stands 48 feet tall. Automated in 1982, its DCB-224 optic flashes white at a focal-plane height of 80 feet. The light station is only occasionally opened to the public, but can be seen from nearby roads.

The First Pair

The original twin towers at Chatham were built of wood in 1808. They stood 40 feet tall and lasted 33 years, before being replaced by brick towers that were erected further from the eroding cliff edge. By the end of 1881, these brick towers had themselves gone over the brink.

34. Sankaty Head Light *Nantucket*

A 70-foot, conical brick tower, painted white with a central red band, this beacon has been lighting the shores near Siasconset since 1850. The current DCB-224 optic flashes white every 7.5 seconds (focal plane 158 feet) and is housed in a black aluminum replacement lantern room (1970). The lighthouse stands on a bluff that is threatened by erosion. The grounds are open to the public.

SPOTTER'S NOTE
Nantucket Cliff Range Lights (1838–1912) were sold, but the white beacons now stand on private property on Bathing Beach Road.

BELOW: *Brant Point Light.*

35. Brant Point Light *Nantucket*

This 26-foot, white, conical wooden lighthouse of 1910, with its black cast-iron lantern, is the latest beacon at America's second-oldest light station (1746). Its immediate predecessor stands nearby. The current Brant Point Light's 250-mm optic emits a red light that eclipses every 4 seconds. The grounds of the lighthouse are open to the public.

36. Bass River Light *West Dennis*

Also known as West Dennis Light, this 1855 lighthouse (deactivated 1914) has served as a private aid to navigation, with a flashing white signal, since 1989. The white, conical iron tower, topped by a red lantern, rises to 44 feet from the roof of a white wooden house (now an inn and restaurant).

37. Point Gammon Light
Point Gammon

This 70-foot, conical fieldstone tower (1816) has narrow windows in its stone lantern room, and no gallery. Deactivated in 1858, it was replaced by the Bishop and Clerk's Light (*see* Spotter's Note). The tower and grounds are privately owned.

38. Hyannis (Range Rear) Light
Hyannis

Also known as Hyannis Harbor Light and South Hyannis Light, this 19-foot, white, conical brick tower, with a black lantern, was built in 1849. Deactivated in 1929, it is now privately owned.

SPOTTER'S NOTE
Just off Hyannis, in Nantucket Sound, a 30-foot pyramidal day beacon stands guard where a lighthouse, known as Bishop & Clerks Light, shone for nearly a century until it was destroyed in 1952.

39. West Chop Light   *West Chop*

At the entrance to Vineyard Haven Harbor, this 45-foot lighthouse, also known as Holmes Hole light, has a fourth-order Fresnel lens that emits an occulting white light (with red sector, focal plane 84 feet). The white, cylindrical brick tower (1881) is not open to the public, but can be seen from a nearby road.

40. East Chop (Telegraph Hill) Light   *Oak Bluffs*

Established in 1878 (automated 1933), this 40-foot, white, cast-iron conical lighthouse, with a black lantern, sends out an alternating green signal (focal plane 79 feet). The grounds are open to the public, and there are tours on summer Sundays.

> **SPOTTER'S NOTE**
> For many years the East Chop lighthouse was painted brown and was known as the "Chocolate Lighthouse."

41. Edgartown Harbor Light   *Edgartown*

Located at the eastern end of Martha's Vineyard, this 1875 lighthouse was relocated from Ipswich in 1939. The 45-foot, conical cast-iron tower (painted white, with a black lantern) has a solar-powered optic that sends out a flashing red signal. The grounds of this popular tourist attraction are open to the public.

42. Cape Poge (Pogue) Light   *Chappaquidick Island*

This 35-foot, white, conical, wood-shingle tower of 1893 has a black cast-iron lantern; its 300-mm optic emits a flashing white signal (focal plane 65 feet). The grounds are open to the public, but perhaps the easiest way to visit the light is with a tour (offered by the Cape Poge Wildlife Refuge).

BELOW: *Cape Poge Light.*

43. Gay Head Light   *Martha's Vineyard*

This unpainted, conical brick tower with a black cast-iron lantern was built in 1856 and stands 51 feet tall on a clifftop site. Its DCB-224 optic emits an alternating red and white signal (focal plane 170 feet). The lighthouse is easily viewed from a scenic overlook on the nearby road and is occasionally opened to visitors in summer.

44. Tarpaulin Cove Light   *Naushon Island*

This 38-foot, white, conical brick tower (1891, automated 1941) has a black cast-iron lantern and a flashing white signal (focal plane 78 feet). The light is best seen by boat.

45. Nobska Point Light *Woods Hole*

Built in 1876, this 40-foot, white, conical cast-iron tower with a black cast-iron lantern still holds its 1888 fourth-order Fresnel lens: its signal is a flashing white beam with a red sector (focal plane 87 feet). The lighthouse is occasionally opened in summer, and its grounds are open daily.

46. Wing's Neck Light *near Pocasset*

This deactivated lighthouse is located at the east side of Buzzard's Bay. Built in 1889, it served until 1945 and was subsequently privately bought. The white, hexagonal-pyramidal wooden tower, with a black cast-iron lantern, has a white keeper's house attached (1870s), which was originally built at the Ned Point Light. The tower is best seen by boat, but may be rented by arrangement with the Wings Neck Lighthouse Trust.

47. Cleveland East Ledge Light
offshore, Buzzard's Bay

This 1943 white Art Deco structure is a 70-foot, cylindrical reinforced-concrete tower erected above a square dwelling, which in turn sits on a concrete caisson. A white light flashes every 10 seconds from the 190-mm optic (focal plane 74 feet). The lighthouse is best seen by boat.

48. Bird Island Light *Bird Island*

This lighthouse was built on Bird Island, in Buzzard's Bay, in 1819. The light was deactivated from 1933 until 1997 (when it was automated) and it now serves as a private aid to navigation. The 31-foot, conical stone tower is painted white, and its black lantern houses a solar-powered optic that emits a flashing white signal (focal plane 37 feet). There is no public access to the lighthouse, which is managed by Bird Island Light Preservation Society, but it is visible in the distance from the shore near Marion Center.

ABOVE: *Nobska Point Light.*

BELOW: *Bird Island Light.*

ABOVE: *Ned's Point Light.*

49. Ned's Point Light *Mattapoisett*

This lighthouse was constructed at the entrance to Mattapoisett Harbor in 1838. The 39-foot, white, conical stone tower has a black lantern. Automated in 1923, but inactive from 1952 until 1961, it now holds a 250-mm optic (focal plane 41 feet). This site is open to the public.

50. Palmer Island Light *New Bedford*

Deactivated in 1963, Palmer Island Light (1849) was abandoned and fell into disrepair until it was renovated in the late 1970s. Relit as a private aid to navigation in 1999, the 24-foot, white, conical stone tower has a black cast-iron lantern. Its solar-powered optic sends out an alternating white signal (focal plane 34 feet). Occasionally opened to the public, the tower may also be visited by special arrangement.

51. Butler Flats Light *New Bedford*

Standing offshore on a caisson, this 1898 lighthouse was given a new rotating beacon on its one-hundredth birthday (flashing white signal). A 53-foot, white, cylindrical brick tower with a black cast-iron lantern, it resembles the cast-iron spark-plug lighthouses of its era. It can be seen from the waterfront in New Bedford or from the New Bedford–Martha's Vineyard ferry.

52. Clark's Point Light *New Bedford*

This 1869 lighthouse at Fort Taber consists of a lantern rising from the center of the roof of a rectangular stone building (white-painted upper half). Inactive from 1898 until 2001, its optic emits a fixed white light. The grounds around the fort are open as a public park.

53. Borden Flats Light *offshore, Fall River*

This active offshore lighthouse was first lit in 1881 and was automated in 1963. The white, conical, spark-plug tower stands 50 feet tall on a caisson. In 1997, the original fourth-order Fresnel lens was replaced with a 250-mm optic, which has a flashing white signal. The lighthouse is best viewed from the Borden Light Marina in the city of Fall River.

RHODE ISLAND

The Ocean State may be the nation's smallest, but it has a long coastline and many historic lights, from caisson-mounted spark-plug lights to onshore masonry towers.

1. Sakonnet Point Light
Little Compton
Established in 1884, this 66-foot, white, conical cast-iron lighthouse, built on a caisson, was deactivated in 1955 because of hurricane damage. It was relit privately in 1997 and now emits a flashing white signal, with a red sector. The lighthouse can be seen from the beach at Sakonnet Point.

2. Castle Hill Light *Newport (overleaf)*

3. Ida Lewis (Lime Rock) Light
Newport
Built in 1856, the white, square, 13-foot brick tower is attached to the two-story granite keeper's house, now a club. It is a private aid to navigation that operates seasonally. Renamed for a courageous former keeper, the best views of this historic light are from the water.

ABOVE: *Newport Harbor Light.*
BELOW: *Rose Island Light.*

4. Newport Harbor Light *Goat Island*
This white, octagonal granite tower (1842), with a black cast-iron lantern, stands 35 feet tall on a harbor pier. Automated in 1963, its signal is a fixed green light. The lighthouse can be viewed from near the Hyatt Regency Hotel, Newport.

5. Rose Island Light *Newport*
Established in 1870, this lighthouse consists of an octagonal wooden tower with a black lantern on the roof of the keeper's dwelling. The light functions as a private aid to navigation, flashing white every 6 seconds (focal plane 48 feet). The building houses a museum and is available for overnight accommodation. Rose Island is accessible by ferry from Newport or Jamestown.

Castle Hill Light

Description: conical rubblestone tower
Markings: white upper; black lantern
Lens: 300 mm
Height: 34 feet (tower); 42 feet (focal plane)

BELOW: *This scenic light is unique in design.*

Rocky Road

This robust beacon was built on the grounds of Harvard zoologist Alexander Agassiz's summer home, despite his objection: he believed that the fog signal would disturb the marine life he was studying. A conical granite-block tower (1890) whose top half is painted white, the lighthouse is thought to have been designed by noted architect Henry Hobson Richardson. The 34-foot light marks the entrance to Narragansett Bay: it has a a black, cast-iron lantern (focal plane 40 feet) that emits a red alternating signal. The lighthouse is closed, but the adjacent grounds of Castle Hill Inn are open to the public.

6. Prudence Island (Sandy Point) Light *Portsmouth*

The oldest lighthouse in Rhode Island, this 25-foot, white, octagonal-pyramidal granite tower, with a black birdcage lantern, was built on Newport Harbor's Goat Island in 1823. It was moved to Prudence Island in 1851, and its flashing green signal (focal plane 28 feet) was automated in 1972. The grounds may be visited (within 20 minutes' walking distance from the ferry landing).

SPOTTER'S NOTE
Prudence Island's neighbors in Narragansett Bay include three small islands named Patience, Hope, and Despair.

BELOW: *Hog Island Shoal Light.*

7. Hog Island Shoal Light *Portsmouth*

Built in 1901 on an offshore caisson, this white, conical cast-iron tower was automated in 1964. Its alternating white signal shines at a focal-plane height of 54 feet above sea level. The lighthouse is best seen by boat.

8. Bristol Ferry Light *Bristol*

This 1855 lighthouse stands at the foot of Mount Hope Bridge. The 34-foot, square brick tower is white, with a black lantern, and is attached the keeper's house. Deactivated in 1927, the building is now a private residence. There is no public access, but the building can be seen from the end of Ferry Road.

BELOW: *Bristol Ferry Light.*

SPOTTER'S NOTE

The lighthouse at Pomham Rocks is named for a Narragansett chief who fought in King Philip's War and was killed in 1676. C.H. Salisbury was the first keeper at the lighthouse, which originally included a parlor with a piano, a hall containing a large library, and a flower and vegetable garden. The Salisburys lived there with their daughter and a dog named Sailor.

BELOW: *Dutch Island Light.*

9. Nayatt Point Light *Barrington*

This 25-foot lighthouse is a white, square brick tower (1856) with a black, red-roofed lantern, attached to the former keeper's house (1826). It was deactivated in 1868, and the property is now a private home. The light can be seen from the street nearby.

10. Pomham Rocks Light (Old)
East Providence

This 40-foot lighthouse, built in 1871, consists of an octagonal wooden tower with a black cast-iron lantern that rises from the red roof of the white keeper's dwelling. Located on a small island, the lighthouse is privately owned and has been inactive since 1974. It can be seen from the cycle path that runs from Providence to Bristol.

11. Conimicut Shoal Light *Warwick*

This 58-foot, conical, white cast-iron tower (1883) stands offshore on a rocky ledge. Its black lantern houses a 250-mm optic that emits a flashing white signal. The lighthouse can be seen in the distance from Conimicut Point Park, Warwick, and the area around Nayatt Point, Barrington.

12. Warwick Light *Warwick*

This 1932 lighthouse is a 51-foot white, conical steel tower, topped with a black cast-iron lantern. The tower was moved in 1939 after erosion caused by the 1938 hurricane. It was automated in 1985 and has a green flashing signal (focal plane 66 feet). The Victorian keeper's dwelling, which dates from 1889, stands nearby. The site is not open to the public, but the light can be seen from the perimeter fence of the grounds.

ABOVE: *Plum Beach Light.*

13. Poplar Point Light *North Kingstown*

One of the oldest wooden lighthouses in the United States (1831, deactivated 1894), this building has been privately owned since 1894. The white, octagonal wooden tower rises from the roof of the keeper's house and is topped with a black lantern. The lighthouse is not open to the public, but can be seen from the breakwater at Sauga Point.

14. Conanicut Island Light (Old) *Jamestown*

Established in 1886, this red, square wooden tower attached to a two-story keeper's house (red with white trim) was deactivated in 1933 and has had its lantern removed. The property is privately owned and can only be seen by boat; an automated light is now mounted on a skeleton tower nearby.

15. Plum Beach Light *North Kingstown, Washington County*

Deactivated between 1941 and 2003, this 1889 offshore lighthouse has been restored as a private aid to navigation. The 53-foot, conical cast-iron tower has a white lower portion, a red upper, and a black lantern and supporting caisson. The original fourth-order Fresnel lens is still in use and flashes white every 5 seconds. The lighthouse is near Jamestown Bridge and is best seen by boat.

16. Dutch Island Light *Jamestown*

This 1857 light is a 42-foot, white brick tower with black trim. Deactivated in 1979, it is now under renovation. It can be seen from the Fort Getty Recreation Area.

ABOVE: *Beavertail Light stands in a state park and is accessible by car.*

SPOTTER'S NOTE
Point Judith Light underwent an extensive renovation in the summer of 2000.

BELOW: *Point Judith Light.*

17. Beavertail Light *Jamestown*

This 45-foot tower, which is square in shape, made of granite, and topped with a black, cast-iron lantern, was built in 1856. It sends out a white flash every 6 seconds (focal plane 68 feet) from its DCB-24 optic. The previous fourth-order Fresnel lens is on display at the Beavertail Lighthouse Museum, housed in the former assistant keeper's house (1898). The tower is not open to the public.

18. Point Judith Light *Narragansett*

This 51-foot, octagonal-pyramidal brownstone tower (bottom half white, top half brown) with a black cast-iron lantern was built in 1857. It was automated in 1954 but retains its original fourth-order Fresnel lens, which emits a white signal (focal plane 65 feet). The grounds may be visited, but the lighthouse itself is closed.

19. Block Island (North) Light

Block Island

This light is one of a series built in the Long Island Sound in the 1860s to the same design (*see* page 146). Its octagonal tower with red cast-iron lantern rises from the gable end of a granite keeper's house. The station was deactivated between 1970 and 1990; it now emits a flashing white light (focal plane 61 feet). There is a museum (North Light Interpretive Center) in the lighthouse building, but visitors cannot climb to the lantern.

SPOTTER'S NOTE
North Light is mostly powered by a combination of solar energy and a wind generator. Ecologically minded visitors and lighthouse spotters can enjoy Block Island without their cars: cycle rentals are available near the ferry terminal.

20. Block Island (Southeast) Light *Block Island*

The Coast Guard deactivated this unusual lighthouse (operational 1875–1990) to move it back 300 feet from the edge of the cliff. Relighted in 1994, it emits a green flash every 5 seconds (focal plane 261 feet). The 52-foot, unpainted octagonal-pyramidal brick tower with black lantern is attached to a brick keeper's house. There is a small museum in the lighthouse, and the tower is open for tours during the summer.

21. Watch Hill Light *Watch Hill (overleaf)*

BELOW: *Block Island (Southeast) Light became a National Historic Landmark in 1997.*

Watch Hill Light

LEFT: *Watch Hill's tower resembles the one at Beavertail.*
BELOW: *The museum is located in the former oil house.*

Lookout Point

Colonists used this beautiful resort area during the French and Indian War, giving the town, and the light (then a rudimentary beacon), their names. Today's lighthouse is a square, unpainted granite tower with a white cast-iron lantern that rises to 45 feet. Built in 1856, the light was automated in 1986 and uses a VRB-25 optic to produce its alternating red-and-white signal (focal plane 61 feet). The lighthouse grounds and the Watch Hill Lighthouse Museum in the station's oil house are open to the public.

Description: square granite tower
Markings: unpainted; red and white lantern
Lens: VRB-25
Height: 45 feet (tower); 61 feet (focal plane)

CONNECTICUT

Connecticut's historic beacons light the Long Island Sound, once a busy thorough-fare for whalers and traders, and now a recreational area.

1. Stonington Harbor Light
Stonington

This 1840 lighthouse consists of a 35-foot, octagonal granite tower attached to the stone keeper's dwelling. The light was deactivated in 1889, and the building has housed a museum since 1925.

2. Mystic Seaport Light
Mystic Seaport

Located on the grounds of the historic village of Mystic Seaport—a large maritime museum—this lighthouse is a replica of Nantucket's Brant Point Light. The white, conical wooden tower has a black lantern that houses a fourth-order Fresnel lens, which is operational, although it is not an official aid to navigation.

3. Morgan Point Light   *Noank*

Built in 1868, this light is one of a series constructed in this style in Long Island Sound (*see* page 146). The inactive light tower rises to 61 feet; it has been a private residence since 1922. It is best viewed by boat.

4. Avery Point Light   *Groton*

Built to memorialize America's lighthouse keepers and located on the Avery Point campus of the University of Connecticut, this 41-foot, brown, octagonal concrete tower, with a wooden lantern (*see* Spotter's Note), guarded the shores between 1944 and 1967. The Avery Point Lighthouse Society is working to restore the tower; its grounds are open to the public.

5. New London Ledge Light
New London (overleaf)

ABOVE: *Stonington Harbor Light.*
BELOW: *Mystic Seaport Light.*

SPOTTER'S NOTE
In December 2001 Avery Point's wooden lantern was removed from the tower. A duplicate is being constructed by the West Mystic Wooden Boat Building Company.

New London Ledge Light

Description: integrated lantern and square brick keeper's house
Markings: red; white trim and lantern
Lens: VRB-25
Height: 58 feet (focal plane)

A Haunted Mansion

Built in 1909, this handsome offshore lighthouse was designed in the French Second Empire style. The red building, with white trim, is made of brick and granite and served as the keeper's house, with the red-roofed lantern room rising from the roof. Automated in 1987, its solar-powered VRB-25 optic emits a cycle of three white flashes and one red flash every 30 seconds. The original Fresnel lens is now on display at the Custom House Museum of Maritime History in New London. A keeper named Ernie is said to haunt the building; he supposedly jumped to his death after learning that his wife had run off with the captain of the Block Island ferry. There are plans to open the lighthouse as a museum, possibly offering overnight accommodation. It is best seen by boat: tours are run by Project Oceanology.

BELOW: *This is the only lighthouse built to this design.*

LEFT: *New London Harbor Light.*
BELOW: *Saybrook Breakwater Light.*
BOTTOM: *Lynde Point Light.*

6. New London Harbor Light *New London*

Standing sentinel at the water's edge, this is Connecticut's oldest (1801) and tallest (89 feet) light tower. Octagonal-pyramidal in shape, it was built of brick-lined brownstone and has been painted white, with a black lantern. In 1863 the keeper's house was built alongside the tower, but this has been a private residence since 1912. The original fourth-order Fresnel lens is still in use, sending out an alternating white signal, with a red sector. The station is closed to the public and best viewed from the water (the Block Island ferry passes nearby).

7. Saybrook Breakwater Light
Old Saybrook

At the mouth of the Connecticut River, this 49-foot, brick-lined cast-iron tower (1886), which is white with black trim, emits a flashing green signal (focal plane 58 feet). The keepers lived inside the lighthouse, which was was automated in 1959 and now uses a 300-mm optic. The breakwater lighthouse is not open to the public but can be seen disntantly from various points on the coast.

8. Lynde Point (Saybrook Inner)
Light *Old Saybrook*

This 65-foot, white, octagonal-pyramidal brownstone tower with a red-roofed cast-iron lantern was built in 1838 (automated 1975). The fifth-order Fresnel lens (1980) sends out a fixed white beam (focal plane 71 feet). The lighthouse is not open to the public but can be seen from the area near the South Cove Bridge at Saybrook Point.

BELOW: *Five Mile Point Light is a popular tourist attraction in New Haven.*

9. Faulkner's Island Light *Guilford*

Located on an island in the scenic Thimble Islands chain, this 1802 lighthouse is the state's second-oldest. The white, octagonal-pyramidal tower stands at 46 feet (focal plane 94 feet) and is constructed of brick-lined brownstone, with a black cast-iron lantern. The solar-powered VRB-25 optic emits a white flash every 10 seconds. Also on site are several outbuildings, although the keeper's house burned down in 1976. There is an open house each September; the light can be viewed by boat or in the distance from Guilford.

10. Southwest Ledge (New Haven Breakwater) Light *New Haven*

(opposite)

11. Five Mile Point (Old New Haven) Light *New Haven*

This lighthouse, constructed in 1847, is located in Lighthouse Point Park; it was deactivated in 1877, when it was replaced by Southwest Ledge Light. It is a 70-foot octagonal-pyramidal, white brownstone tower with brick lining and a black, cast-iron lantern, which originally held a fourth-order Fresnel lens (1855). The grounds are open to the public, and there are occasional tours of the tower itself.

12. Stratford Shoal (Middle Ground) Light *Bridgeport*

This 1877 lighthouse is an octagonal granite tower rising to 35 feet and integrated with the granite keeper's quarters; the light stands on a platform built over an offshore rocky shoal. Automated in 1970, it currently houses a VRB-25 optic that flashes white every 5 seconds (focal plane 60 feet). Closed to the public, the light can be seen from the Bridgeport–Port Jefferson (NY) ferry.

Southwest Ledge Light

Description: octagonal cast-iron tower
Markings: white; black lantern
Lens: VRB-25
Height: 45 feet (tower); 57 feet (focal plane)

A New Haven Monument

This 1877 white cast-iron tower stands on a concrete caisson and is 45 feet tall. A VRB-25 optic is currently in use, sending out a red flash every 5 seconds (focal plane 57 feet). The lighthouse is closed to the public but can be seen from New Haven's Lighthouse Point Park.

Pride of Place

The plan for a new offshore beacon at the end of the hazardous Southwest Ledge became viable with advances in caisson technology. Once assembled, the tower was not dispatched to its intended site immediately, however, being first displayed in Pennsylvania, at the 1876 Centennial Exposition hosted by Philadelphia. This indicates the pride that both the Lighthouse Board and its manufacturers took in this cutting-edge, French Second-Empire–style manifestation of offshore building expertise. The structure's durability has proved equal to its elegance, and the light continues to perform its duties today.

ABOVE: *The mile-long breakwater.*
ABOVE, LEFT: *An elegant design.*
BELOW: *A cross-section.*

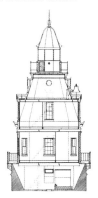

SPOTTER'S NOTE
Southwest Ledge Light was built in Baltimore and is the identical twin of Ship John Shoal Light in Delaware Bay.

ABOVE: *Stratford Point Light.*
BELOW: *Black Rock Harbor Light.*

SPOTTER'S NOTE
Tongue Point Light was moved in 1919 when the breakwater upon which it was built was partially dismantled in order to widen the shipping channel in the harbor.

13. Stratford Point Light *Stratford*

This striking 35-foot cast-iron tower is white with a central red band, topped with a red-roofed lantern. The lighthouse was built in 1881 alongside the wooden keeper's house, which now provides housing for a Coast Guard Family. A double flash of white light is emitted every 20 seconds from the VRB-25 optic (focal plane 52 feet). The station is closed to the public, and the best views are by boat.

14. Tongue Point (Bridgeport Breakwater) Light *Bridgeport*

Also known as Bug Light, this 31-foot, black, conical cast-iron tower (1895) stands on a concrete foundation and sends out a flashing green light every 4 seconds (focal plane 31 feet). A 155-mm optic has replaced the original sixth-order lens. The lighthouse is closed but can be seen from nearby beaches and from the Bridgeport–Port Jefferson (NY) ferry.

ABOVE: *Penfield Reef Light.*

15. Black Rock Harbor (Fayerweather Island) Light *Bridgeport*

This 47-foot, white, octagonal-pyramidal stone tower of 1823, which has a black lantern and trim, was renovated in 1998 but has not been operational since 1933 (the solar-powered light installed in 2000 is not an official aid to navigation). The lighthouse is part of a nature reserve, and the grounds are open to the public.

16. Penfield Reef Light *Fairfield*

At the entrance to Black Rock Harbor, this white wood-and-granite tower rises from the upper section of the granite keeper's dwelling that sits on an artificial island. The 35-foot lighthouse dates from 1874; a VRB-25 optic emits a flashing red beam every 6 seconds. The lighthouse is closed but can be seen from beaches in Fairfield and Bridgeport. The best views are to be found by boat, however.

17. Peck Ledge Light *Norwalk*

BELOW: *Peck Ledge Light.*

This 54-foot, conical cast-iron tower (1906), white with a brown band, is built on a black cast-iron caisson in the long entrance channel to Norwalk Harbor. Automated in 1933, the original fourth-order Fresnel lens was in use until 1988, when a 250-mm optic was installed; this sends out a flashing green light every 2.5 seconds. The lighthouse can be seen from Calf Pasture Park in South Norwalk.

ABOVE: *Sheffield Island Light.*

18. Sheffield Island (Norwalk) Light *Norwalk*

Also known as Smith Island Light, this is one of a series built to the same design in the sound. The tower dates from 1868 and rises to 44 feet. It was deactivated in 1902 (when it was replaced by Greens Ledge Light) and now functions as a museum. Tours are available spring through early fall; the boat departs from a dock next to South Norwalk's Maritime Aquarium.

19. Greens Ledge Light *Norwalk*

Standing 52 feet tall, this cast-iron tower, which has a red-brown lower section and a white upper and lantern, was built over an offshore reef marking the entrance to the Norwalk Harbor channel in 1902. It was automated in 1972 and a VRB-25 is currently in use, emitting alternate red and white flashes every 20 seconds (focal plane 62 feet). The lighthouse is closed to the public but can be seen from Rowayton's Pine Point.

20. Stamford Harbor (Chatham Rocks) Light *Stamford*

This 1882 lighthouse was officially decommissioned in 1953 and has been privately owned and operated ever since. The 60-foot offshore cast-iron tower, white on a red base, uses a 200-mm optic and beams out a white flash every 4 seconds. The lighthouse is not open to the public but can be seen from Shippan Point.

21. Great Captain Island Light *Greenwich*

This 1868 lighthouse is one of a series built in the Long Island Sound of the same design (*see* Sheffield Island, above). The station was deactivated in 1970. The island is part of a town park that is open to Greenwich residents only; nonresident visitors can only view the light by private boat.

BELOW: *Greens Ledge Light appears briefly in the 1999 remake of* The Thomas Crown Affair.

NEW YORK

The Empire State's Long Island, Hudson River, and Upstate lights are listed here, not including those that illuminate Lakes Ontario, Erie, and Champlain.

LONG ISLAND AND NEW YORK CITY

1. Latimer Reef Light   *Fishers Island Sound*

A 49-foot cast-iron lighthouse dating from 1884, this white tower, with a central red band, still uses its original fifth-order Fresnel lens, which flashes white light every 6 seconds. The offshore lighthouse is not accessible but can be seen from Dubois Beach, near Stonington Harbor Lighthouse, in Connecticut.

2. North Dumpling Light
North Dumpling Island

This 31-foot, octagonal, shingled red-brick tower was built in 1871 and is attached to the keeper's house. The station was replaced with a nearby skeleton tower in 1959 (*see* photograph, below) but was renovated, modified, and relit in 1980 and still sends out its fixed white beam, which has a red sector. The lighthouse and island are privately owned and are not open to the public; viewing is only possible by boat.

> **SPOTTER'S NOTE**
> During Prohibition, islands in this area were often used for trafficking bootlegged alcohol. The keeper of North Dumpling Light came under scrutiny after reports of "strange lights," but no evidence was found.

BELOW: *North Dumpling Light.*

ABOVE: *The lantern room at Little Gull Island Light.*

ABOVE: *Race Rock Light.*
BELOW, RIGHT: *Plum Island Light.*

3. Little Gull Island Light
Fishers Island

An unpainted, conical granite tower with a red-and-white lantern, this 1869 lighthouse rises to 91 feet. Automated in 1978, it emits a flashing white signal. Its original second-order Fresnel lens is on display at the East End Seaport Maritime Museum in Greenport, which runs occasional cruises that include views of this light.

4. Race Rock Light *Fishers Island*

A testament to the engineering skills of the time, this 1879 lighthouse, eight years in the making, was among the earliest lighthouses built on a caisson foundation. The square, granite tower, with a white lantern, is attached to the keeper's dwelling and stands 45 feet tall on an artificial island over a dangerous reef near Fishers Island. Automated in 1978, the new DCB-24 optic emits a flashing red signal. The light can be seen from the ferry between New London and Block Island or, distantly, from Watch Hill, Rhode Island, and points along the Connecticut coast.

5. Plum Island (Plum Gut) Light
Orient

This 1870 lighthouse is one of a series built to the same design in the Long Island Sound during this period. It has been deactivated and abandoned; there is no access to the island.

SPOTTER'S NOTE
The architect of Race Rock Light was Francis Hopkinson Smith, an engineer who was also responsible for construction of the foundation of the Statue of Liberty and the sea wall on Governors Island, New York.

6. Orient Point Light *Orient Point*

Located on an offshore reef, this 1899 lighthouse is known locally as the "Old Coffee Pot." A 45-foot conical cast-iron tower, it is white with black lantern, trim, and base, built on a caisson. A 190-mm optic replaced the original fifth-order Fresnel Lens. The lighthouse, which leans at a 5-degree angle, can be seen from the ferry landing at Orient Point.

7. Horton Point Light *Southold*

Dating from 1857, this light was deactivated in 1933, when a new skeleton tower replaced it. Following a major restoration effort, the historic tower was relit in 1990, and the lighthouse now serves as both an active aid to navigation and a museum. Visitors may climb the square, white, stuccoed masonry tower, which stands at 58 feet and is attached to the rectangular, white keeper's house. The flashing green light has a height of focal plane of 103 feet above sea level.

8. Long Beach Bar ("Bug") Light *Greenport*

This 1990 building is a replica of the 1870 lighthouse that withstood the 1938 hurricane but was destroyed by arsonists in the 1960s. Marking the end of a long sandspit, the tower is square in shape, with beveled edges, and rises from the roof of the keeper's dwelling, which stands on screwpile foundations. Closed to the public, the lighthouse can be seen from the shore.

9. Cedar Island Light *Sag Harbor*

This square, unpainted granite tower (1864), which is integral to the large keeper's house and rises to a height of 40 feet, was deactivated in 1934 and has since been abandoned, but efforts to restore it are underway. The light, which still has its red lantern, can be seen from Cedar Point County Park.

TOP: *Orient Point Light.*
ABOVE: *Horton Point Light.*

SPOTTER'S NOTE
The ferry between Orient Point and New London, Connecticut, provides good views of both the Orient Point and Plum Island lights.

SPOTTER'S NOTE
The East End Seaport Museum in Greenport features exhibits on lighthouses in the Long Island Sound.

ABOVE: *Montauk Point Light.*

BELOW: *Stepping Stone Light and the Throgs Neck Bridge.*

10. Montauk Point Light   *Montauk*

The fourth-oldest active lighthouse in the United States, and New York's oldest, this 110-foot, octagonal-pyramidal sandstone tower of 1796 was built under the direct orders of George Washington, because of its strategic location. A distinctive daymark, it is painted white with a central brown band and a black cast-iron lantern. The lighthouse emits a flashing white light every 5 seconds (focal plane 168 feet). Located in Montauk State Park, the light station is open to the public, and there is a museum in the keeper's house (1860).

11. Montauk Yacht Club Light
Lake Montauk

A 60-foot replica of Montauk Point Light, this tower is a private aid to navigation.

12. Fire Island Light   *Fire Island*
(opposite)

13. Stepping Stone Light   *Kings Point*

This 38-foot, integrated square red-brick tower (1877), topped with a white lantern, is attached to a Second Empire–style brick keeper's dwelling built on an offshore concrete-and-granite pier. The beacon sends a green flash every 4 seconds (focal plane 46 feet). Visible from the Throgs Neck Bridge, the lighthouse is not open to the public.

Fire Island Light

Description: tapered
cement-coated tower
Markings: black and
white bands; black
lantern
Lens: DCB-224
Height: 168 feet (tower);
167 feet (focal plane)

LEFT AND BELOW: *The historic
landmark at Fire Island National
Seashore.*

Old Flame

A 168-foot, tapered, cement-coated brick tower
(1858), painted with black and white bands and
topped with a black cast-iron lantern, this lighthouse was scheduled for demolition in the early
1980s, but was saved by the strenuous efforts of
conservationists. Deactivated between 1974 and
1986, it now emits a white flash every 7.5 seconds from the DCB-224 optic (focal plane 167
feet). In addition to its function as a navigational
aid, it is a museum, and guided tours enable visitors to climb the tower itself. The reborn light
station is now a major tourist attraction.

SPOTTER'S NOTE
Fire Island Light (open
daily, 9 a.m. to 5.30 p.m.)
can sometimes be seen
from commercial flights
on the approach to John
F. Kennedy International
Airport, especially in the
darkness, when its signal can
be seen up to 25 miles away.
Flights from Northern
Europe frequently offer
views of the light.

ABOVE: *Jeffrey's Hook Light.*

BELOW: *Blackwell Island Light.*

14. Whitestone Point Light
Whitestone Point

This navigational aid consists of a lantern mounted on a skeletal tower, emitting an alternating white light with green and red sectors. It stands on the site of an 1889 wooden bell tower with a light mounted on top.

15. Jeffrey's Hook ("Little Red") Light *Manhattan*

This much-photographed, bright-red landmark stands underneath the George Washington Bridge in a city park. The conical cast-iron tower, with black lantern, uses a 300-mm optic to produce its signal; it is a private navigational aid (although the building of the bridge rendered the light unnecessary for navigation). The lighthouse is open to the public, and scheduled tours are offered seasonally.

16. Blackwell (Welfare) Island Light *Roosevelt Island*

This 50-foot gray, octagonal stone tower (1872) was built with the labor of prisoners. It is no longer operational but serves as a popular tourist attraction in the city's Lighthouse Park. The island is accessible via a bridge at 36th Avenue and Vernon Blvd. in Astoria, Queens, or via tram from Second Avenue and 60th Street, Manhattan.

17. Titanic Memorial Light
Manhattan

This cylindrical, white steel light tower, built in 1913, stands at the entrance to the South Street Seaport Museum, having been moved in 1976 from its original location on top of the Seaman's Church Institute.

18. Statue of Liberty Light *New York Harbor (officially in New Jersey Waters)* *(opposite)*

Statue of Liberty Light

Enlightening the World

The Statue of Liberty is among the world's most famous landmarks. Built in 1886, the statue is 151 feet tall (or 305 feet including the pedestal foundation), and the signal beamed from its torch was visible for 24 miles. It was a gift from the people of France, but was deactivated in 1902. Following a series of closures and safety concerns, the statue was reopened to the public in August 2004, but visitors are advised to check in advance.

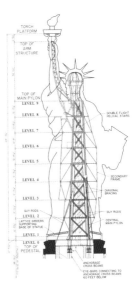

ABOVE: *A cross-section.*
LEFT: *A famous symbol of freedom.*
BELOW: *Lady Liberty's torch under restoration in 1984.*

Description: copper sculpture
Markings: patinated green
Lens: fourth-order Fresnel
Height: 151 feet (statue); 305 feet (from base)

ABOVE: *Fort Wadsworth Light and the Verrazano Narrows Bridge. The National Lighthouse Museum is located nearby at the St. George Ferry Terminal.*

19. **Fort Wadsworth Light** *Staten Island*

This lighthouse, which was built on top of a fort wall in 1903, was deactivated in 1965 when construction of the Verrazano Narrows Bridge made its signal unnecessary. The building fell into disrepair, but, following a restoration program, the light was reactivated in 2003. The brick tower is square-shaped and has a white cast-iron lantern (focal plane 75 feet). The complex is part of a national park.

20. **Coney Island (Norton's Point) Light** *Brooklyn*

A white, skeletal steel tower with black trim and a black cast-iron lantern, this 1890 lighthouse stands 70 feet tall and marks the main channel into New York Harbor. The 190-mm optic flashes a red light every 5 seconds at a focal-plane height of 75 feet. The keeper's house was built in 1896 and was home to a civilian caretaker until 2003. The light station is located in the private, gated community of Seagate.

21. **West Bank Range Front Light** *Staten Island*

Serving as a range light in tandem with Staten Island Light, this waveswept, brown spark-plug tower uses a solar-powered optic and has a height of focal plane of 59 feet above sea level. The tower was built on a caisson foundation in 1901 and, since being heightened seven years later, rises to 55 feet. It can be seen from South Beach (Staten Island) and from the boardwalk at Coney Island.

22. Staten Island Range Rear Light *Staten Island*

This 90-foot, octagonal, buff-colored brick tower (1912), with a black, cast-iron lantern (focal plane 231 feet), is built on a limestone foundation and marks the entrance to New York Harbor's Ambrose Channel. It serves in tandem with the West Bank light. There is no public access to this lighthouse.

23. New Dorp (Swash Channel Range Rear) Light *Staten Island*

This lighthouse was deactivated in 1964 and has been privately owned as a residence since 1974. The 80-foot, white, square wooden tower (1856) rises from the integral keeper's dwelling. The property is not open to the public.

24. Elm Tree (Swash Channel Range Front) Light *Staten Island*

This unpainted octagonal concrete tower (1939), with its lantern removed, was once the front light of a pair of range lights. Deactivated in 1964, it can be seen in Miller Field.

25. Old Orchard Shoal Light *Staten Island*

A 35-foot, spark-plug lighthouse (1893) with a white upper and lantern and a dark brown lower section, this tower is built on an offshore caisson. It uses a 250-mm optic (focal plane 51 feet) and can be seen from Great Kills Park.

26. Prince's Bay Light *Staten Island* *(officially New Jersey Waters)*

Built in 1864 and deactivated in 1992, this conical brownstone tower (lantern removed) is located in a nature reserve that is open to the public, though the grounds that immediately surround the tower and former keeper's residence are closed. At the time of this writing, it appears that the light may be restored and reactivated in the future.

ABOVE: *Staten Island Range Rear Light.*

SPOTTER'S NOTE
Staten Island Range Rear Light is one of the last brick lighthouses built in the United States. Today, only half of the original bivalve second-order Fresnel lens is in use, and there is an additional light mounted on the gallery replacing the former signal from the New Dorp Light.

SPOTTER'S NOTE
For many years, Prince's Bay Light was adjacent to the Mount Loretto Mission of the Immaculate Virgin, and a statue of the Virgin Mary was on the tower in place of the lantern for some years.

ABOVE: *Sands Point Light.*
BELOW: *Execution Rocks Light.*

27. Sands Point Light *North Hempstead*

This octagonal brownstone tower (1809), now fitted with a replica lantern, and the brick colonial former keeper's house (1868) are privately owned. The tower has not been in operation since 1922 and there is no public access to the site. A skeletal tower off Sands Point has replaced its function.

28. Execution Rocks Light
New Rochelle

This attractive landmark, built on a reef a mile offshore on the northeastern approach to New York Harbor, is a 60-foot, white, conical granite tower with a central brown band, attached to the stone keeper's dwelling (1850). It was designed by Alexander Parris, a Massachusetts–based architect who was known principally for his Greek Revival buildings. The light, which still emits a flashing white signal, can be seen from Sands Point, but there is no public access.

29. Cold Spring Harbor Light
Cold Spring Harbor

A white, square-pyramidal wooden tower (1890), this light was built on an offshore caisson but now stands 35 feet tall on the lawn of a private residence. It has not been in operation since 1965 and there is no public access.

30. **Huntingdon Harbor Light** *Huntingdon*

This 42-foot, square concrete tower (1912) is attached to the concrete, castlelike keeper's dwelling, which is built offshore on a concrete crib. The lighthouse is accessible by boat and is open seasonally for tours, weather permitting. The owners plan to open a museum at the lighthouse in the future.

31. **Eatons Neck Light** *Huntingdon*

This 73-foot, white, octagonal-pyramidal field-stone tower of 1799, attached to a workroom, is one of just six surviving eighteenth-century U.S. light stations. It still uses the original third-order Fresnel lens, which is housed in the red-roofed lantern room and has a focal-plane height of 144 feet. The light station is not open to the public, but permission to visit is occasionally granted by appointment with the Coast Guard.

> **SPOTTER'S NOTE**
> Eaton's Neck Light was designed by John J. McComb, a prominent architect who was responsible for New York's City Hall (1803–12) as well as the old Cape Henry lighthouse.

32. **Old Field Point Light** *Port Jefferson*

This lighthouse is one of a series built in the Long Island Sound (*see* page 146). The black lantern tower rises to 35 feet, and its optic produces alternate red and green flashes every 10 seconds (focal plane 74 feet). The light is not open to the public, but can be seen from the Bridgeport (CT)–Port Jefferson ferry.

BELOW: *Huntingdon Harbor Light.*

HUDSON RIVER

1. Tarrytown Harbor (Kingsland Point) Light *Tarrytown*

This white, conical cast-iron tower (1882, now inactive), with a red base and black trim, is located in Kingsland Point Park in Sleepy Hollow, near the Tappan Zee Bridge.

2. Stony Point Light *Stony Point*

A 30-foot, white, octagonal stone tower (1826), with a black lantern, this light overlooks the Hudson at a focal-plane height of 178 feet. It is still operational and is located at a public historic site that commemorates a battle in the Revolutionary War.

3. Esopus Meadows Light *Esopus*

This 1872 white, integral wooden structure, a keeper's dwelling with a tower rising from the center, stands on a small island in the Hudson. It is also known as Middle Hudson River Light and Maid of the Meadows. The building is under restoration and was relit as a private light in 2003 after almost forty years of darkness.

4. Rondout Creek (Kingston) Light *Kingston*

This handsome light is an off-white brick keeper's dwelling with a 48-foot square tower attached, with black lantern, built on a concrete pier. Its signal is a white flash every 6 seconds. The Hudson River Maritime Museum offers tours.

5. Saugerties Light *Saugerties*

Built in 1869, this substantial keeper's dwelling with attached square brick tower, topped with a black lantern, is easily accessible from the town of Saugerties and, while still emitting its occulting white signal, doubles up as a bed-and-breakfast inn. The lighthouse was fully restored from its dilapidated state and relit in 1990 after almost half a century of darkness.

BELOW: *Saugerties Light.*

6. Hudson-Athens (Hudson City) Light *Hudson City*

This stone-and-red-brick lighthouse, an integrated keeper's dwelling with tower attached, stands on a square stone caisson (with one corner shaped to prevent ice damage) and is the northernmost of the Hudson River lights. It is 30 feet tall, and its flashing green signal (automated in 1949) has a focal-plane height of 46 feet. The light can be seen from the riverbank and is occasionally opened to visitors.

UPSTATE NEW YORK

For other Upstate New York lighthouses, *see* the Great Lakes chapter and Lake Champlain.

1. Cooperstown Marina Light
Otsego Lake
This cylindrical white tower, with a central red band and a black lantern, is an operational light and an attraction at the marina in which it stands (one block from the Baseball Hall of Fame).

2. Cayuga Inlet Light   *Ithaca*
This 25-foot, white steel-clad tower (1917) is still active, though its lantern has been removed and replaced with a modern plastic optic. It can be seen from a viewpoint near the public marina on Pier Road.

3. Cayuga Inlet Breakwater Light
Ithaca
This 25-foot, red, conical steel tower (1927) is still an active beacon on the Erie Canal System. It can be seen from the state marina; the break-water on which it stands is almost completely submerged.

> **SPOTTER'S NOTE**
> Daily boat tours of Otsego Lake are available aboard *The Glimmerglass Queen*, although times may vary according to season. Departure is from the Lake Front Motel on Fair Street. Private chartered parties are also available.

> **SPOTTER'S NOTE**
> Although closed to the public, the Cayuga Inlet Light is accessible on foot, though the pier running to it is narrow and hazardous. The parking lot for the east side of the marina and the public golf course is less than a mile from the pier.

4. Shoal Point Light   *Fourth Lake*
This tapering octagonal lighthouse dating from the 1890s, painted red with a white, green-roofed lantern, has been restored and relit (2001) as a private navigational aid at this scenic location in the Adirondacks. It is not open to the public.

5. Frenchman's Island Light   *Frenchman's Island*
This 105-foot structure consists of an 85-foot, white concrete tower topped with a 20-foot skeletal steel tower, which holds a modern signal. It functions as an Erie Canal System navigational aid. The island is situated on Oneida Lake near Cicero.

6. Sylvan (Verona) Beach Light   *Verona Beach*
This 85-foot white cylindrical tower (1917) lights the eastern end of Oneida Lake on the Erie Canal System; its lantern has been removed, and a small modern optic installed. The tower is not easily viewed, because it is surrounded by private homes.

NEW JERSEY

New Jersey's low-lying, sandy Atlantic coastline is illuminated by a number of impressively tall towers built in the nineteenth century, as well as smaller beacons marking inlet and harbor entrances, and the twin fortress lights at Highlands. Cottage-style beacons and cast-iron offshore lights can be found in the Delaware Bay.

1. Robbins Reef Light   *Staten Island*

Also affectionately known as Kate's lighthouse, for Kate Walker, the keeper from 1886 until 1919, this 45-foot, conical cast-iron structure (1883) has a brown lower half, a white upper, and a black lantern. It stands on a granite caisson, and its modern optic emits a green flash every 6 seconds at a focal-plane height of 56 feet from the west side of the main channel in the Upper New York Bay. There are good views of this light from the Staten Island Ferry.

2. Romer Shoal Light   *Staten Island*

A 54-foot, cast-iron spark-plug lighthouse (1898) built on a caisson, the lower part is white and the upper part and lantern, red. It can be seen from the north point of Sandy Hook, and its optic emits two white flashes every 15 seconds (focal plane 54 feet).

3. Great Beds Light   *South Amboy*

A 60-foot, white, conical cast-iron tower (1880) built on a caisson in Raritan Bay, this lighthouse sends out a red flash every 6 seconds from its 155-mm optic. There is no public access to the light, but it can be seen from Front Street in Perth Amboy.

4. Conover Beacon (Chapel Hill Front Range Light)   *Leonardo*

This skeletal tower with a central cylinder (1941), white with a red central band and lantern, stands 40 feet tall in Sandy Hook Bay. It has not been operational since 1957. The beach near Roop Avenue in Leonardo, New Jersey, offers close-up views.

SPOTTER'S NOTE

The *Liberty* (*Winter Quarter*) lightship was built in Bath, Maine, in 1923 at a contract price of $200,000. Retired from duty in 1968, she now functions as the Lightship Bar and Grill, located at Liberty Landing Marina (open seven days).

---

5. Chapel Hill Range Rear Light
Leonardo

This 31-foot lighthouse (1856) consists of a square wooden tower that rises from the roof of the white keeper's dwelling. Originally a range light in tandem with Conover Beacon, it was deactivated in 1957 and is now a private residence, with no public access.

6. Sandy Hook Light   *Sandy Hook*
(opposite)

Sandy Hook Light

A Venerable Monument

This lighthouse tower—the oldest in the United States (1764)—reopened in 2000 after a major restoration program. The 85-foot, white rubble-stone structure is octagonal-pyramidal in shape and is topped with a red lantern. The original third-order Fresnel lens is still in use and has a height of focal plane of 88 feet above sea level. The 1883 keeper's house stands near the tower; the lighthouse is a National Historic Landmark, and the complex is part of the Gateway National Recreational Area.

ABOVE: *Sandy Hook Light.*
BELOW: *The light's location and restored keeper's house.*

Description: octagonal-
  pyramidal rubblestone
  tower
Markings: white; red
  lantern
Lens: third-order Fresnel
Height: 85 feet (tower);
  88 feet (focal plane)

Navesink (Highlands) Twin Lights

Description: octagonal
  brownstone towers
Markings: natural; brown
  lantern
Lens: sixth-order Fresnel
  (north tower)
Height: 73 feet (tower);
  246 feet (focal plane)

RIGHT AND BOTTOM: *This site, with
its elevated location, has been used
for signaling since 1746, but these
towers were built in 1862.*
BELOW: *One of the ornate, crown-
like lanterns.*

Twin Towers

The Navesink Twin Lights, also known as
Highland Lights, consist of two identical brownstone towers connected by a fortresslike structure. The octagonal towers rise to 73 feet and
have a height of focal plane of 246 feet above sea
level. Today, only the north tower is operational;
it uses a sixth-order Fresnel lens dating from
1962. In 1841 these lights became the first in
the United States to be fitted with Fresnel
lenses. The complex is now a museum, and visitors can climb the north tower.

7. Navesink Twin Lights *Highlands*
   (opposite)

8. Sea Girt Light *Sea Girt*
Deactivated between 1955 and 1983, this light-house, which resembles a seaside home, has been fully restored and now operates as a private navigational aid. The 44-foot square tower (1896) is integral to the red-brick Victorian–style keeper's house and has a black cast-iron lantern. Its third-order Fresnel lens sends out its signal at a focal-plane height of 60 feet above sea level. The lighthouse and its small museum are open to the public seasonally.

ABOVE: *Sea Girt Light.*
BELOW: *Barnegat Light.*
BOTTOM: *Absecon Lighthouse.*

9. Barnegat Light *Barnegat*
This striking 172-foot, conical brick tower (1857) is painted red on its upper part and white on the lower. It is known locally as "Old Barney." The light, whose signal was visible for up to 30 miles, was deactivated in 1944 and is now a museum; visitors may climb the tower.

10. Absecon Lighthouse
   Atlantic City
A conical brick tower, painted pale yellow with a central black band and a black lantern, this 169-foot lighthouse, first lit in 1857, is the third-tallest in the United States and has a venerable history. It was deactivated in 1933 but was refurbished in 1997 and is now a National Historic Landmark, complete with a museum and visitor center, attracting many tourists in its location near Atlantic City's boardwalk. The historic keeper's dwelling was destroyed by fire in 1998, but it is hoped that this will be reconstructed. No longer an offi-cial aid to navigation, the original first-order Fresnel lens is back in use (now powered by an electric light) to help replicate the light-house in its heyday.

11. Hereford Inlet Light *North Wildwood*

This 1874 lighthouse consists of a square tower atop a Swiss Gothic keeper's dwelling. Deactivated between 1964 and 1986, the lighthouse signal is now a white flash every 10 seconds (focal plane 57 feet), and the keeper's dwelling serves as a museum.

12. Cape May Light *Cape May*

This off-white conical brick tower (1823) with a red cast-iron lantern rises to 157 feet and has a height of focal plane of 165 feet. Still active, its solar-powered aero-beacon emits a white flash every 15 seconds. The lighthouse is open to the public, as is the brick oil house (1893) that serves as a visitor center.

13. East Point (Maurice River) Light *Maurice River*

This 40-foot lighthouse (1849) consists of an octagonal brick tower that rises from the red roof of a stone keeper's dwelling (250-mm optic, focal plane 43 feet). The building has been undergoing restoration since it sustained fire damage in 1971, and is occasionally opened to visitors.

14. Brandywine Shoal Light *Delaware Bay*

This 45-foot, white, cylindrical cast-iron tower (1914) on a caisson foundation marks a treacherous offshore shoal 8 miles northwest of Cape May. Its red lantern houses a 250-mm solar-powered optic (focal plane 60 feet). The light can only be seen by boat.

15. Miah Maull Shoal Light *Downe*

Surrounded by open water, this 45-foot, red, conical cast-iron tower (1913) with integral keeper's quarters was built on a caisson foundation. Its original fourth-order Fresnel lens (focal plane 59 feet) is still in use. The light can only be seen from the water.

LEFT: *Hereford Inlet Light.*

SPOTTER'S NOTE
Now located at Pyne Poynt Marina in Camden, the *Barnegat* lightship was built in 1904 and served until 1967.

RIGHT: *Cape May Light.*

16. Elbow of Cross Ledge Light *Delaware Bay*

Located 3 miles northwest of Miah Maull Shoal, this red, square skeletal tower (1954) rises from a caisson that provided the foundation for the original lighthouse that stood here in 1910. The light is operational, and can only be seen by boat.

17. Ship John Shoal Light *Delaware Bay*

This distinctive, 45-foot, red-brown cast-iron tower (1877) has a mansard roof and stands offshore on a caisson foundation; the tower is linked to its boat landing by a short walkway. Automated in 1973, it has a solar-powered optic (focal plane 50 feet), and can only be seen from the water.

18. Finns Point Range Rear Light *Pennsville*

Deactivated since 1950, this lighthouse is a 115-foot, black, hexagonal skeletal tower with a central cylinder (1877). It stands in a wildlife refuge and is open to visitors once each month. The range front light has been destroyed.

19. Tinicum Island Range Rear Light *Billingsport*

This 83-foot, black, hexagonal skeletal tower with a central cylinder (1880) is still active; its fixed red signal has a focal-plane height of 112 feet. It can be viewed at close range and is occasionally open to the public. The front range light served two separate rear range signals—the second one being Fort Mifflin Bar Cut Rear Range Light (destroyed)—and was deactivated in 1982 when it was replaced by a skeleton tower; it has since been destroyed.

DELAWARE

The waterways of the western half of the Delaware Bay have been served by off-shore beacons marking underwater shoals and several pairs of range lights. The southernmost point of the Atlantic shore in Delaware boasts a tall masonry tower that is typical of those built along the low-lying coastlines of the Eastern Seaboard.

1. Marcus Hook Range Lights *Bellefonte*
The Marcus Hook Range Rear Light (1918) rises to 100 feet and has a height of focal plane of 250 feet above sea level. The square tower is built of reinforced concrete and is unpainted. The front range light is an 85-foot skeletal tower. These lights are active, but the former keeper's dwelling is now a private residence, and there is no public access to the site.

2. Bellevue Range Rear Light *Wilmington*
This 1909 lighthouse is a 104-foot, black, square-pyramidal, cast-iron skeletal tower with a central cylinder. The light was deactivated and its optic removed from the tower in 2001. The light can only be accessed via the landfill site on which it stands; limited visiting is possible at the time of writing. The former range front light was deactivated in the 1980s and has been destroyed.

3. Liston Range Lights *Port Penn*
The rear range light is a 127-foot, black, hexagonal-pyramidal, skeletal iron tower with a central cylinder. It was built in 1877 and relocated to its present site in 1906. Its fixed signal beam is emitted from a 1906 second-order Fresnel lens at a height of focal plane of 176 feet above sea level. The front range light is mounted on a 45-foot steel structure at the front of the original lighthouse, which is a white keeper's dwelling with a lantern room on its roof.

RIGHT: *The Lightship* Overfalls.

SPOTTER'S NOTE
Located in the Overfalls Maritime Museum, Lewes, the *Overfalls* was the last lightship to be built by the United States Lighthouse Service (1938). Considered "state of the art," it served a distinguished career before its decommission in 1972.

ABOVE: *Delaware Breakwater Light.*

4. Reedy Island Range Rear Light *Taylor's Bridge*

This active lighthouse is a 110-foot, black, square skeletal tower with a central cylinder, located on the grounds of a private home (it can be seen from Highway 9). The keeper's house burned down in 2002. The range front light, an integrated cottage-style building and lantern, was replaced by a post light in 1951 and destroyed.

5. Fourteen Foot Bank Light *Delaware Bay*

A large, white, two-story keeper's residence secures the tower that rises to a height of 40 feet at this 1888 light station that was built offshore on a black caisson at a site once served by a lightship. The solar-powered optic has a focal-plane height of 59 feet. The lighthouse can only be seen from the water.

6. Mispillion Light *Milford*

This 1873 cottage-style beacon, with a shingle tower and red lantern, once marked the entrance to the Mispillion River but was deactivated in 1929. It was severely damaged by a lightning strike in 2002, and dismantled, but a campaign to build a replica has been launched.

7. Delaware Breakwater Light *Lewes Harbor*

This 45-foot, red-brown, conical cast-iron tower with a black lantern stands at the end of a breakwater; it can be seen from Cape Henlopen State Park and from the Cape May–Lewes ferry. Deactivated in 1996 and renovated in 1999, it is closed to the public.

ABOVE: *The Harbor of Refuge (South) Breakwater Light.*
BELOW: *Fenwick Island Light.*

8. Harbor of Refuge (South) Breakwater Light *Lewes Harbor*

Built on a black caisson on the outer breakwater at Lewes Harbor, this white cast-iron tower (1926) rises to a height of 76 feet and is topped with a black lantern. Its solar-powered VRB-25 emits a white flash every 5 seconds. There are occasional public tours, and the light can be seen from Cape Henlopen State Park and from the Cape May–Lewes ferry.

9. Fenwick Island Light
Fenwick Island

The original third-order Fresnel lens is still in use as a private navigational aid in this 84-foot brick tower (1859) that stands at the eastern end of the Delaware–Maryland state line. The lighthouse is white with a black trim and is open to the public: a small museum operates in the base of the tower. There are several surviving outbuildings, including the keeper's house.

MARYLAND

Maryland's lighthouses are situated on the Chesapeake Bay; there are no beacons on the state's Atlantic coastline. Among the Chesapeake's lighthouses in 1900 were as many as forty-five cottage-style screwpile beacons, but these were prone to ice damage, and just three survive today, many having been replaced by caisson-mounted structures.

1. Solomons Lump Light   *Crisfield*
Standing on a black caisson several miles offshore (near Cherry Island), this 1895 white, square brick tower reaches a height of 35 feet and is topped with a black lantern, which emits a flashing white light with two red sectors (focal plane 47 feet). The keeper's quarters no longer exist, and the tower stands off-center on what now looks like an oversized foundation. It can only be seen by boat.

2. Hooper Island Light   *Hoopersville*
This offshore spark-plug lighthouse is a 35-foot, white conical tower (1902) with a black lantern, rising from a red caisson. With a focal-plane height of 63 feet, its signal guides vessels past submerged shoals. The light can only be seen by boat.

3. Sharps Island Light   *Fairbank*
This 35-foot, red-brown cast-iron lighthouse (1882), surrounded by water, is severely endangered: ice damage (1976–77) caused it to tilt, and it now leans at a 20-degree angle. It is still operational, however; it uses a 250-mm optic (focal plane 54 feet). The future of the lighthouse, which was built on the site of a screwpile light that also succumbed to ice, is uncertain; it is best viewed by boat.

4. Bloody Point Bar Light   *Claiborne*
Also known as the Coffee Pot, this brown, conical cast-iron tower (1882) is 40 feet tall and stands on a caisson almost a mile offshore. Its solar-powered optic emits a white flash every 6 seconds at a focal-plane height of 54 feet. The lighthouse is not open to the public.

5. Hooper Strait Light   *St. Michaels*
This 41-foot, white, octagonal screwpile lighthouse (1879) was deactivated in 1966 and relocated from Tangier Sound a year later, thus saving it from demolition. It is now part of the Chesapeake Bay Maritime Museum at St. Michaels and can be visited year round.

BELOW: *Hooper Strait Light.*

6. Pooles Island Light *Aberdeen*

This 40-foot, white, conical stone tower (1825), with a black lantern, has been inactive since 1939. It was restored in 1997, but Pooles Island is part of a U.S. Army facility and there is no public access; the site contains unexploded bombs.

7. Turkey Point Light *Elk Neck*

The 38-foot lighthouse (1833) that marks the entrance to Elk River, at the head of the Chesapeake Bay, is a white, conical brick tower with a black lantern. Its history is unusual for the fact that it was tended by female keepers during much of the period before its 1947 automation. Deactivated in 2000, it was relighted as a private aid to navigation in 2002, using its original fourth-order Fresnel lens (focal plane 129 feet). The light stands on a bluff in Elk Neck State Park and is accessed on foot.

ABOVE: *Turkey Point Light.*
BELOW: *Concord Point Light.*

8. Concord Point (Havre de Grace) Light *Havre de Grace*

This compact white, conical stone tower (1827), with a black lantern, marks the mouth of the Susquehanna River and is the oldest continuously operating lighthouse in Maryland (in recent years, as a private aid to navigation and historic site). The tower stands in Concord Point Park, and weekend tours are available seasonally.

> **SPOTTER'S NOTE**
> The Friends of Concord Point Lighthouse are working to restore the keeper's house at this station, and they plan to establish a maritime museum at the site. The grounds are open all year.

9. Fishing Battery Light *Havre de Grace*

The original 1853 integrated brick keeper's house with a black lantern rising from its roof was painted white, but it has fallen gradually into disrepair since its 1921 deactivation (it was replaced then by a skeletal tower that is still in operation). There is no public access to its Fishing Battery Island site.

> **SPOTTER'S NOTE**
> After Duxbury Pier Light in Massachusetts, the front-range light of the Lower Craighill Channel pair is the second-oldest spark-plug lighthouse in the United States and the only such light with single-story keeper's quarters, making its design unique.

10. Craighill Channel Lower Range Lights *Baltimore*

The front range light is an offshore 35-foot, red, spark-plug lighthouse (1873), with white trim and a black lantern, standing on a red caisson. It has two solar-powered lights, one of which works in tandem with the rear range light (1873), a 105-foot, square-pyramidal skeletal tower with a central cylinder. The upper part of this tower is a faded red and the lower part, white. The range lights can be seen distantly from North Point State Park, Edgemere, but are best seen by boat.

11. Craighill Channel Upper ("Cutoff Channel") Range Lights *Sparrow's Point*

The front range light is a bright-red 25-foot, octagonal brick tower (1886) with a central white band. A fixed red beam shines out from an opening near the top of the tower (focal plane 15 feet). The white, 80-foot rear range light (1886) consists of a square wooden tower supported by a pyramidal iron frame. This light also has a fixed red signal (focal plane 74 feet). Neither is open to the public or easily seen except by boat.

12. Lazaretto Point Light *Baltimore*

This 1985 structure is a replica of the 1831 white, conical lighthouse that was replaced by a skeleton tower in 1926. The light is located on a pier near the eastern end of the I-95 bridge over the Patapsco River; there is no immediate access to the site.

Seven Foot Knoll Light

Description: cylindrical wrought-iron keeper's dwelling on screwpile foundation
Markings: red; black lantern and trim
Lens: removed
Height: 40 feet (tower); 40 feet (focal plane)

RIGHT: *A photograph taken in 1900.*
BELOW: *The former optic.*

BELOW, LEFT: *The fog bell.*
BELOW, RIGHT: *The light today, at the Baltimore Maritime Museum.*

Museum Piece

The oldest surviving screwpile lighthouse (1856) from the Chesapeake Bay, this 40-foot red structure was deactivated in 1987 and relocated the following year from the harbor entrance to form an exhibit at the Baltimore Maritime Museum, which is open year round. Now a National Historic Landmark, the renovated lighthouse consists of a single-story cylindrical keeper's residence topped with a black lantern, supported on its screwpile legs.

LEFT: *The* Chesapeake *Lightship, and Baltimore waterfront at Harbor Place.*

> **SPOTTER'S NOTE**
> Now docked in Baltimore Harbor Place, the lightship *Chesapeake* (1930) served for almost 40 years before her decommission in 1970. She is open to the public.

12. Seven Foot Knoll Light *Baltimore* (*opposite*)

13. Fort Carroll Light *Baltimore*

This wooden tower, square-shaped and topped with a black lantern, was built in 1898 on the walls of Fort Carroll, which is on a small island in the Patapsco River. Deactivated in the 1940s, the light has fallen into severe disrepair. It can be seen distantly from Fort Amistead Park.

14. Baltimore Light *Baltimore*

The last lighthouse built on the Chesapeake Bay, this 38-foot beacon (1908) consists of an integrated white octagonal brick keeper's residence on a red caisson, crowned with a black lantern (focal plane 52 feet). The light still marks the entrance to the Magothy River; it is best viewed by boat but can be seen from Gibson Island.

15. Sandy Point Shoal Light *Skidmore*

This 37-foot offshore lighthouse (1883) is built on a black caisson. The red, octagonal, Empire-style keeper's dwelling forms the main body of the light and is topped with a black lantern. A 300-mm solar-powered optic is in use and has a height of focal plane of 51 feet above sea level. Good views can be found from Sandy Point Park.

16. Thomas Point Shoal Light *Annapolis* (*overleaf*)

17. Cove Point Light *Lusby*

This 45-foot, conical brick tower (1828) is coated with concrete and painted white, with a black lantern, and stands adjacent to the keeper's dwelling. The original fourth-order Fresnel lens is still in use (focal plane 45 feet). The lighthouse is open to the public; buses transport passengers from the Calvert Marine Museum to the site.

Thomas Point Shoal Light

Description: wooden
tower and integral
hexagonal keeper's
dwelling on screwpile
foundation
Markings: white with red
roof; black lantern
Lens: solar-powered
modern optic
Height: 25 feet (tower);
43 feet (focal plane)

RIGHT AND BELOW: *Views of the
light and its Chesapeake
surroundings.*

The Survivor

A wooden tower emerges from the red roof of
the white, hexagonal wooden dwelling, which is
secured by screwpile foundations. The solar-
powered optic in the black lantern emits a white
flash every 5 seconds (focal plane 43 feet),
marking a submerged shoal. The 1875 light station is the only surviving cottage-style screwpile
light in its original location in the Chesapeake
Bay and is now a National Historic Landmark. It
can be seen from Thomas Point Park.

18. Drum Point Light *Solomons*

This lighthouse was built in 1883 on the Patuxent River; it has not been operational since 1962 and is on show at the Calvert Marine Museum, where it was moved in 1975. From the white, octagonal keeper's house rises the wooden tower that holds its black cast-iron lantern; it measures 47 feet including the screw-pile legs. The original fourth-order Fresnel lens is on display, and the lighthouse has been fully restored and furnished with period antiques.

19. Point No Point Light *Dameron*

This 1905 lighthouse consists of a white, octagonal brick keeper's house, rising to three stories, mounted on a red caisson near the entrance to the Potomac River and topped with a black lantern, which has a height of focal plane of 52 feet. The light is still operational and can only be seen from the water.

ABOVE: *Drum Point Light.*

20. Point Lookout Light *Scotland*

An octagonal red tower rises from an off-white (with red trim), square, two-story keeper's house. The 36-foot lighthouse (1883) is no longer operational and is an attraction at Point Lookout State Park. The tower itself is open to the public once yearly.

SPOTTER'S NOTE
Piney Point Light was designed by John Donahoo of Havre de Grace. He was responsible for building twelve lighthouses in total, of which seven are still extant.

---

21. Piney Point Light *Piney Point*

This 35-foot, white, conical brick tower (1836), with a black lantern, now functions as a museum, which is open daily. The light (deactivated 1964) is also known as the "Lighthouse of Presidents," because several U.S. presidents have paid visits.

22. Fort Washington Light

Fort Washington National Park

Still an active aid to navigation, this 32-foot, white, square-pyramidal structure is a modified fog-signal tower dating from 1901. The red triangle on one face bears the number "80" that identifies it as a channel marker for vessels navigating the Potomac. The tower can be viewed from close range.

SPOTTER'S NOTE
The Fort Washington Light is the only surviving fog-signal tower of its type on the Chesapeake Bay.

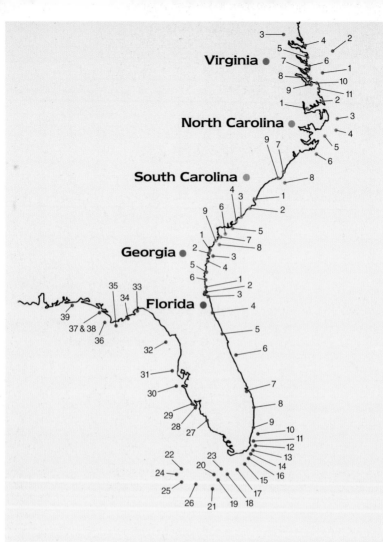
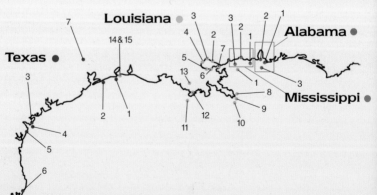

THE SOUTH

VIRGINIA

The historic lighthouses of Virginia stand on the low-lying shores of the Atlantic and the Chesapeake Bay, or offshore in these waters. They range from onshore lights dating from the early lighthouse years to nineteenth- and twentieth-century screwpile and caisson-mounted offshore structures.

ABOVE: *Assateague Light.*

1. Cape Charles Light *Smith Island*

The tallest skeletal lighthouse in the United States, the 191-foot Cape Charles Light is located on the southernmost tip of Smith Island. It is not open to the public and is accessible only by boat. Built on the site of an earlier (1828) stone tower and subsequent (1864) brick structure, the octagonal, cast-iron skeleton tower with a central cylinder was erected on concrete piers in 1895. It is white, with a black lantern, and its solar-powered optic, automated in 1963, has a focal-plane height of 180 feet.

2. Assateague Light *Assateague Island*

A red-and-white-striped, conical brick tower, this light measures 142 feet. Erected in 1867 as a replacement for its 1833 predecessor, it is now lit by a DCB-224 optic (focal plane 154 feet). It is open to the public and is situated in the Chincoteague National Wildlife Refuge.

3. Jones Point Light *Alexandria*

Situated in Jones Point Park, this beacon aids navigation on the Potomac River. Although the lighthouse, whose gray, conical lantern is integrated into the white, wooden keeper's house, has been standing on this strategic site since 1856, the erection of a steel skeletal lighthouse nearby signaled its deactivation in 1926. Since 1995, when a new optic (focal plane 60 feet) was installed, the building has again been functioning as a lighthouse. It is open to the public.

4. Smith Point Light *Smith Point*

Situated at the entrance to the Potomac River, this lighthouse is accessible only by boat and is closed to the public. Its white-painted, brick, octagonal keeper's dwelling perches atop a red base and submerged caisson, its square tower in turn supporting the black lantern that houses a DCB-24 optic (focal plane 52 feet). This light station was automated in 1971.

5. Wolf Trap Light *Chesapeake Bay*

This 52-foot light was constructed of brick on a brown cylinder atop a caisson foundation in 1894. Rising above the octagonal, two-story, red keeper's dwelling is a square tower and black lantern, with a solar-powered Vega VRB-25 (1996, automated in 1971). It is closed to the public and can only be viewed by boat.

6. New Point Comfort Light *Mathews*

Having survived a violent hurricane in 1933, it is feared that the New Point Comfort Light could succumb to erosion (the keeper's dwelling has already been swept away). The 58-foot, white, octagonal sandstone tower was raised on a small island at the entrance to Mobjack Bay in 1806. It was deactivated in 1963, when it was replaced by an offshore beacon, but was fitted with a new beacon in 1999. This historic lighthouse was renovated in 1989 and is today open to the public.

7. Thimble Shoal Light *Hampton Roads*

An offshore, conical spark-plug light with integral keeper's quarters, this beacon has beamed out a signal from the top of its cast-iron-and-concrete-caisson foundation since 1914. The light was initially equipped with a fourth-order Fresnel lens, but now holds a solar-powered RB-355 optic (focal plane 55 feet), backed up by a horn fog signal. The red-painted, cast-iron tower is 40 feet high. Automated in 1964, the lighthouse is closed to the public and accessible only by boat, but can be viewed from points along the Virginia shore (Norfolk and Fort Monroe).

SPOTTER'S NOTE
Today's Smith Point and Wolf Trap lights have managed to survive the ice to which their predecessors succumbed: no fewer than four towers (dating from 1802, 1807, 1828, and 1868) were destabilized by erosion at Smith Point.

SPOTTER'S NOTE
The remains of the screwpile foundation that supported the original Thimble Shoal Light—housed in a wooden cottage—can still be seen near the current lighthouse. This light served from 1872 until 1880, when it suffered fire damage. A replacement cottage dating from 1891 also burned down.

BELOW: *Jones Point Light front elevation.*

8. **Old Point Comfort Light** *Fort Monroe*

This octagonal, white-painted sandstone tower has stood at the entrance to Hampton Roads Harbor in Chesapeake Bay since 1802 (light station established 1774). The green, red-roofed lantern houses a fourth-order Fresnel lens with a focal-plane height of 54 feet (which is also the height of the tower), emitting a flashing red signal. The wood-framed keeper's house was built in 1900, in the Queen Anne style, and is today the official residence of the Command Sergeant Major at Fort Monroe. Despite being situated on a U.S. Army base, the grounds of this lighthouse are open to the public.

ABOVE: *Old Point Comfort Light.*

SPOTTER'S NOTE
The lightship *Portsmouth* served as an active navigational aid from 1916 to 1964. Originally known as the lightship *Charles*, she was renamed several times before coming to rest at Portsmouth's waterfront where she is now a museum.

9. **Newport News Middle Ground Light** *Newport News*

This offshore lighthouse is inaccessible except by boat (and is closed to the public), but it can be seen from Route I-664 where the Interstate crosses Hampton Roads and the James River. This conical, cast-iron, red-painted spark-plug structure, which rises above a caisson foundation, measures 35 feet in height and has a focal-plane height of 52 feet. It projects its flashing white light by means of a 375-mm optic.

10 & 11. **Cape Henry Lights**
Virginia Beach *(opposite)*

Cape Henry Lights (Old & New)

Heralds of the Chesapeake

No longer operational, the old Cape Henry Light still stands at the entrance to the Chesapeake Bay. Notable for being the first lighthouse to be constructed under the auspices of the federal government of the United States, the tower was completed in 1792 and lit with Argand lamps and reflectors. Despite having been equipped with a new lens in 1855, worries about the worsening cracks in its structure sealed its fate during the 1870s, and it was finally deactivated in 1881, when the new Cape Henry Light became operational.

The new light is the tallest of its kind in the United States. Clad with iron plates, the tower is painted in a striking black-and-white pattern of vertical stripes. Its original, first-order Fresnel lens is still operational and was automated in 1984. A two-story, wood-framed keeper's house and various outbuildings share its Fort Story site, which is open to the public. Visitors can climb the old tower, but there is no access to the new light.

Description: New: octagonal masonry tower. Old: octagonal sandstone-and-brick tower

Markings: New: black and white vertical stripes; black lantern room and trim. Old: unpainted; copper lantern

Lens: New: first-order Fresnel. Old: first-order Fresnel; originally Argand

Height: New: 163 feet (tower); 164 feet (focal plane). Old: 90 feet (tower); 172 feet (focal plane)

BELOW: *The new and old towers stand sentinel, about 350 feet apart.*

NORTH CAROLINA

The combination of the treacherous Diamond Shoals off the Outer Banks and the collision of the cold Labrador Current with the warm Gulf Stream gave the waters off North Carolina their reputation as the "graveyard of the Atlantic." Several tall towers, three of which were built by Dexter Stetson (1815–99), help mariners avoid the fate of at least 2,000 vessels that came to grief here.

1. Roanoke River Light *Edenton*

Originally constructed offshore in 1903, atop iron screwpile foundations in Abermarle Sound, the white wooden structure was relocated to its current onshore location in 1955. It incorporates keeper's quarters, a square tower, and a lantern with a focal-plane height of 35 feet, housing a fourth-order Fresnel lens (deactivated in 1941). It is today a private residence that is not open to the public.

ABOVE: *Currituck Beach Light.*
BELOW: *Bodie Island Light.*

2. Currituck Beach Light
Whale Head Bay

This 162-foot lighthouse on the Outer Banks was constructed of red brick in 1875, and the original first-order Fresnel lens still operates in the black lantern room today (automated in 1939) at a focal-plane height of 158 feet. The Stick-style keeper's duplex remains on site. This lighthouse is open to the public, offers magnificent views from the gallery, and has a museum store which is open Easter through Thanksgiving.

3. Bodie Island Light *Oregon Inlet*

The black- and white-painted bands make this 170-foot landmark (1872) eye-catching. This is the third lighthouse to be situated on Bodie Island (the first was erected in 1848, and the second—which was blown up during the Civil War—in 1859). The first-order Fresnel lens, installed in its black cast-iron lantern room over a century ago, still shines at a focal-plane height of 156 feet and can be seen up to 22 miles away. The light was automated in 1954, and the former keeper's accommodation today functions as a visitor's center. Recently restored and staffed by volunteers, only the lower part of the lighthouse is open to the public.

4. Cape Hatteras Light *Buxton*
   (overleaf)

5. Ocracoke Island Light *Ocracoke*

The conical, mortar-dressed, white-painted brick tower that rises to a height of 65 feet was constructed in 1823, making it North Carolina's oldest functioning lighthouse. It replaced a tower on Shell Castle Island that operated from 1803 to 1818, when it was destroyed by lightning. The current optic is a fourth-order Fresnel lens dating from 1899 (when the light, which had been extinguished in 1862, was relit), with a focal-plane height of 75 feet; it was automated in 1955. The two-story brick keeper's cottage today provides accommodation for National Park Service employees. The grounds are open to the public.

ABOVE: *Ocracoke Island Light.*
BELOW: *Cape Lookout Light.*

6. Cape Lookout Light *Core Banks*

The first lighthouse (1812) to stand sentinel on Core Banks Island was replaced with the 169-foot-tall lighthouse that still stands today. The Cape Lookout Light was initially equipped with a first-order Fresnel lens; since 1967, however, a DCB-24 optic has beamed out its light at a focal-plane height of 156 feet. The black and white diamonds with which this conical brick tower is painted make it a striking daymark for sailors negotiating the "Horrible Headland," as an old map once justifiably designated Cape Lookout. This light, whose grounds are open to the public, was automated in 1950, and the brick, keeper's house (1873), which has recently been restored, is now a visitors' center.

Cape Hatteras Light

America's Tallest Light

As their nickname, "the graveyard of the Atlantic," suggests, the waters to the east of Cape Hatteras are extremely dangerous: more than 2,000 vessels have come to grief here. The United States' tallest lighthouse was raised in 1870 (succeeding an 1803 tower) and fitted with a first-order Fresnel lens whose light could be seen 27 miles away. Threatened by erosion, the light was deactivated in 1936, when an automated skeleton tower took over its duties, until 1950, when it was re-exhibited. The National Historic Landmark was moved 2,900 feet inland from its original position in 1999 to avert its destruction by the encroaching Atlantic, at a cost of $12 million.

Cape Hatteras Today

The original two-story brick keeper's house, which was built in 1871 in the Victorian style, is now a visitors' center, while the 1854 assistant keepers' house serves as a museum; cisterns and an oil house dating from 1892 can also be seen on site. The lighthouse itself is open to the public, except during the winter and at times when the weather constitutes a safety risk.

ABOVE: *Cape Hatteras Light.*
RIGHT: *The cast-iron spiral stairway inside the tower. There are nine flights making a total of 248 steps to the lantern room (see cross-section).*

Description: conical brick tower
Markings: alternating white and black spirals; black lantern
Lens: DCB-24
Height: 193 feet (tower); 208 feet (focal plane)

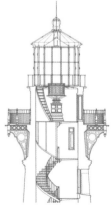

7. Price's Creek Range Front Light
Price's Creek

Also known as Price's Creek Light, this abandoned lighthouse north of Southport, on the west bank of the Cape Fear River, was built in 1849, but deactivated during the 1860s. Of several range lights that once lit the river, only this 20-foot, conical brick tower still stands, and it is not open to the public. It can, however, be glimpsed from the Bald Head Island ferry.

8. Bald Head Light *Bald Head Island*

At 100 feet high, "Old Baldy" has dominated this site overlooking the Cape Fear River since 1817, though there has been a lighthouse here since the mid-1790s (the first was felled by an 1812 tornado). Called the Cape Fear Light until 1903, it is North Carolina's oldest extant lighthouse, but it is no longer functioning, having had its lantern removed in 1935. Imposing rather than breathtaking, the octagonal-pyramidal brick structure that remains is covered with mottled stucco plasterwork. Of the original outbuildings, only a brick oil house still stands, which now functions as restrooms, while the keeper's house—actually a replica constructed in 2000—serves as a museum.

ABOVE: *"Old Baldy."*
BELOW: *Oak Island Light.*

9. Oak Island Light *Caswell Beach*

Erected in 1958, the Oak Island Light, which soars 155 feet above the entrance to the Cape Fear River, is notable for being the United States' second-tallest reinforced-concrete lighthouse. The top third of the tower is painted black; the central section, white; and the bottom third, gray. A total of eight 480-volt mercury arc bulbs produce four flashes every ten seconds, at a focal-plane height of 169 feet, a signal that can be seen from a distance of approximately 27 miles. Apart from the occasional open day, this lighthouse is closed to the public.

SOUTH CAROLINA

The continual battle against erosion is an ongoing concern for South Carolina's venerable lighthouses, because of the shifting, sandy foundations on which most were erected.

ABOVE: *Georgetown Light.*
BELOW: *Charleston Light.*
BOTTOM: *Morris Island Light.*

1. Georgetown Light *Winyah Bay*

This 87-foot beacon (focal plane 85 feet) is also known as the North Island Light and has aided navigation around North Island since 1812, making it the state's oldest operational lighthouse. The conical, white brick tower replaced a wooden structure that was destroyed in 1806. Its black lantern has housed a solar-powered VRB-25 optic since 1999. Automated in 1986, this lighthouse is closed to the public, but it can be viewed from a boat; trips depart from Georgetown.

2. Cape Romain Lights (Old and New) *Lighthouse Island*

The old, conical Cape Romain Light, which was erected of brick by Winslow Lewis in 1827, was equipped with eleven lamps and 21-inch reflectors in 1847, but the light that they produced was deemed inadequate, and today, only 65 feet of the truncated light tower remain. The new, 150-foot lighthouse (erected 1858) is an octagonal brick structure with a focal-plane height of 161 feet; the top two-thirds are painted in black-and-white vertical stripes, while the lower third is white. Deactivated in 1947, the light from its first-order Fresnel lens could be seen from 22 miles away. The grounds are open to visitors.

3. Charleston Light *Sullivan's Island*

Also known as Sullivan's Island Light, this tower was raised near Fort Moultrie in 1962 to replace the Morris Island Light. Built from reinforced concrete and clad in a steel-and-aluminum-alloy skin, the 140-foot triangular beacon (focal plane 162 feet, range 30 miles) holds a DCB-24 optic. Before its automation in 1975, its keeper must have been the envy of those who tended older lights because of its elevator and air-conditioning, both features being unique to this lighthouse. The Charleston Light is closed to the public.

4. Morris Island Light *Morris Island*

Also known as the Old Charleston Light, this beacon funtioned from 1673 to 1962. The tower seen today is the third on the site. The brown-and-white striped, conical, dressed-stone 1876 tower rises to 161 feet (focal plane 158 feet). Erosion threatens it, however: the wooden keeper's quarters succumbed in 1939, and by 1948 the lighthouse was encircled by water. Closed to the public, it can be viewed from the beach.

5. Hunting Island Light *Hunting Island*

The first lighthouse on this island (1859) was demolished during the Civil War; it is not known whether erosion or Confederate troops destroyed it. The second, a 136-foot cast-iron, brick-lined conical tower was erected in 1875 and moved 1 mile inland in 1889. The second-order Fresnel lens (focal plane 140 feet) was deactivated in 1933, but a modern optic was installed in 1994 and the lighthouse continues to serve as a distinctive daymark, its top third being painted black above a white base. The lighthouse is situated in a state park.

6. Hilton Head Rear Range Light
Hilton Head Island

Also known as the Haig Point or Leamington Light, this was originally one of a pair of range lights on Hilton Head Island. The hexagonal, wooden lantern of the white-painted, cast-iron 1880 skeletal tower is supported by a central cylinder and six braced, iron "legs," and rises to a height of 94 feet (focal plane 136 feet). Deactivated in 1932, the beacon was restored in 1985. Now part of the Palmetto Dunes Resort, it can be viewed by prior arrangement.

ABOVE: *Hunting Island Light.*
BELOW: *Hilton Head Rear Range Light.*

RIGHT: *Harbour Town Light.*

7. Harbour Town Light *Hilton Head Island*

This red-and-white-banded beacon (1970) was built as a private aid to navigation marking the Inland Waterway and Caliboque Sound. The lantern room atop the 90-foot tower boasts a gift store as well as a flashing white optic.

8. Bloody Point Bar Front Range Light *Daufuskie Island*

The steel, tripod-style skeletal tower of the rear range light in this pair no longer exists, but the Bloody Point Bar Front Range Light (1883) now marks the spot where the rear light stood, beach erosion having prompted its repositioning in 1899. A two-story keeper's dwelling, the light from its fixed reflector lens was projected from a second-story window until 1922, when it was deactivated. The privately owned structure is not accessible to the public.

9. Haig Point Rear Range Light
Daufuskie Island

The Haig Point Rear Range Light (1872, deactivated 1934–87), which has a fifth-order Fresnel lens, operates as a private aid to navigation. A square tower rises from a wooden, white-painted, two-story keeper's cottage, its lantern having a focal-plane height of 70 feet. Restored in 1986, the building is now a private club; it can be viewed from the cruise ships that depart from Shelter Cove Harbor.

GEORGIA

Of Georgia's six surviving lighthouses, just three remain active aids to navigation; these are all located on small, low-lying islands just off the mainland.

1. Savannah Harbor Range
Rear Light *Emmet Park, Savannah*

Also known as the Old Harbor Light and the Beacon Range Light, this beacon guided vessels into Savannah Harbor from 1858, but today lights up only its patch of Bay Street. Restored in 2000, its gas-fueled light is contained within a glass lantern supported by a cast-iron pole measuring 25 feet in height.

2. Cockspur Island Light
Cockspur Island

This conical, white-painted, 46-foot brick lighthouse overlooking the Savannah River (once called the South Channel Light) was built on an oyster-shell foundation in 1857 and is a reconstruction of the 1849 original. Deactivated in 1909 and now part of the Fort Pulaski National Monument, this restored lighthouse is accessible only by boat. It is not open to the public, but can be seen from Fort Pulaski and off Route 80, east of the Lazaretto Creek Bridge.

3. Tybee Island Light *Tybee Island*
(overleaf)

4. Sapelo Island Light *Sapelo Island*

This conical brick tower was built in 1820 by Winslow Lewis to guide vessels into Doboy Sound and was deactivated in 1905. Following a major restoration program, it is identifiable by its six red and white horizontal bands below the black cast-iron lantern. The 70-foot tower was relit privately in 1998. Visitors to the lighthouse can also see the Sapelo Island Front Range Light, a 25-foot skeleton tower that is no longer active.

ABOVE: *Savannah Harbor Light.*
BELOW: *Cockspur Island Light.*

Tybee Island Light

Description: octagonal-pyramidal brick tower
Markings: black and white bands; black lantern
Lens: first-order Fresnel
Height: 145 feet (tower); 144 feet (focal plane)

BELOW: *Tybee Island Light's previous color scheme.*

A Phoenix Rising

The black-white-black-banded, octagonal-pyramidal brick tower that rises 145 feet at the entrance to the Savannah River is the fourth incarnation of Tybee Island Light. The first was a 90-foot-tall, wood-framed structure, a daymark that stood from 1736 until 1741 before succumbing to a storm. Erosion was the fate that, in 1767, befell the 90-foot wood-and-stone tower that replaced it as a daymark in 1742. A 100-foot-tall brick tower was constructed in 1773, which was later equipped with lamps and 16-inch reflectors. Having received a second-order Fresnel lens in 1857 before being damaged during the Civil War, its lower 60 feet were eventually used as the foundation for the light tower that can be seen today, which was completed in 1867.

Pride of Georgia

Automated since 1972, the original first-order Fresnel lens continues to operate at a focal-plane height of 144 feet, with a range of around 23 miles. During a late-1990s renovation program, the markings were changed from the scheme shown here to a black lower section, with a white band above and small black band at top, with black lantern room. A red-roofed workroom juts out of the lighthouse's base, but the two-story keeper's quarters (Stick style, 1881), a brick summer kitchen (1812), the first assistant keeper's house (1885), the second assistant keeper's home (once a Confederate barracks), a brick fuel-storage building (1890), cistern, and garage (1936) are separate structures. Operated as a museum by the Tybee Island Historical Society, Inc. since 2002, this historic lighthouse is open to the public as well as continuing as an active aid to navigation.

RIGHT: *The keeper's dwelling attached to St. Simons Island Light now serves as a museum documenting the area's maritime history.*

SPOTTER'S NOTE
There was once a lighthouse at the southern end of Little Cumberland Island, too, namely a brick tower erected by Winslow Lewis in 1820; having been made redundant in 1838, this was deconstructed and reconstructed on Florida's Amelia Island, where it continues to operate to this day (*see* overleaf).

5. St. Simons Island Light   *St. Simons Island*

The first lighthouse to overlook St. Simons Sound was erected in 1811 as an octagonal, brick-and-coquina, tabby-covered tower measuring 75 feet in height. It was destroyed in the Civil War and replaced with today's white-painted, cylindrical brick light tower (104 feet tall). A third-order Fresnel lens was installed in its cast-iron lantern room on its completion in 1872; automated in 1954, its focal-plane height is 106 feet and range, 23 miles. A two-story keeper's dwelling is attached to the light. As well as serving as an active aid to navigation, this light houses a museum.

6. Little Cumberland Island Light   *Little Cumberland Island*

Situated at the northern end of the island, this lighthouse was deactivated in 1915. The 60-foot, white-painted, conical brick tower, with a black lantern, was built in 1838. No associated structures survive. The lighthouse was renovated during the 1960s and 1990s, but remains closed to the public (as does the island). It can, however, be viewed by boat.

FLORIDA

The Atlantic shores of Florida are lit by several tall masonry towers, while screw-pile lights predominate in the waters from the Keys to the Panhandle. The lighthouses of this region are built to withstand hurricane-force storms.

ABOVE: *Amelia Island Light.*
BELOW: *St. Johns River Light.*

1. Amelia Island Light *Amelia Island*

This 64-foot white, conical stucco tower (1820) was dismantled at its original location on Georgia's Little Cumberland Island and rebuilt here, on Fernandina Beach, in 1838. Its third-order Fresnel lens was installed in 1903. Automated in 1956, and with a focal-plane height of 107 feet, this optic flashes a signal with red and white sectors. Recently restored, and used as a residence for Coast Guard personnel, it is closed to the public, but the light can be seen from the beach.

2. St. Johns River Light *Mayport*

Also known as the Mayport Light, it is situated at the mouth of the St. Johns River and was in use from 1859 until 1929, when the third-order Fresnel lens within its white lantern was deactivated. The 81-foot conical, red-painted brick tower (focal plane 77 feet) remains, though its base is now invisible as it is buried in 20 feet of fill material, so that its entrance is now a window. Situated on the U.S. Naval Air Station Jacksonville, this lighthouse is not open to the public.

3. St. Johns Light *Mayport*

This light was erected in 1954 some 2 miles southeast of the decommissioned St. Johns River Light (*see* above). Built of concrete blocks, and octagonal in shape, this 64-foot light tower has an Art Deco concrete keeper's dwelling attached to it. Its Crouse-Hinds FB-61 optic, which emits four white flashes every 20 seconds, has a focal-plane height of 83 feet above sea level and a range of 22 miles. Part of the U.S. Naval Air Station Jacksonville, this lighthouse is closed to the public.

4. St. Augustine Light   *Anastasia Island*

This 165-foot brick lighthouse (1874) has a focal plane of 161 feet and replaced the harbor light of 1823. A revolving first-order Fresnel lens was installed in its red lantern room (1874, *see* Spotters' Note). The tower's black and white spirals make it a striking daymark. The site includes a garage (1936); U.S. Coast Guard barracks (1941); and a keeper's house (1876), which now houses a museum. The lighthouse and grounds are open to the public.

5. Ponce de Leon (Mosquito) Inlet Light   *Ponce Inlet*

This conical, 175-foot red-brick tower, south of Daytona Beach, was completed in 1887 with a first-order, fixed Fresnel lens in its black, copper-roofed lantern room. The 1933 third-order Fresnel lens was restored and relit in 2004, producing six white flashes every 15 seconds (focal plane 164 feet). Deactivated from 1970 to 1982, it was recommissioned privately. Visitors can tour the museums housed in the three restored keepers' cottages.

6. Cape Canaveral Light   *Cocoa Beach*

This 145-foot lighthouse (1868) was moved here in 1894. A conical, brick-lined building clad in cast-iron plates, its six black and white horizontal bands are topped by a black lantern room that has held a DCB-224 optic since 1993. Its signal is white and flashing (focal plane 137 feet). Located within the Cape Canaveral Air Force Station, this light station is closed to the public, but the tower can be seen from the nearby Kennedy Space Center.

7. Jupiter Inlet Light   *Jupiter (overleaf)*

8. Hillsboro Inlet Light   *Pompano Beach (page 195)*

ABOVE: *St. Augustine Light.*

SPOTTER'S NOTE
The first-order Fresnel lens that serves St. Augustine Light was damaged by a vandal's rifle fire in 1986. Now repaired, it is enclosed in bullet-proof glass.

BELOW: *Ponce de Leon Inlet Light.*

Jupiter Inlet Light

Description: cylindrical brick tower
Markings: red; black lantern room and base
Lens: revolving first-order Fresnel
Height: 108 feet (tower); 146 feet (focal plane)

ABOVE: *A Period photograph of the view from the gallery.*
RIGHT: *Jupiter Inlet Light's flashing white signal is visible for 25 miles.*

SPOTTER'S NOTE
George Meade was later the general in command of the Union troops that defeated Robert E. Lee's Confederate force at the Battle of Gettysburg in 1863. Both men served as engineers with the U.S. Army in earlier, more peaceful times, and Lee had surveyed the site on which Meade built the Jupiter Inlet Light, which was extinguished for much of the Civil War.

The Loxahatchee Landmark

The Jupiter Inlet Light was raised near the town of Jupiter in 1860, to the design, and under the supervision, of George Meade. Constructed from brick on an oyster-shell foundation, its deep-red paintwork below its black lantern and above a black base, as well as its imposing height of 108 feet, make this conical tower an eye-catching daymark. Its cast-iron lantern room contains the original optic, a revolving first-order Fresnel lens that has a focal-plane height of 146 feet and has been automated since 1987. Recently restored, the Jupiter Inlet Light is open to the public, and though the keeper's accommodation was destroyed by fire in 1927, the oil house—now a museum—remains standing.

Hillsboro Inlet Light

Skeleton Service

Erected on iron pilings, an iron framework supports the central cylinder and lantern, which houses the original second-order Fresnel lens (focal plane 136 feet). The tower was made at a foundry in Chicago and transported by barge down the Mississippi River to St. Louis, where it was exhibited at the 1904 Exposition. Following its purchase by the U.S. government, the 137-foot tower and lens (automated in 1974) were assembled at their current location on Pompano Beach in 1907. This active light station, which is occasionally opened to the public, encompasses a number of outbuildings, including a wood-framed keeper's house dating from 1907.

ABOVE: *Hillsboro Inlet Light can be seen from the A1A bridge over the inlet.*

Description: Octagonal, skeletal iron tower
Markings: lower half white, upper half black; black lantern room
Lens: second-order bivalve Fresnel
Height: 137 feet (tower); 136 feet (focal plane)

ABOVE: *Cape Florida Light.*

9. Cape Florida Light *Biscayne Bay*

The current 95-foot lighthouse (1846), situated on a coral reef, is a whitewashed, conical brick tower with a black-painted lantern room (focal plane 100 feet). It was deactivated from 1878 (when the Fowey Rocks Light assumed its duties) until 1978 (when it was relit and automated), and again from 1990 to 1996. Now a private aid to navigation, the restored lighthouse is open to the public, and a replica keeper's dwelling houses a museum.

10. Fowey Rocks Light
Cape Florida, Key Biscayne

Constructed offshore on straightpile-and-disk foundations, over 10 miles south of Cape Florida, in 1878, this brown-and-white cast-iron skeleton tower can only be viewed by boat. The original optic was a first-order drum Fresnel lens, tended by a keeper whose quarters were integral to the structure. Automated in 1974, the present optic is a solar-powered Vega VRB-25 that operates at a focal-plane height of 110 feet.

11. Pacific Reef Light *Elliot Key*

First established at its offshore station 3 miles southeast of Elliott Key in 1921, the Pacific Reef Light is a square-pyramidal skeletal tower that rises 44 feet above its screwpile foundations. It continues to function as an active aid to navigation, emitting a white flash every 4 seconds. It is inaccessible to the public.

12. Key Largo Light *Oleander Circle, off Ocean Way, Key Largo*

This 1959 structure is purely decorative. A square-pyramidal tower painted in a distinctive checkerboard pattern, its cast-iron lantern was salvaged from the original Rebecca Shoal Light in 1953, when this offshore lighthouse (which operated east of Garden Key, Dry Tortugas, from 1886) was demolished. Although it is closed to the public, the "faux" lighthouse can be admired from the street.

13. Carysfort Reef Light *John Pennekamp Coral Reef State Park*
(opposite)

Carysfort Reef Light

The Exposed Screwpile Prototype

The Carysfort Reef Light, which stands northeast of Key Largo, is notable for having been the first massive, exposed screwpile lighthouse to go into operation off the Florida Keys. Its offshore location was first established in 1825, when a lightship took up position above the reef. The lighthouse was erected to the design of I.W.P. Lewis under the supervision of George Meade between 1848 and 1852. Originally equipped with a first-order revolving Fresnel lens, the light was automated in 1960 and refurbished in 1996. Accessible only by boat and closed to the public, it continues to act as an important aid to navigation. The area around it is now the John Pennekamp Coral Reef State Park, a marine sanctuary.

Description: iron screwpile reef lighthouse, partly skeletal; integrated keeper's quarters
Markings: red; red lantern
Lens: solar-powered Vega VRB-25
Height: 120 feet (tower); 100 feet (focal plane)

BELOW: *The flashing signal of Carysfort Reef Light has a range of 15 miles.*

14. **Molasses Reef Light** *John Pennekamp Coral Reef State Park*

This 1921 square-pyramidal daymarker has rested on its steel footplates, screwpiles, and legs since it was established at its current offshore position 8 miles southeast of Key Largo. A small navigation beacon flashes red every 10 seconds at a focal-plane height of 45 feet. It is inaccessible except by boat and is not open to the public.

15. **Alligator Reef Light** *Alligator Reef, 4 miles east of Indian Key*

Situated offshore, the 136-foot skeletal iron tower that has served as a light station since 1873 can only be visited by boat and is closed to the public. Recognizable by its black lantern, platform, and legs, white central cylinder, integral former keeper's quarters, and crossbracing, this reef lighthouse can be viewed from between Mile Marker (M.M.) 80 and M.M. 77 on the Overseas Highway (there is an off-road vantage point at M.M.79). Since 1997, a solar-powered VRB-25 optic has generated the beacon's white-and-red flashing light, which can be seen from up to 12 miles away (focal plane 136 feet).

16. **Tennessee Reef Light** *east of middle Florida Keys, south of Long Key*

This offshore lighthouse is an exposed screwpile structure that was established in 1933. An octagonal-pyramidal skeletal tower, its optic continues to operate from within a closed lantern. It has no integral keeper's quarters and is closed to the public.

17. **Sombrero Key Light** *south of Marathon Key*

Constructed in 1858 on iron-pile-and-disk foundations, this brown-painted, cast-iron, octagonal-pyramidal skeletal tower is the tallest of Florida's reef lights. At 160 feet, its solar-powered VRB-25 optic (installed 1997) has a focal plane of 142 feet. The beacon was automated in 1960, spelling the end of the line of keepers who once occupied the one-story, integral keeper's quarters. This offshore light station is closed to the public, but can be viewed from Sombrero Beach State Park, while the first-order Fresnel lens that was originally installed in its lantern room can today be inspected at the Key West Lighthouse Museum in Key West.

18. **American Shoal Light** *Summerland Key*

Located 15 miles east of Key West, the American Shoal Light could easily be mistaken for its close contemporary, the Fowey Rocks Light. Established above iron straightpile-and-disk foundations in 1880, this octagonal-pyramidal skeletal tower is painted brown, with a white central cylinder and a solar-powered Vega VRB-25 optic with a focal-plane height of 109 feet above sea level. Earlier in its history, the keeper who tended the original first-order drum Fresnel lens was housed in the lighthouse's integral two-story accommodation; automation made this position redundant in 1963, however. The light is not open to the public and remains an active aid to navigation.

19. Sand Key Light *off Key West*

The second lighthouse constructed on this sandy key about 7 miles southwest of Key West was a cast-iron screwpile structure designed by I.W.P. Lewis and raised by George Meade that has stood firm since 1853. Painted red, with black trim, this 120-foot square-pyramidal skeletal tower with a central cylinder houses a Vega VRB-25 optic (focal plane 109 feet). The light was automated in 1938, but deactivated between 1989 and 1998, following a devastating fire in the (now demolished) single-story keeper's quarters. Closed to the public, it can be glimpsed from Key West.

ABOVE: *Sand Key Light.*
BELOW: *Key West Light.*

20. Key West Light *Whitehead's Point*

In 1846, a hurricane flattened the first Key West Light, killing the keeper and his family. This second structure—a white-painted, conical brick tower—was built to a height of 60 feet the following year, and later heightened, giving the now 86-foot-high beacon a focal-plane height of 91 feet. Automated in 1915, the light was deactivated in 1969. The structure underwent a restoration program during the late 1980s, and though it was fitted with an operational optic, it is not an official aid to navigation. As well as climbing the light tower, visitors can view various outbuildings, including the 1887 keeper's house, which today house a museum.

21. Cosgrove Shoal Light
south of the Marquesas Keys, southwest of Key West

In 1935, a 54-foot hexagonal-pyramidal skeletal light tower was the first beacon to be established here. Subsequently replaced with a similar structure, this lighthouse (which has always been unstaffed and is closed to the public) continues to function as an active offshore aid to navigation.

> **SPOTTER'S NOTE**
> For centuries Key West's wreckers made a lucrative living from salvaging and selling the cargoes given up by the thousands of vessels that came to grief on the surrounding reefs and shoals. With the construction of the offshore lights, the wreckers had to look elsewhere for their livelihood.

BELOW: *Tortugas Harbor Light.*

22. Pulaski Shoal Light   *Pulaski Shoal*

An unmanned 56-foot, hexagonal-pyramidal skeletal light station was established here, offshore, north of the Dry Tortugas Islands in the Gulf of Mexico, and 30 miles northwest of Key West, during the 1930s. The present structure is not the original, although it appears the same, and is closed to the public.

23. Smith Shoal Light   *Smith Shoal*

This offshore aid to navigation, 11 miles northwest of Key West, is not the original, unmanned tower that was erected in 1933, but closely resembles it. The 54-foot, hexagonal-pyramidal skeletal tower is closed to the public.

24. Tortugas Harbor Light
Fort Jefferson

Also known as the Fort Jefferson Light and the Garden Key Light, it is set in a parapet of the nineteenth-century Fort Jefferson, on the Dry Tortugas Islands' Garden Key. Although there has been a light station here since 1825 (*see* Spotters' Note), this 82-foot hexagonal, black-painted iron tower (open to the public) was constructed in 1876. Today it serves as a private aid to navigation, its lantern having been equipped with three 75-watt incandescent bulbs (focal plane 86 feet).

25. Dry Tortugas Light   *Loggerhead Key*

Also known as the Loggerhead Key Light, it was erected on this part of the Dry Tortugas Islands, to compensate for the poor performance of the lighthouse situated on the nearby Garden Key. Constructed to a height of 157 feet (focal plane 151 feet), the lantern room at the apex of the conical brick tower holds a solar-powered Vega VRB-2 that can be seen 20 miles away. A radio room abuts the base of the tower, whose top half is painted black, and bottom half, white. The tower (still active) is not open to the public.

26. Twenty-eight-foot Shoal Light *south of the Tortugas, west of Sand Key*

Situated in the Gulf of Mexico, the Twenty-eight-foot Shoal Light is a 53-foot, hexagonal-pyramidal skeletal tower. Its light flashes white every 4 seconds and can be seen 9 miles away. This offshore beacon is only accessible by boat.

27. Sanibel Island Light *Point Ybel*

The 102-foot, brown-painted, square-pyramidal skeletal iron tower that soars over eastern Sanibel Island was erected in 1884. The lantern, which is supported by a central cylinder, has held a 300-mm optic since 1965, whose flashing white light can be seen up to 13 miles away at a focal-plane height of 98 feet. It was the Sanibel Island Light's original third-order Fresnel lens that was first automated in 1949, however, while a Swedish 500-mm drum lens operated here for three years from 1962. The one-story keeper's quarters, which were constructed of wood on iron piles in a West Indian style, are contemporaneous with the lighthouse, as are the second keeper's accommodation, cistern, and oil house. The former keepers' bungalows are today occupied by employees of Sanibel City (which leases the light station from the U.S. Coast Guard), who maintain the site. The grounds are open to the public.

ABOVE: *Sanibel Island Light.*

BELOW: *Gasparilla Island Light.*

28. Gasparilla Island Light *Gasparilla Island State Park*

Before its name was officially changed in 2003, the white-painted, cast-iron hexagonal skeletal tower was known as the Boca Grande Entrance Range Rear Light. Before that, it was the Delaware Breakwater Rear Range Light, having served at Lewes, Delaware, from 1881 until it was deactivated in 1918 and dismantled in 1921. Erected at its current location in 1927, and lit in 1932, the central cylinder of this 105-foot tower supports a lantern containing a 250-mm optic. This active aid to navigation is closed to the public, although visitors can explore the surrounding parkland.

29. Port Boca Grande Light *Gasparilla Island*

Known as the Gasparilla Island Light until 2003, the 44-foot keeper's house that bears a black lantern first went into operation in 1890. Automated in 1950 and deactivated in 1966, it was relit in 1986; its light can be seen up to 12 miles away (focal plane 41 feet). This functioning lighthouse and museum welcomes visitors.

30. Egmont Key Light *Egmont Key State Park*

This 87-foot, conical brick tower was constructed in 1858 on stone foundations. The Egmont Key Alliance plans to enclose the current DCB-224 optic (focal plane 85 feet) within a lantern some day soon. Automated in 1989, the former keeper's quarters remain standing nearby. The grounds are only accessible by boat and are open to the public, as, on occasional weekends, is the bottom of the tower. Lighthouse spotters can also view the lighthouse from Fort DeSoto State Park.

31. Anclote Key Light *Anclote Key State Reserve*

First lit in 1887 and automated in 1952, this 102-foot, cast-iron skeletal light dominates the mouth of the Anclote River. Following an intensive restoration program, a TFB-220 optic was installed in its black lantern room, atop the brown central cylinder, and lit in September 2003. Now a private aid to navigation, its flashing white signal (focal plane 110 feet) can today be spotted from 19 miles away. Although the lighthouse is closed to the public, visitors can explore its grounds (accessible only by boat).

32. Cedar Keys Light *Seahorse Key*

Once known as the Seahorse Key Light, this one-story brick keeper's dwelling, with a hexagonal white tower protruding from its center supporting the lantern room was built on a platform above granite-pile foundations in 1854. The 23-foot, elevated structure gave its fourth-order Fresnel lens a focal plane of 75 feet. Deactivated in 1915, the renovated building currently serves as a dormitory for the University of Florida's marine laboratory and is closed to the public. It can, however, be viewed by prior arrangement with the Florida Lighthouse Association.

LEFT: *Port Boca Grande Light.*

SPOTTER'S NOTE
In 1922 the Seahorse Reef Light took over from the Cedar Keys Light. A 51-foot, white, square skeleton tower constructed on piles, its light flashes white every 6 seconds (focal plane 31 feet).

33. St. Marks Light *Appalachee Bay*

This 73-foot, white, conical brick tower overlooks the eastern side of the entrance to the St. Marks River. It replaced the first tower (1831) in 1842, its lantern housing a fourth-order Fresnel lens. Civil War damage prompted the reparation and modification of the tower in 1867, when it was equipped with a new black, cast-iron lantern and fifth-order Fresnel lens. Although this lens remains in situ, the light signal is today generated by a solar-powered 250-mm optic fixed to the gallery's railing (focal plane 82 feet). Before the light's automation in 1960, the keeper occupied an attached brick house. The grounds, today a national wildlife refuge, are open to the public.

34. Crooked River Light *Carrabelle*

Towering 100 feet above the Crooked River, the square-pyramidal skeletal lighthouse that was erected near Carrabelle (hence its alternative name, the Carrabelle Light) in 1895 was decommissioned in 1995. The section of the lighthouse immediately below the black lantern is painted red, while the bottom half is white. The keeper's dwelling has since been relocated 2 miles to the west and is today a private residence. The Crooked River Light is, at present, closed to the public.

ABOVE: *St.Marks Light.*

SPOTTER'S NOTE
The Crooked River Light's fourth-order Fresnel lens is today on display at the U.S. Coast Guard station in New Orleans, Louisiana.

BELOW: *Crooked River Light.*

BELOW: *Cape San Blas Light.*

35. Cape St. George Light

Cape St. George, Little St. George Island

A combination of beach erosion and hurricanes may one day finally topple the Cape St. George Light, a 70-foot, conical, white-painted brick lighthouse that has been situated at this location since 1852. (Its Winslow Lewis–designed predecessor of 1833 succumbed to a hurricane in 1851.) No longer operational (it was deactivated in 1994), it once accommodated a third-order Fresnel lens in its black, cast-iron lantern (focal plane 72 feet). Now leased to the Cape St. George Lighthouse Society, the "Leaning Tower of Florida" (as it was nicknamed in 1999) is on the Lighthouse Digest Doomsday List of endangered lighthouses, and an ongoing battle is being fought to keep it stable. Its grounds are accessible to the public.

36. Cape San Blas Light

Cape San Blas

The only light at Cape San Blas to have survived (though it is no longer operational) was erected on iron piles in 1885. A cast-iron, pyramidal skeleton tower whose supporting structure and central cylinder are painted white, the black lantern at the apex of the 90-foot-high edifice still contains the third-order bivalve Fresnel lens that it received in 1906, which had a focal-plane height of 101 feet. The light was automated in 1981, and its flashing signal was extinguished in 1996. The two-story frame keeper's quarters, which date from 1919, along with the second keeper's dwelling (both of which have been moved from their original position) and a 1939 radio beacon can be seen near the lighthouse, which is today located within an U.S. Air Force base. Only its grounds are currently open to the public, but Gulf County, which has leased it, is working on restoring the Cape San Blas Light and establishing a museum in the former keeper's cottage.

37. St. Joseph Bay Light
St. Joseph Bay

The lighthouse that assumed the duties of the St. Joseph Point Range Rear Light (*see* below) is a steel skeletal tower that was raised in 1960. Still operational, its 300-mm optic has a focal-plane height of 78 feet above sea level.

38. St. Joseph Point Range Rear Light   *Simmons Bayou*

Also known as the Beacon Hill Light, this now defunct lighthouse originally served as an aid to navigation on Beacon Hill, Port St. Joe, from 1902 until its deactivation in 1960. After being used as a barn, the square, two-story wooden keeper's house, whose square, wooden tower rises to a height of 41 feet and once supported a third-order Fresnel lens (focal plane 63 feet) was moved here, south of Port St. Joe, in 1979. This white-painted building, which has a red roof and verandas, is now a private residence that is closed to the public.

39. Pensacola Light   *Penascola Bay*

There has been a beacon at this bay entrance, in the Florida Panhandle, since 1825, but the first tower was demolished upon the completion, in 1859, of the conical brick lighthouse that continues to serve as an aid to mariners to this day. The top two-thirds of the 150-foot tower are painted black, and the bottom third, white, and a workhouse is attached to its base. The Henry Lepaute revolving lens that flashes white every 20 seconds (focal plane 191 feet) was installed in 1869 and auto-mated in 1965. The two-story brick keeper's quarters of 1868 are among the surviving outbuildings in what is now a U.S. Navy air station (which is why an aircraft-warning light is mounted 171 feet up the lighthouse). The former keeper's house is now a U.S. Navy Command Display Center that is open to the public. The lighthouse itself is open for tours on summer weekends.

ABOVE: *Pensacola Light*

SPOTTER'S NOTE

The first lighthouse to be erected on the St. Joseph Peninsula was the old St. Joseph Bay Light, a 55-foot white, conical brick tower (1839–46). The decreased trading activity in St. Joseph Bay that ultimately snuffed out this beacon had a tragic cause: a yellow-fever epidemic that killed many citizens of St. Joseph (now Port St. Joe) in 1841.

ALABAMA

BELOW: *The old Mobile Point Light.*

Recent hurricane damage has further endangered one of Alabama's three surviving lights, which was already in poor condition, while another is in storage awaiting restoration.

1. Mobile Point Light
Fort Morgan State Park

Today a state historic site, the old Mobile Point Light served at the entrance to Mobile Bay from 1873 to 1966. The 30-foot black, iron skeletal structure was dismantled in 1979 and re-erected near Fort Morgan's visitors' parking lot, where it is open to the public. It was replaced by a 120-foot skeletal tower in 1966 (DCB-24, flashes white every 10 seconds, focal plane 125 feet, range 24 miles).

2. Mobile Middle Bay Light
Mobile Bay

Deactivated in 1967, this beacon was recently dismantled and taken into storage. A replica of Maryland's Hooper's Strait Lighthouse, the screwpile structure, whose 1905 wooden, white-painted keeper's dwelling rested on a platform surmounting the red piles, went into service in 1885. The 54-foot hexagonal tower will eventually be restored and reassembled.

3. Sand Island Light   *Sand Island*

This 131-foot, conical, Gothic-style brownstone tower sits at the entrance to Mobile Bay, 3 miles south of Dauphin Island. Its black, cast-iron lantern held a second-order Fresnel lens (focal plane 132 feet) until its deactivation in 1933. Now on the Lighthouse Digest Doomsday list of endangered lighthouses and having sustained serious damage by Hurricane Ivan (2004), the tower is closed to the public. The old lens can still be admired at the Fort Morgan Museum.

MISSISSIPPI

This state has two lighthouses that have survived as private aids to navigation and a third that is being rebuilt after being destroyed in a 1998 hurricane.

1. Round Island Light *Pascagoula Bay*

The existing light took over the original structure's duties in 1859. The 50-foot, conical brick tower was equipped with a fourth-order Fresnel lens (automated 1944). Deactivated around 1949, and all but destroyed by Hurricane George in 1998, the remains are now under restoration.

2. Biloxi Light *Biloxi*

This 61-foot, white conical tower was raised in 1848. Long since automated, its keeper's cottage was destroyed by Hurricane Camille in 1969. On its completion, the tower's brick body was encased in cast iron, and a fifth-order Fresnel lens was installed; the current fifth-order lens (1926) has a focal-plane of 48 feet. Today it is a private aid to navigation that stands between lanes on the busy U.S. Highway 90.

3. Ship Island Light *Ship Island*

The current optic flashes white every 6 seconds atop a skeleton tower 80 feet high, which was erected on this spot overlooking Mississippi Sound in 1971. A 70-foot, square-pyramidal wooden tower stands nearby; it looks old, but appearances can be deceptive, and the structure is, in fact, a modern replica of the Ship Island Lighthouse that stood here between 1886 and 1972, when it was destroyed by fire. Funded by the Friends of the Gulf Islands National Seashore, the construction of the replica lighthouse was completed in 2000, and it today operates as a private aid to navigation, its light flashing white every 10 seconds; it is also open to the public. The 1886 lighthouse was the second beacon on Ship Island.

ABOVE: *Biloxi Light.*

SPOTTER'S NOTE

Three women have served as the Biloxi Light's keeper: Mary J. Reynolds (1854–61); Maria Younghans (1867–1918); and her daughter, Miranda Younghans (1918–29).

LOUISIANA

Several of the lighthouses of Louisiana are endangered, sinking gradually into the soft, muddy ground on which they stand. Thus, none are open to the public, though some can be glimpsed from dry land.

ABOVE: *Tchefuncte River Range Rear Light.*

1. Chandeleur Island Light
Chandeleur Island

The 100-foot, red-brown skeleton lighthouse that today soars above Chandeleur Sound is the third to have been erected on this island. The iron structure, constructed on pile foundations in 1896, has survived all that the sea and sky have thrown at it for over a century (though the surrounding land was washed away by Hurricane George in September 1998). An automated 300-mm optic (focal plane 99 feet) was installed in 1966, but deactivated when a new skeleton tower took over as the active aid to navigation (2001). The recently retired lighthouse is inaccessible to the public.

2. Barataria Bay Light *Fort Livingstone*

The existing lighthouse at this site was first lit in 1897. The 66-foot square-pyramidal, wooden skeletal tower has a 200-mm optic (focal plane 77 feet) and is not open to the public.

3. Tchefuncte River Range Rear Light *Madisonville*

This active light station, with its vertical black stripe on a white background, is also a striking daymark. Constructed on stone foundations in 1868, the 43-foot conical brick tower now houses a 250-mm optic (focal plane 49 feet). The structure is owned by the town of Madisonville, which has plans to make a museum of it one day (at the time of writing, it is closed to the public, however). A range front light was erected nearby in 1903 in the form of a pile-supported skeletal tower, automated in 1952.

4. Pass Manchac Light   *Ponchatoula*

The 40-foot, cylindrical brick tower (1857) that overlooks Pass Manchac between Lake Maurepas and the western shore of Lake Pontchartrain was deactivated in 1987 when a new tower assumed its duties. Automated in 1941, and installed with a modern beacon in 1952, this dilapidated, listing lighthouse is closed to the public and is accessible only by boat. Its owner, the State of Louisiana, along with the Lake Maurepas Society, hope to restore and open it some day.

5. New Canal Light   *New Orleans*

When built in 1901, the 32-foot, white-painted, red-roofed, two-story integral keeper's dwelling and square light tower that today stands sentinel at West End Boulevard and Lakeshore Drive, at the entrance to the Lake Pontchartrain Canal, was located offshore, above pile foundations. It was moved to its current location in 1910, from which it has continued to beam out its signal—a white flash every 10 seconds—ever since, firstly with the help of a fifth-order Fresnel lens, and latterly by means of a 190-mm optic (focal plane 52 feet). This light is a U.S. Coast Guard station and is not open to the public.

ABOVE, RIGHT: *New Canal Light.*
BELOW: *Port Pontchartrain Light.*

6. Port Pontchartrain Light
Ponchartrain Beach, Milneburg

The brick lighthouse that stands on the shore of Lake Pontchartrain is unusual in having a shape that is reminiscent of an hourglass. The reason for this is that 7 feet were added to the original, 40-foot, conical structure in 1880, causing it to flare upward and outward. When this white-painted tower (the third beacon at its location, whose exterior visitors can today walk around) was first raised in 1855, it was located over 2,000 feet off-shore and had keeper's quarters attached (which no longer survive). That it is today on dry land is due to a series of subsequent landfill projects. Its lantern received a fifth-order Fresnel lens in 1857, whose light, prior to its deactivation in 1929, had a focal-plane height above sea level of 42 feet. Its current owner is the University of New Orleans.

7. **West Rigolets Light**   *Fort Pick*

This 1855 lighthouse near New Orleans was raised on columns by 6 feet in 1917 and deactivated in 1945. The integrated, one-story, square keeper's quarters and rooftop lantern still survive, but the light is privately owned and closed to the public.

8. **Pass à L'Outre Light**   *Delta National Wildlife Refuge*

This abandoned 1855 tower (third-order Fresnel, deactivated 1930) is slowly sinking into the Mississippi Delta. Only 50 feet of this once 85-foot, conical cast-iron lighthouse are visible today (only by boat or airplane). It is on the Lighthouse Doomsday List of endangered lighthouses.

> **SPOTTER'S NOTE**
> Two abandoned light towers still stand at the Southwest Pass entrance to the Mississippi River, one a conical tower (1839), and the other its skeletal replacement (1873). Both called the "Southwest Pass Light" in their day, the 1839 structure took over from an 1832 tower constructed by Winslow Lewis.

9. **South Pass Range Lights**   *Venice*

The rear light, a 116-foot, iron skeletal tower, was erected on pilings in 1881. It is painted white below the lantern's gallery (focal plane 108 feet) and black above it. The front light—also a skeletal tower—was raised in 1947.

10. **Southwest Pass Entrance Light**   *entrance to Mississippi River*

Originally called the South Pass East Jetty Light, this light station was enlarged and renamed in 1953. The Texas Tower-style, 85-foot lighthouse was completed on pile foundations in 1962 (automated 1985). It is a white-painted, hexagonal concrete keeper's dwelling, from the center of which rises a hexagonal tower. The DCB-224 flashes white every 10 seconds (focal plane 95 feet). A radiobeacon and attached helicopter pad are also part of this offshore complex, which is closed to the public.

11. **Ship Shoal Light**   *10 miles south of Grand Isle*

This historic 125-foot lighthouse (first lit 1859, deactivated 1972) can only be seen from a boat. Its central cylinder is supported by a brown, octagonal, cast-iron skeletal framework on screwpiles. Automated in 1950, the integral keeper's quarters are uninhabited. The abandoned beacon is now listing to one side.

BELOW: *Ship Shoal Light before its condition deteriorated: it is now endangered.*

ABOVE: *Southwest Reef Light.*

12. Point Au Feu Light *Eugene Island*

This 44-foot, gray, steel skeletal tower was erected on pile foundations in Atchafalaya Bay in 1975. The third lighthouse to stand here, it is inaccessible to the public. It flashes white every 5 seconds (focal plane 44 feet, range 13 miles) and is also equipped with a horn that blasts every 10 seconds from November 1 to April 30.

13. Southwest Reef Light *Everett S. Berry Lighthouse Park, Berwick*

Deactivated in 1916, this lighthouse stood neglected in Atchafalaya Bay until moved to its current location in 1987 and renovated. Today this Egyptian Revival-style lighthouse—constructed of iron plate, on iron piles, with two platforms—is open to the public. The lantern (focal plane 49 feet) now stands empty above the 40-foot square-pyramidal tower, as does the integral keeper's residence.

14. Sabine Pass East Jetty Light *offshore, Louisiana Point*

A modern cylindrical tower on pile foundations, its optic flashes white every 5 seconds, while a horn emits two blasts every 20 seconds from November 1 to April 30. The original, 1924 structure was a skeletal tower atop the roof of a rectangular fog-signal building that was in turn elevated by piles.

15. Sabine Pass Light *Sabine Pass (overleaf)*

Sabine Pass Light

Description: octagonal
  brick tower supported
  by eight buttresses
Markings: faded bands;
  black lantern
Lens: removed; originally
  third-order Fresnel
Height: 74 feet (tower),
  85 feet (focal plane)

RIGHT AND BELOW: *There are
plans to renovate this light and
turn it into a museum.*

A Space Age Structure from the Victorian Era

If it weren't for its Victorian-era lantern, the Sabine Pass Light could easily be mistaken for a lighthouse built during the 1960s, the decade when space exploration became a major inspiration for architects and designers. From the cone-like tip of its lantern to the eight "shellcrete" (a form of concrete) buttresses that support it, four of which extend for 20 feet, and four for 18 feet, this light tower looks like a rocket ship. Many people are therefore surprised to learn that construction of this lighthouse was actually completed in 1856, and that its designer, Danville Leadbetter, was an engineer employed by the U.S. Army who subsequently served as a Confederate general.

An Endangered Monument

Deactivated in 1952, the Sabine Pass Light continues to act as a striking daymark at its location on the Louisiana side of the Sabine Pass, near the southeastern border with Texas. It can be seen from Sabine Pass, Texas, and its former Fresnel lens can be viewed at the Gulf Coast Maritime Museum in Port Arthur, Texas. The keeper's quarters were burned to the ground in 1976.

TEXAS

The long Gulf Coast of Texas has relatively few lights, but still boasts a handful of venerable towers that have withstood the onslaught of many a storm, Point Bolivar Light having saved 125 refugees when a devastating 1900 hurricane claimed 8,000 lives.

1. Sabine Bank Light *off Sabine Pass*

Now replaced by a skeletal tower (2002), the original, conical, rusty-red, cast-iron spark-plug tower, with integral keeper's quarters, stood 15 miles south of the Louisiana–Texas border from 1906 to 2001, when it was deactivated. Constructed above a submerged caisson on a dangerous shoal, it rose 72 feet above a cylindrical pier. Now dismantled, the lantern can be seen in Lion Park, in Sabine Pass.

2. Point Bolivar Light *Galveston Bay*

The old lighthouse, a 116-foot, black, brick-lined, cast-iron conical tower has stood on the Bolivar Peninsula since 1872. The third in the area, it was originally equipped with a third-order Fresnel lens (focal plane 117 feet). Decommisioned in 1933 and now privately owned, the old lighthouse is closed to the public, but can be seen from the Bolivar–Galveston ferry.

ABOVE: *Old Point Bolivar Light.*

> **SPOTTER'S NOTE**
> The ruins of Galveston Jetty Light are still visible. A storm swept away the pilings under the abandoned black-and-white tower in 2000.

ABOVE: *Half Moon Reef Light.*
BELOW: *Matagorda Island Light.*
BOTTOM: *Lydia Ann Light.*

3. Half Moon Reef Light
Port Lavaca's Bay Front Park

This hexagonal keeper's cottage was constructed in 1858 above iron-screwpile foundations. Supported by a rudimentary tower that protrudes from the roof of the keeper's quarters, its lantern once held a fourth-order Fresnel lens, but has housed a decorative, flashing bulb since 1990. Decommissioned in 1942 (when it was partly demolished by a storm), it was moved here in 1980 and restored. The white-painted, green-trimmed structure is today a tourist attraction.

4. Matagorda Island Light
Matagorda Bay

This 79-foot black, conical lighthouse was built in 1852 and has held a solar-powered optic since 1977 (focal plane 90 feet). In 1873, the brick-lined cast-iron tower was moved to minimize the risk of erosion. Deactivated from 1995 to 1999, is is now leased to Calhoun County, which oversaw a renovation program in 2004. No associated structures survive. Visitors can explore the grounds, and Matagorda Island can be reached by ferry from Port O'Connor.

5. Lydia Ann Light *Harbor Island*

This light station overlooks the Lydia Ann Channel, at the northwest entrance of the Aransas Pass. The lantern that surmounts the 65-foot, octagonal brick tower (erected 1855 on timber pilings) held a fourth-order Fresnel lens (focal plane 65 feet) when it was first lit in 1857. Deactivated in 1952, this optic is now on display at the Port Aransas Civic Center. The lighthouse was decommissioned in 1952, but its keeper's quarters—a bungalow built in 1919 following the destruction of the original by a hurricane in 1916—still stand. This lighthouse, which is closed to the public, has operated as a private aid to navigation since 1988 and displays a flashing white light.

6. Port Isabel Light *Port Isabel*

Situated on the Lower Laguna Madre, overlooking Brazos Santiago Pass in the Gulf of Mexico, this light is today both a private aid to navigation and the centerpiece of the Port Isabel Lighthouse State Historical Park. Raised of brick to a height of 57 feet in 1853, the cast-iron lantern at the apex of this conical, white-painted tower was originally equipped with four lamps, but received fifteen lamps and twenty-one reflectors a year later. The top of the tower has frequently been disturbed: destroyed during the Civil War and rebuilt during the 1860s, it required extending by around 3 feet during the 1880s in order to accommodate a third-order Fresnel lens, which was deactivated in 1905. After an extended period of neglect, its current owners have recently funded and presided over a comprehensive restoration program, including the construction of a replica of the 1855 keeper's quarters. Today the Port Isabel Light's light signal again flashes white at a focal-plane height above sea level of 91 feet.

ABOVE: *Port Isabel Light.*

7. Lake Conroe Lighthouse *Lake Conroe*

Also known as the Harbour Town Lighthouse, there has been a light on this lake, 40 miles north of Houston, since 1977, but the current 90-foot, stucco-covered octagonal tower (painted with red and white bands) with a copper top dates from 1999. After a tornado cut a swath through the lake, the Lake Conroe Lighthouse Association was forced to fund and supervise the repair of the tower. A private aid to navigation, this lighthouse is closed to the public.

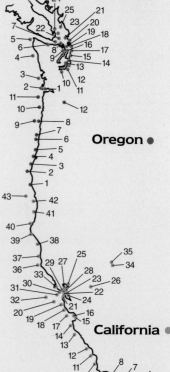

THE WEST

CALIFORNIA

California's rugged coastline is beset with hazards to mariners, including jagged cliffs, treacherous reefs and currents, and fog so dense and pervasive that round-the-clock sound signals are required, while the risk of earthquakes poses additional challenges to lighthouse builders. Unless mentioned otherwise, these lights are closed to the public.

ABOVE: *Los Angeles Harbor Light.*

1. Point Loma Light *San Diego*
(opposite)

2. Long Beach Light *Long Beach*
Nicknamed the "Robot Light" on account of its futuristic appearance, this 1949 lighthouse consists of six cement pilings supporting a concrete building, above which rises a 42-foot, white, rectangular steel tower bearing a square, green daymark. Its optic flashes white every 5 seconds (focal plane 50 feet, range 23 miles).

3. Los Angeles Harbor (Angel's Gate) Light *Los Angeles*
This 69-foot, cylindrical steel-and-concrete tower (with vertical black and white stripes) was built on its pentagonal concrete base at the end of the San Pedro breakwater in 1913. Its solar-powered DCB-24 flashes green every 15 seconds (focal plane 73 feet, range 21 miles). The light can be seen from the San Pedro–Santa Catalina ferry.

4. Point Fermin Light *San Pedro*
Since 1970, the new, post-mounted light flashes white every 10 seconds. The old, integrated, Italianate cottage lighthouse (1874), deactivated 1942, is now a museum, open to the public (*see also* Spotter's Note, page 220).

5. Point Vicente Light *Point Vicente*
Erected in 1926 on the southwesternmost point of the Palos Verdes Peninsula, the 67-foot, cylindrical, white concrete light tower's original third-order Fresnel lens continues to flash white twice every 20 seconds (focal plane 185 feet, range 28 miles). It can be viewed either by appointment or on monthly open-house days (currently the second Saturday of each month).

> **SPOTTER'S NOTE**
> Two private aids to navigation operate at Long Beach. One is a 65-foot, white, conical steel tower in Rainbow Harbor named the Long Beach Lighthouse (2000), which also serves as the harbormaster's office. The second is known either as the Shoreline Marina Entrance Light or as Parkers' Lighthouse (1982). Its beacon shines at a focal-plane height of 71 feet from within a lantern mounted on the roof of a restaurant at the point of Shoreline Village.

Point Loma Light (Old & New)

Lighting Point Loma

The Old Point Loma Light was active from 1855 until 1891, but its focal-plane height—462 feet above sea level—was so high (then the highest of all U.S. lighthouses) that its light was often obscured by fog and low clouds, which is why the decision was taken to replace it at a lower elevation. The old lighthouse is now part of Cabrillo National Monument and is open to the public. A hybrid structure, it consists of a white-painted Cape Cod-style keeper's cottage constructed from sandstone, with a conical tower rising from the center of its roof to a height of 46 feet. Its green lantern still contains the original third-order Fresnel lens.

Constructed in 1891, on concrete foundations at the southern end of Point Loma 18 feet above sea level, the cylinder at the center of the "new" white-painted, pyramidal, steel skeleton tower supports a black-painted lantern. It has a focal-plane height of 88 feet and its flashing white signal can be seen up to 26 miles away.

Description: New: steel skeleton tower; Old: integrated cottage
Markings: New: white with black lantern; Old: white with green lantern
Lens: New: Vega VRB-25; Old: third-order Fresnel
Height: New: 70 feet (tower), 88 feet (focal plane); Old: 46 feet (tower), 462 feet (focal plane)

ABOVE AND BELOW: *The old lighthouse is now a museum.*

ABOVE: *Anacapa Island Light.*

ABOVE: *Old Point Hueneme Light.*
BELOW: *New Point Hueneme Light.*

6. Anacapa Island Light
Anacapa Island

The 40-foot, white, cylindrical, concrete-and-brick lighthouse that guides mariners in and out of the Santa Barbara Channel first went into operation in 1932 (automated 1968). Its black lantern holds a DCB-24 optic (1991) that flashes white twice every 60 seconds (focal plane 277 feet, range 23 miles). A Spanish Revival-style keeper's residence still stands in the grounds, now part of a national park, and open to the public.

7. Point Hueneme Light
Point Hueneme

This 1941 lighthouse is a white, concrete, Art Deco structure with a 48-foot, square light tower. Its original fourth-order Fresnel lens (automated 1972) produces five white flashes every 30 seconds (focal plane 52 feet).

8. Santa Barbara Light
west of Santa Barbara

The current light (1935) is a 24-foot, white tower whose automated signal flashes white every 10 seconds (focal plane 142 feet, range 29 miles). Its predecessor (a two-story Cape Cod-style keeper's dwelling with tower, 1856) operated until 1925, when it was shattered by an earthquake that also killed its keeper.

9. Point Conception Light
Point Conception

This cylindrical, white tower is 52 feet tall, but its flashing white signal has a focal-plane height of 133 feet and a range of 23 miles. Built of brick, wood, and stucco on stone foundations in 1882, this is the second lighthouse to serve here. The light was automated in 1973, but the one-story, Spanish-style, brick-and-stucco keeper's quarters (1911) remain, as do a generator building and additional dwelling, both dating from the 1960s.

10. Point Arguello Light *Point Arguello*

This navigational aid is an optic mounted on a 20-foot post (flashes white every 15 seconds, focal plane 100 feet). Its predecessors included an integrated, Cape Cod light of 1901, which was demolished in the 1940s.

11. San Luis Obispo (Port Harford) Light

San Luis Obispo Bay

The first lighthouse—a white-painted, wood-frame structure consisting of a 40-foot, square tower and octagonal lantern, attached to a red-roofed keeper's quarters—was erected on Avila Beach in 1890 and today stands in the Diablo Nuclear Power Plant reservation (due to security, check for access status). Deactivated in 1975, its duties were transferred to a nearby cylindrical structure, which flashes white every five seconds (focal plane 116 feet, range 23 miles).

12. Piedras Blancas Light

northern entrance to San Simeon Bay

This privately maintained, 74-foot, white, conical brick tower was constructed in 1875. Its lantern was removed in 1949 and the VRB-25 optic (2002) that flashes white every 10 seconds (focal plane 142 feet) is exposed to the elements. Apart from the occasional tour, this light is closed, but it can be spotted from Highway 1, about 1 mile north of San Simeon.

13. Point Sur Light *Moro Rock, Point Sur*

This lighthouse's 48-foot, square sandstone tower atop a fog-signal building holds a DCB-224 (flashes white every 15 seconds) with a focal plane of 250 feet. The Richardson Romanesque structure, constructed in 1889, is now part of the Point Sur State Historic Park and is open to the public. An active aid to navigation, all of its associated buildings have survived intact.

ABOVE: *Piedras Blancas Light.*
BELOW: *Point Sur Light.*

SPOTTER'S NOTE
The sandstone cliff on which the Point Sur Light stands is so steep that it was necessary to build a railroad track on which to transport men and materials before work on the lighthouse's construction could begin.

14. Point Piños Light *southern entrance to Monterey Bay*

This 1855 lighthouse is typical of the Cape Cod-style, integral lighthouses that were raised along the Californian coastline during that decade. It is the oldest operational lighthouse on the West Coast, having survived the 1906 San Francisco earthquake. Its cast-iron lantern is supported by a 43-foot, white-painted conical tower that protrudes from the keeper's dwelling. Automated in 1975, its original third-order Fresnel lens has a white signal that occults every 4 seconds (focal plane 89 feet, range 20 miles). Now housing a maritime museum, it is open to the public Thursdays through Sundays.

SPOTTER'S NOTE
The U.S. Coast Guard once maintained a light at Point Santa Cruz. This served from 1869 until 1941, when it was decommissioned. It was demolished in 1948.

15. Santa Cruz West Breakwater (Walton) Light *Santa Cruz*

A 42-foot, conical concrete tower, painted white with red and black trim, this lighthouse was erected in 2001 on the end of a jetty at the harbor entrance. It was funded by private donations and displays an occulting green signal.

16. Santa Cruz Light *West Cliff Drive, Point Santa Cruz*

Following the death of a surfer here in 1965, his parents funded the erection of this lighthouse (1967), which is also known as the Mark Abbott Memorial Light. The white-painted, cast-iron lantern (which originally graced the now defunct Oakland Harbor Light, *see* page 225) sits atop a 39-foot, square brick tower that adjoins a brick building that houses a surfing museum. The light that it exhibits flashes white every 5 seconds at a focal-plane height of 60 feet.

17. Año Nuevo Island Light *Año Nuevo Island*

Ruins are all that remains of this light station, whose most recent light was a partly enclosed skeleton tower of 1948 (demolished 1976). The island is now a state nature preserve and is closed to visitors.

BELOW: *The last Año Nuevo Island Light before its demolition (1976).*

ABOVE: *Pigeon Point Light before its 1974 automation.*

18. Pigeon Point Light   *southern entrance to San Francisco Bay*

This active lighthouse (1872) was named for the vessel *Carrier Pigeon*, which came to grief on the shoals below in 1853. Its 115-foot, white-painted, conical brick tower with black trim is attached to a one-story workroom. Its original, first-order Fresnel lens is lit once a year (November 15), and its current DCB-24 flashes white every 10 seconds (focal plane 148 feet, range 28 miles) from the balcony rail. The four keepers' dwellings (1960) now serve as a hostel; the site is a state historic park.

19. Point Montara Light   *Point Montara*

This 30-foot, white-painted, conical steel light tower was erected in 1928. Automated in 1970, its octagonal, cast-iron lantern houses an FA-251 aerobeacon that flashes white every 5 seconds (focal plane 70 feet). Now a hostel, visitors are welcome to visit the grounds, where they will see a two-story, wood-framed keeper's cottage in the Victorian Gothic style (1875).

20. Mile Rocks Light   *offshore,*
San Francisco Bay

Spotters can see this beacon from Lincoln Park as it flashes white every 5 seconds (focal plane 49 feet). The modern optic is mounted atop an orange-striped, white-painted, steel-and-concrete caisson (1906) near the Golden Gate. In 1966 the two upper sections of the steel, three-tier structure were removed and a helipad was instituted on the remaining tier.

ABOVE AND BELOW: *Mile Rocks Light before and after 1966.*

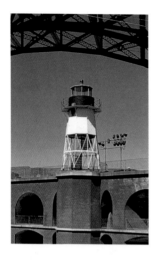

21. Fort Point Light *San Francisco Bay*

This 27-foot, nine-sided, white-painted, iron part-skeletal tower was erected at the entrance to the harbor, on a stairway tower in Fort Winfield Scott, in 1864, and given a fourth-order Fresnel lens (focal plane 110 feet). Deactivated in 1934, visitors can explore the fort around it.

22. Alcatraz Island Light
San Francisco Bay

This 84-foot, gray, octagonal-pyramidal concrete lighthouse occupies the site on which the West Coast's first "official" lighthouse was constructed in 1854. Damaged by the 1906 earthquake, that structure was replaced with the present tower. Automated in 1963, its DCB-24 optic flashes white every 5 seconds (focal plane 214 feet, range 26 miles). The Alcatraz Island Light is closed to the public, unlike its grounds, which are now part of a national park.

23. Yerba Buena (Goat) Island Light *San Francisco Bay*

This 1875 light is a 25-foot, white-painted, octagonal wood-framed tower with a fifth-order Fresnel lens (focal plane 95 feet, range 16 miles). The signal is a white light that occults every 4 seconds. Automated in 1958, the Gothic-style keeper's residence of 1873 still stands (and is now used to accommodate the U.S. Coast Guard's district commandant) alongside a fog-signal building (1875) and an oil house. The light station can be viewed from the Bay Bridge.

Top: *Fort Point Light.*
Above: *Alcatraz Island Light's tower and the ruined prison warden's house.*
Right: *A period photograph of Yerba Buena Island Light and its outbuildings.*

24. Oakland Harbor Light

Embarcadero Cove, Oakland

Operational in Oakland Harbor from 1903 until 1966, this two-story, wooden keeper's quarters with tower was re-erected on concrete pilings at its new location in 1984 and is now enjoying a second career as a restaurant. Lighthouse spotters in Oakland will also now find the lightship *Relief* (1951–75), which is open to the public.

25. Carquinez Strait Light

Elliott Cove

This lighthouse once stood sentinel at the entrance to the Carquinez Strait, around 20 miles east of San Francisco Bay. The square, cream-painted wooden structure was built atop a wooden pier in 1910. Sold to a private owner following its deactivation in 1951, the keeper's dwelling was relocated to its current location in Vallejo, where it forms part of the Glen Cove Marina complex. Automated in 1963, a beacon sited at the end of a pier today aids navigation through the Carquinez Strait.

ABOVE: *The old Southampton Shoals Light before it was moved to its new location at a Stockton yacht club.*

26. Southampton Shoals Light   *Tinsley Island, Stockton*

The current Southampton Shoals Light is a white, cylindrical tower with an automated alternating red signal (focal plane 32 feet, range 7 miles). The old beacon was raised here, off Angel Island, in 1905. Its square tower and integral keeper's quarters had a fifth-order Fresnel lens (focal plane 52 feet). This optic was deactivated in 1960 and can now be inspected at the Angel Island Interpretive Center. The supporting structure—or the top two stories of it, at least—was later moved to the privately owned Saint Francis Yacht Club, Stockton. Members of the public can view the interior by appointment.

27. East Brother Island Light   *East Brother Island, San Francisco Bay*

The buff, square tower on a two-story, Stick-style dwelling that has stood here, off Point San Pablo, since 1874, was automated in 1969. The lantern that surmounts the 48-foot wooden tower once contained a fourth-order Fresnel lens, but the light that flashes white every 5 seconds (focal plane 61 feet) is today produced by an FA-251 optic. Not only is the East Brother Island Light (which the East Brother Light Station, Inc. leases from the U.S. Coast Guard) open to the public, but it offers bed-and-breakfast accommodation, too.

28. Point Blunt Light   *Angel Island*

Active since 1915, this beacon flashes green every 5 seconds (focal plane 60 feet, range 15 miles). It comprised a small, square, white-painted, wood-framed tower with supporting piles, extended in the 1960s to include accommodation for four keepers and their families. Visitors to Angel Island are permitted to view the Point Blunt Light from the outside.

29. Lime Point Light   *Lime Point, entrance to San Francisco Bay*

A post light was established here in 1900, next to the Golden Gate Bridge. The current, solar-powered 250-mm lens (mounted on a fog-signal building) flashes white every 4 seconds (focal plane 15 feet). The grounds are open to the public.

30. Point Diablo Light   *entrance to San Francisco Harbor*

Sitting atop a square, white fog-signal building is this white, isophase beacon (focal plane 85 feet). This light station is inaccessible to the public.

31. Point Bonita Light   *entrance to San Francisco Harbor*

The first lighthouse here was completed in 1856 (when it received the West Coast's first ever fog signal). The current lighthouse (1877, automated 1980) holds both the original lantern and second-order Fresnel lens from the first lighthouse, and this is still operational. Its white, occulting light is exhibited every 4 seconds (focal plane 124 feet, range 21 miles). The 33-foot, white, brick-and-cement, hexagonal tower is mounted on a brick fog-signal building. Visitors can still view several buildings dating from the late-nineteenth and early-twentieth centuries. The light now stands within a national park and is accessible to the public (a hike is required) at weekends.

BELOW: *Point Bonita Light is perched on sheer cliffs.*

RIGHT: *Point Reyes Light.*

32. Farallon Island Light   *South Farallon Island*

Perched outside the entrance to San Francisco Bay since 1855, this 41-foot, white, conical brick tower (automated 1972) holds a Vega VRB optic, which flashes white every 15 seconds (focal plane 358 feet). As the island is now a national wildlife refuge, closed to the public, the tower can only be seen from the water.

33. Point Reyes Light   *Point Reyes*

The current lighthouse dates from 1975, when an automated beacon (white flash every 5 seconds) was mounted on a cylindrical support on an old fog-signal building (elevation 37 feet, focal plane 265 feet, range 28 miles). The first light (a 35-foot, white, brick-lined, sixteen-sided, cast-iron pyramidal tower with red-roofed lantern) was raised in 1870. Its first-order Fresnel lens (deactivated in 1975), remains in situ. It is open to visitors Thursdays through Mondays.

34. Rubicon Point Light   *Lake Tahoe, southwestern shore*

This 12-foot wooden structure (1916, now inactive) has an elevation above sea level of 6,300 feet—the highest of any U.S. beacon. It can be reached by a 2-mile hiking trail.

35. Sugar Pine Point Light   *Lake Tahoe, western shore*

This pole-mounted, solar-powered optic (flashes white every 5 seconds, focal plane 35 feet) and daymark replaced Rubicon Point Light in 1921.

36. Point Arena Light   *2 miles north of Point Arena*

Two years after the 1906 earthquake destroyed the original 1870 lighthouse, its lantern was moved to a new 115-foot, white, cylindrical concrete tower. Automated in 1977, and still active, a DCB-224 now flashes white every 15 seconds (range 29 miles, focal plane 155 feet). This lighthouse is open to the public, and the former keeper's houses are available for vacation rentals).

ABOVE: *Old Cape Mendocino Light.*

37. Point Cabrillo Light

north of Mendocino (*opposite*)

38. Cape Mendocino Light

Shelter Cove

An optic mounted on a post today flashes white every 15 seconds (focal plane 515 feet, range 22 miles). The original lighthouse that served here 1868–1951 can be viewed at Point Delgado, having been moved there in 1998. This 43-foot, white-painted, cast-iron, sixteen-sided, pyramidal light tower is the twin of Point Reyes Light (*see* page 227) and is now an attraction in Mal Coombs Park.

39. Punta Gorda Light   *Punta Gorda*

A lighted whistle buoy today serves offshore as the Punta Gorda Light. The original, 27-foot, reinforced-concrete lighthouse (1912–51) still stands 12 miles south of Cape Mendocino, though its fourth-order, bull's-eye Fresnel lens has been removed from the lantern. The lighthouse can be visited by members of the public.

40. Table Bluff Light   *Woodley Island Marina, near Eureka, Arcata Bay*

During its working days (1892–1961), this 35-foot, square, white-painted wooden light tower with integral two-story keeper's quarters held a fourth-order Fresnel lens (focal plane 176 feet, automated 1953) that aided navigation in and out of Humboldt Harbor from the South Spit. Relocated in 1987, it is privately owned and closed to the public.

41. Trinidad Head Light   *Trinidad Harbor* (*page 230*)

42. Battery Point (Crescent City) Light   *Battery Point Island* (*page 231*)

43. St. George Reef Light   *offshore, Point St. George*

Constructed over a period of ten years at the then astronomical cost of $704,634 (the United States' most expensive), 6 miles offshore on a concrete pier, the 90-foot, square-pyramidal, whitewashed granite lighthouse atop an integral fog-signal building and keeper's quarters has been active since 1892. Since 2002 it has held a solar-powered optic (focal plane 144 feet), but the official beacon here is a lighted whistle buoy. The old light is visible from Point St. George.

Point Cabrillo Light

A Treasure Restored

The original rotating, bull's-eye, third-order Fresnel lens at Point Cabrillo Light (1909) is today again flashing white every 10 seconds at a focal-plane height of 81 feet. (A DCB-224 aerobeacon mounted on the integral fog-signal building had assumed this duty for thirty years or so from 1969.) Situated in what is now a nature preserve, the light is an octagonal, wooden tower 47 feet high, with black lantern, protruding from the end of a wooden, white-painted, Cape Cod-style building that once housed the fog signal. Various outbuildings remain at the site. Visitors are welcome here, and guided walks take place on Sunday mornings from May through September.

Description: integrated Cape Cod-style light
Markings: white with gray-brown trim and red roof; black lantern
Lens: third-order Fresnel
Height: 47 feet (tower); 81 feet (focal plane)

BELOW: *Point Cabrillo Light was much sought-after by keepers because it was relatively close to "civilization." The aerobeacon, now replaced by the original lens, can be seen on the roof.*

Trinidad Head Light

Description: square-
 pyramidal light tower
Markings: white; red-
 roofed lantern
Lens: 375 mm
Height: 25 feet (tower);
 196 feet (focal plane)

BELOW: *Hiking trails lead to
Trinidad Head Light, and visitors
can see the lantern from a viewing
platform above.*

Cliff Hanger

The Trinidad Head Light was constructed from
brick on stone foundations in 1871, its white,
square-pyramidal sides and lantern rising to a
height of 25 feet. Its light was once focused by a
fourth-order Fresnel lens, but since 1947 it has
been a 375-mm optic with an occulting white
signal. The original keeper's quarters were
demolished during the 1960s, and the wood-
frame, triplex replacement (1969) now houses
U.S. Coast Guard personnel. The nearby frame
fog-signal building dates from 1900. This light
station can be seen from close range, and visitors
can also see a replica at the end of Trinity Street
in Trinidad. The replica Trinidad Memorial
Light is so called because a wall adjacent to the
lighthouse has been inscribed with the names of
local people who have died at sea.

Battery Point (Crescent City) Light

Power Point

Because it is situated close to Crescent City's A Street, this lighthouse is also known as the Crescent City Light. Constructed in 1856, it is a square, masonry, Cape Cod-style keeper's dwelling, painted white, from the center of whose red roof a cylindrical tower rises, elevating its lantern to a height of 45 feet (focal plane 77 feet). Having been deactivated in 1965, the fifth-order lens remained dark until 1982, when the Del Norte County Historical Society set it operating again, and today it continues to flash white every 30 seconds. This privately maintained aid to navigation and museum is open to the public from the beginning of April until the end of September (tides permitting).

ABOVE: *Battery Point Light is situated close to the Oregon border. It is particularly popular with visitors at sunset, when views are often dramatic.*

Description: integrated keeper's dwelling and cylindrical light tower
Markings: white with red roof; red-roofed lantern
Lens: fifth-order Fresnel
Height: 45 feet (tower); 77 feet (focal plane)

OREGON

Most of Oregon's spectacularly sited lighthouses are at relatively high elevations and are located on public parkland or can be viewed from nearby vantage points.

1. Pelican Bay Lighthouse
Brookings Harbor

The house that Bill and Jo Ann Cady built in 1990 is unusual in that it has a white-painted, 35-foot, octagonal light tower attached to it. The optic within the black lantern acts as a private aid to navigation with a flashing white signal (focal plane 141 feet, range 13 miles). The light can be seen from nearby.

2. Cape Blanco Light *Sixes*

Completed in 1870, this is Oregon's oldest operational lighthouse. Its 59-foot whitewashed, conical brick tower is attached to a workroom and supports a green-painted, red-domed lantern that has accommodated a second-order Fresnel lens since 1936. Automated in 1980, and lit continuously, this beacon flashes white every 20 seconds (focal plane 245 feet, range 30 miles). Members of the public are welcome to tour the lighthouse, which today stands in Cape Blanco State Park.

ABOVE: *Cape Blanco Light.*
BELOW: *Coquille River Light.*

Above: *The third—and only surviving—incarnation of Cape Arago Light.*

3. Coquille River (Bandon) Light *Bandon*

Also known as the Bandon Light, this 1896 lighthouse consists of a 40-foot, white, conical, stucco-clad brick tower built above a jetty and attached to an eight-sided sound-signal building. The optic in the black lantern (focal plane 47 feet) was deactivated in 1939, but the tower was relit in 1991 as a historic attraction, now part of Bullards Beach State Park (the old light is open to the public). The Coquille River entrance now has a lighted whistle buoy that flashes red every 4 seconds.

4. Cape Arago Light *Gregory Point, Coos Bay, near Charleston*

Also known as the Cape Gregory Light, this, the third at its location, was erected in 1934 from reinforced concrete. It comprises a 44-foot, white-painted, octagonal tower attached to a fog-signal building. Its green lantern has a red dome and once housed a fourth-order Fresnel lens, which it inherited from its predecessors. Since 1998, a solar-powered VRB-25 continually produces three white flashes every 30 seconds (focal plane 100 feet, range 20 miles). The light station is closed to the public, but can be seen from a parking area near Cape Arago State Park.

BELOW: *Umpqua River Light now stands in Umpqua River State Park; tours are available in summer.*

5. Umpqua River Light
Winchester Bay, near Reedsport

This 1894 lighthouse is a 61-foot, white, stucco-covered, conical brick tower with an attached workroom. The first-order Fresnel lens that sits beneath the red dome of the green lantern operates continuously, with alternating white and red lights (focal plane 165 feet, range 23 miles). Automated in 1966, it is open to the public during the summer, and there is a museum.

6. Heceta Head Light *Siuslaw National Forest, near Florence (opposite)*

7. Cleft of the Rock Light
Cape Perpetua, near Yachats

Built in 1976, 10 miles north of Heceta Head, by a former lighthouse keeper, this light exhibits an alternating white–red signal (focal plane 110 feet). A 31-foot, white, square-pyramidal wooden tower with red trim, it was formally recognized as a private aid to navigation in 1979. It was modeled on Vancouver's Fiddle Reef Lighthouse. Also a private residence, this beacon can be seen from Highway 101 nearby.

8. Yaquina Bay Light
mouth of Yaquina River, near Newport

The red lantern room atop the short, square tower rising to 51 feet from the center of the roof of the white, red-trimmed, wooden, two-story keeper's house (1871) was deactivated in 1874, but was finally relit privately in 1996 with a 250-mm optic (focal plane 161 feet). It was the construction of the lighthouse at Yaquina Head that rendered this beacon redundant, and during its years of inactivity, it served as a crew station for the U.S. Lifesaving Service. The light is the oldest building in Newport and is now part of Yaquina Bay State Park, where it is open to the public and houses a museum.

Heceta Head Light

Description: conical brick tower
Markings: whitewashed; green lantern and red dome
Lens: first-order Fresnel
Height: 56 feet (tower); 205 feet (focal plane)

ABOVE AND BELOW: *Heceta Head's light and view.*

Point of Light

Although the U.S. Coast Guard has access to the optic—still the original first-order Fresnel lens of the 56-foot-tall, conical brick tower of 1894—the Heceta Head Light is now maintained by Oregon State Parks and Recreation, while the U.S. Forest Service runs its restored keeper's quarters as a bed-and-breakfast inn. The whitewashed, stucco-covered tower supports a green lantern with a red dome, and its light (automated in 1963) continuously flashes white every 10 seconds at a focal-plane height of 205 feet above sea level; this can be seen up to 32 miles from its dramatic position on a cliff near Florence. Visitors are welcome at the lighthouse, which is now part of the Siuslaw National Forest, along with the integral workroom and wooden, two-story, Queen Anne-style keeper's accommodation.

RIGHT: *Yaquina Head Light is Oregon's tallest.*

BELOW: *Cape Meares Light.*

9. Yaquina Head Light *Newport*

Unlike its neighbor at Yaquina Bay (page 234), this lighthouse, north of Newport, has operated continuously since 1873, when its fixed, first-order Fresnel lens was first lit (automated 1966). It flashes white twice every 20 seconds (focal plane 162 feet, range 22 miles). The 93-foot, conical, white-painted, brick tower that supports the green lantern and its red dome is the tallest lighthouse in Oregon. It is open to the public.

10. Cape Meares Light *Tillamook Bay*

Today's flashing white signal comes from a 17-foot-tall building, while the old lighthouse (1890) is open to the public. Before retirement (1963), its first-order Fresnel lens beamed out its signal (focal plane 217 feet) from the black lantern room atop the 40-foot, white, brick-lined, octagonal iron tower.

11. **Tillamook Rock Light** *1 mile off Tillamook Head, near Seaside*

Today a lighted whistle buoy marks the approach to the Columbia River, but between 1881 and 1957 the lighthouse perched on Tillamook Rock guided navigators negotiating the often tempestuous, rock-strewn waters below. The white-painted structure, which was raised from basalt, brick, and iron, consists of a 62-foot, square tower crowned with a lantern that once accommodated a first-order Fresnel lens (focal plane 133 feet) and integral keeper's quarters. Now privately owned, this historic, weather-battered lighthouse can be spotted from Ecola State Park.

12. **Warrior Rock Light** *Sauvie Island, Columbia River*

Warrior Rock Light is a whitewashed, octagonal-pyramidal tower raised during the 1930s, which, despite having been rammed by a runaway barge in 1969, still stands. The optic mounted on top of the 25-foot structure (which lacks a lantern) flashes white every 4 seconds at a focal-plane height of 28 feet and has a range of 8 miles. The light can be seen from the marina in Saint Helens, where there is also a replica of the former lighthouse (1889).

ABOVE: *Tillamook Rock Light was a technical triumph for builder George Ballantyne.*

SPOTTER'S NOTE
Tillamook Rock Light, once nicknamed "Terrible Tilly," is currently used as a columbarium (a place where the ashes of the dead are preserved).

SPOTTER'S NOTE
The lightship *Columbia* was established in 1892 to mark the mouth of the Columbia River and was the first to serve on the Pacific coast. In 1979, after several ships had served here, a navigational buoy finally took over and the west coast's last lightship was retired. The last *Columbia* is now at Astoria's Columbia River Maritime Museum.

WASHINGTON

This state is home to twenty-five lighthouses, many of which are open to visitors: there are eight fully accessible lighthouses in the Puget Sound area alone.

ABOVE: *The venerable Cape Disappointment Light.*
BELOW: *Grays Harbor Light.*

1. Cape Disappointment Light
North Point Island

This 63-foot, white-painted, conical dressed-stone light tower sports a distinctive black band and has guided vessels through the Columbia River entrance since 1856. The oldest lighthouse in the state, its beacon is lit continuously, its fourth-order Fresnel lens beaming out an alternating white–red signal (focal plane 220 feet) from the black lantern room. Automated in 1962, the grounds are open to the public.

2. North Head Light   Ilwaco   (opposite)

3. Grays Harbor Light   Westport

This 107-foot, brick, octagonal-pyramidal, white-washed tower (1898) is Washington's tallest. The current beacon is an FA-251 aerobeacon that flashes white, and then red, every 30 seconds (focal plane 123 feet). An active aid to navigation, it is owned by the Westport–South Beach Historical Society, which encourages visitors.

North Head Light

Northern Light

The aerobeacon that replaced North Head Light's fouth-order Fresnel lens in 1999 is a VRB-25 that operates continuously, producing two white flashes every 30 seconds, visible up to 30 miles away at a focal-plane height of 194 feet. The 65-foot, conical lighthouse, with its attached red-roofed keeper's quarters, was constructed from brick near Ilwaco, north of the mouth of the Columbia River, and then dressed with stone and painted white. The Washington State Parks and Recreation Commission now leases this active aid to navigation from the U.S. Coast Guard, letting out the former keepers' quarters for vacation rentals and welcoming day trippers here. As well as the lighthouse, visitors to the North Head Light can see two garages, a pair of oil houses, a cistern, a storage building, and a chicken coop.

Description: conical brick tower
Markings: white; red lantern and dome
Lens: VRB-25
Height: 65 feet (tower); 194 feet (focal plane)

ABOVE AND BELOW: *The lighthouse at North Head.*

ABOVE, LEFT: *Destruction Island Light and its surviving outbuildings.*
ABOVE, RIGHT: *New Dungeness Light after modification in 1927.*

4. Destruction Island Light *Destruction Island*

On its completion in 1891, the 94-foot, conical, dressed-stone light tower off the coast of Washington's Olympic Peninsula was painted white, and the gallery surrounding it, black. The lantern is today a solar-powered VRB-25 aerobeacon that flashes white every 10 seconds (focal plane 147 feet). Automated in 1968, a concrete sound-signal building remains. Still active, the light can be seen from Route 101 near Ruby Beach.

5. Cape Flattery Light *Tatoosh Island, Cape Flattery*

This light station has stood sentinel at the entrance to the Strait of Juan de Fuca since 1857 and occupies the northwesternmost point of the United States. The 65-foot, whitewashed, conical sandstone-and-brick tower supports a red-roofed, black lantern. Its VRB-25 optic produces two white flashes every 20 seconds (focal plane 165 feet). Automated in 1977, the Cape Cod-style keeper's dwelling is integral with the light tower. Renovated in 1994, it can be seen from Neah Bay.

BELOW: *Ediz Hook Light in 1908.*

6. Ediz Hook Light *Ediz Hook, Port Angeles Harbor*

Today, the light is an automated optic that continuously beams green and white flashes (focal plane 60 feet) from a skeleton tower atop a hangar. It is closed to the public. This is the third beacon on this spit of land, overlooking the Strait of Juan de Fuca (its predecessors dated from 1865 and 1908). The old keeper's quarters have since been relocated from the site to Fourth and Albert streets in Port Angeles.

7. New Dungeness Light

Sequim, Dungeness Spit

Despite what the name suggests, this lighhouse has stood here since 1857 and is among the oldest lighthouses on the West Coast. Its conical tower was remodeled to incorporate a duplex in 1906, and in 1927 the 37-foot upper section of the tower that protrudes from the red-roofed, white masonry dwelling was removed to avert the danger of collapse, so that it is now 63 feet tall. A VRB-25 aerobeacon flashes white every 5 seconds (focal plane 67 feet). The light station is open, but is accessible only by sailing or hiking there.

> **SPOTTER'S NOTE**
> U.S. Lighthouse Society members can experience a taste of a lighthouse keeper's life by applying for a week-long stint of maintaining New Dungeness Light.

> **SPOTTER'S NOTE**
> A red-roofed keeper's dwelling is all that remains of Clallam Bay's Slip Point Light (1905).

8. Point Wilson Light *Point Wilson*

In 1914, a 46-foot, octagonal masonry tower and integrated white-painted, red-roofed fog-signal building replaced the previous light here. Still active, its original fourth-order Fresnel lens emits an occulting white light and a red flash every 20 seconds (focal plane 51 feet). It is open to the public by arrangement.

9. Marrowstone Point Light *near Port Townsend*

Serving the Admiralty Inlet, this automated 250-mm optic on a square, white fog-signal building has an occulting white light (obscured from 040° to 090°, focal plane 28 feet). Automated in 1962, the 1895 keeper's accommodation is now used as research quarters for the U.S. Geological Survey's Biological Resource Division.

BELOW: *Point Wilson Light is located in Fort Warden State Park.*

ABOVE: *Dofflemyer Point Light.*
BELOW: *Browns Point Light.*

10. **Dofflemyer Point Light**
North of Olympia

Situated on a private beach, this U.S. Coast Guard–operated light station is inaccessible to the public. Sailors entering Budd Inlet are guided by the 6-second isophase white light that sits atop the 1934 lanternless, white, octagonal-pyramidal concrete tower (focal plane 30 feet, range 10 miles).

11. **Browns Point Light**
Commencement Bay, northeastern Tacoma

There has been a beacon marking the bay's eastern entrance in Puget Sound since 1887, but the current light—a 31-foot, square, white-painted concrete tower, without lantern—dates from 1933. Automated in 1963, a VRB-25 aerobeacon flashes white every 5 seconds (focal plane 38 feet). The 1903 keeper's house is rented out by the Points Northeast Historical Society as a guest house. The lighthouse is open to the public.

12. **Gig Harbor Light** *Gig Harbor,*
near Tacoma

This lighthouse is a 15-foot, white, hexagonal concrete structure from the late 1980s. It is a privately maintained aid to mariners, displaying a flashing red light (obscured from 162° to 273°) every 4 seconds (focal plane 13 feet). The grounds are accessible to the public.

13. **Point Robinson Light** *Point*
Robinson, Maury Island, Puget Sound

Before it boasted a beacon, there was a fog signal here that first sounded in 1885. In 1915, a 38-foot, square concrete tower was integrated into the fog-signal building, topped with a red roof, and painted white with green trim, and the fifth-order Fresnel lens was lit for the first time. Today, an automated white light flashes twice every 12 seconds during darkness (focal plane 40 feet). Visitors are welcome at the light station.

14. Alki Point Light *Seattle*

The first signal here (1887) was a kerosene-fueled, brass lantern on the side of a barn. It was replaced in 1913 with a 37-foot, octagonal masonry tower and attached fog-signal building, painted white with red-and-black trim. A VRB-25 aerobeacon flashes white continuously every 5 seconds (focal plane 39 feet, range 17 miles). The Alki Point Light (the official residence of the U.S. Coast Guard's district commander) is open to the public and has a museum.

15. West Point Light *near Seattle*

This lighthouse was built from brick in 1881. Originally configured as a fog-signal building attached to a square, 23-foot tower, a second wing was added in 1906. This hybrid structure is clad in stucco, painted white, and protected by a red roof. The original beacon was a fourth-order Fresnel lens, and a similar optic operates today, with alternating white and red lights every 10 seconds (focal plane 27 feet). The Cape Cod-style keeper's house still stands, and the grounds of the West Point Light—which also acts as a National Oceanic and Atmospheric Administration (N.O.A.A.) monitoring station—are open to the public.

16. Point No Point Light *near Hansville, Kitsap Peninsula (overleaf)*

ABOVE: *Alki Point Light.*
BELOW: *West Point Light.*

SPOTTER'S NOTE
In 1909, Swiftsure Bank, near Cape Flattery, became the location of the final lightship station to be established on the Washington coast. The lightship that today bears the *Swiftsure* name was actually a relief vessel for when its namesake, among other ships, was brought in for maintenance. Decommissioned in 1960, she is now located at the Northwest Seaport Maritime Heritage Center, Seattle, and is the only one to still hold her original steam engines.

Point No Point Light

Description: square tower; integral fog-signal building and office wing
Markings: whitewashed and stucco-covered; white lantern and red dome
Lens: fourth-order Fresnel
Height: 30 feet (tower); 27 feet (focal plane)

BELOW: *Point No Point Light is open to visitors, and the former keeper's house is now leased as a private home.*

Focal Point

The 30-foot-high, square, stucco-covered tower at Point No Point Light is sandwiched between an integral fog-signal building and a single-story office wing, and the whole structure is painted white with black trim and red roofing. The only other structures on this site near Hansville—which Kitsap County Parks and Recreation leases from the U.S. Coast Guard and has opened to the public as a museum—are the former keeper's two-story, wood-frame house (1879) and a metal oil house. A fourth-order Fresnel lens was assigned to this light station in 1898; this was automated in 1977 and still beams out three white flashes every 10 seconds continuously at a focal-plane height of 27 feet.

17. Skunk Bay Light *Hansville,*
3 miles northwest of Point No Point

The Skunk Bay Light, which exhibits a fixed red light at a focal-plane height of 210 feet, is a privately maintained beacon situated near Hansville. This octagonal, white-painted wooden light tower supports a red lantern that once served on Smith Island, which was salvaged when its first, erosion-weakened home—a Cape Cod-style lighthouse constructed in 1858—collapsed during the 1950s. The Skunk Bay Light is inaccessible to the public.

18. Mukilteo Light *Mukilteo*

An aid to navigation on the eastern side of Possession Sound since 1906, it consists of a 30-foot, white-painted, octagonal wooden tower and attached red-roofed fog-signal building. Its fourth-order Fresnel lens flashes white every 5 seconds (focal plane 33 feet). Visitors to this light station can also see two wood-frame keeper's houses, an oil house, and a garage, as well as the fourth-order Fresnel lens that once served at the Desdemona Sands Light (demolished).

19. Admiralty Head Light
near Coupeville, Whidbey Island

The first Admiralty Head Light (1860) was demolished in 1903 to make way for the army fortifications that became Fort Casey. The construction of a conical, brick light tower 30 feet tall, attached to a two-story, California Spanish-style keeper's house was completed nearby in the same year, clad with stucco, and painted white. Its lantern was equipped with a fourth-order Fresnel lens (focal plane 127 feet). This lighthouse was superseded by Point Wilson Light in 1922, however. Its lantern and lens were transferred to the New Dungeness Light in 1927, but the tower now supports a replica lantern and is owned by Washington State Parks. This nonoperational lighthouse is now a museum.

ABOVE: *Mukilteo Light.*

SPOTTER'S NOTE

The Dimick Lighthouse, as it is known, was raised near the Jefferson County Courthouse, in Port Townsend, in 1990. It is a vacation home rather than a lighthouse, and consequently exhibits no light.

20. Bush Point Light *South Whidbey Island*

The lanternless Bush Point Light, which stands on the northwestern coast of South Whidbey Island, was established in 1933. The aerobeacon on the 20-foot, white, square-pyramidal tower flashes white at a focal-plane height of 25 feet (range 13 miles). The lighthouse grounds, maintained by the U.S. Coast Guard, are accessible to the public.

21. Burrows Island Light *Burrows Island*

This white-painted, wooden lighthouse (1906) is configured as an integrated light tower and fog-signal building, with red roof and blue-gray trim. It originally held a fourth-order Fresnel lens in the lantern that crowned its 34-foot-tall, square tower but now a 300-mm optic flashes white every 6 seconds at a focal-plane height of 57 feet. A storage building and two-story, wood-frame keeper's quarters stand apart from the lighthouse, which is inaccessible to the public, but can be seen from ferries from Anacortes.

ABOVE: *Cattle Point Light before its lantern was removed.*
BELOW: *Lime Kiln Light.*

22. Cattle Point Light *San Juan Island*

Situated near Friday Harbor, the present Cattle Point Light has assisted navigation along the southern section of the San Juan Channel since 1935. The white, cylindrical tower rising above a fog-signal building is not the first Cattle Point Light, however, for there has been a navigational aid here since 1888. The beacon flashes white every 4 seconds at a focal-plane height of 94 feet. The grounds are open to the public.

23. Lime Kiln Light *San Juan Island*

The sinisterly named Dead Man's Bay, near Friday Harbor, received a navigational aid in 1914, but it was not until 1919 that the present lighthouse—a whitewashed, concrete structure—was built. The octagonal light tower rises to a height of 38 feet from the red roof of a sound-signal building, and supports a lantern housing a VRB-25 aerobeacon that can be seen up to 20 miles away. This flashes white every 10 seconds at a focal-plane height of 55 feet. The light station was automated in 1962, and the two former keepers' dwellings today house Washington State Parks personnel (their employer owns the lighthouse); the site also serves as a whale-research station run by the Whale Museum. The Lime Kiln Light is open to the public.

24. Turn Point Light *Stuart Island*

Preceded by a light on a sound-signal building (1893), it was not until 1936 that the square, white-painted concrete tower that is now the Turn Point Light was completed and went into service. The optic in its 44-foot-high tower, a 300-mm lens whose light is obscured from 260°30' to 357°, today flashes white at a focal-plane height of 44 feet. The ancillary structures that still stand on this light station include the white, red-roofed wooden keeper's quarters and fog-signal building. The grounds of this active aid to navigation can be reached via a hiking trail from Prevost Harbor.

ABOVE: *Burrows Island Light and associated outbuildings.*

25. Patos Island Light *Eastsound*

The Patos Island Light, near Eastsound, which overlooks Puget Sound's Straits of Georgia, started life as a fog-signal station in 1893, and gradually became increasingly grand. A Greek Revival-style sound-signal building was constructed in 1898 to house a horn, and a square, weatherboard tower was raised above its roof ten years later to a height of 35 feet. Today painted white, with green and gray trim and a red roof, this is the only original building to survive, the keeper's house having been demolished in 1983 and replaced with modern accommodation. The beacon is now a solar-powered 300-mm optic that has two red sectors, but otherwise flashes white every 6 seconds at a focal-plane height above sea level of 52 feet (*see* Spotter's Note). At the time of writing, the grounds of this lighthouse are open to the public, but it can only be accessed by boat.

BELOW: *Patos Island Light is now locateed within a state park.*

SPOTTER'S NOTE

The Patos Island Light's signal consists of one red sector (011.5° to 0.59.5°) covering Six Fathom Shoal; another (097° to 114°) covering Rosenfeld Rock; and a fixed white light that can be seen up to 10 miles away (the red light is visible for 7 miles).

ALASKA

The length of Alaska's coastline exceeds that of the continental United States, but only a few small stretches of the coast are lit, most areas being rarely (or never) navigable. All the state's lighthouses date from the twentieth century—many built in the Art Deco style—and, unless otherwise mentioned below, they are inaccessible to the public.

ABOVE: *Tree Point Light.*

SPOTTER'S NOTE

Situated high on a cliff on Unimak Island is the 1950 skeleton tower of the automated Scotch Cap Light. The original, octagonal wooden structure (1903) was replaced in 1940 by a new, stronger, reinforced-concrete light station, but this was swept away by the great tsunami of 1946, killing five keepers.

1. Tree Point Light *Metlakatla*

Constructed in 1935, this lighthouse overlooks the Revillagigedo Channel, and takes the form of a square, white-painted concrete tower attached to a rectangular fog-signal building. The 66-foot light tower gives its VRB-25 optic a focal plane of 86 feet (range 10 miles). Automated in 1969, the site still includes a Cape Cod-style keeper's cottage that dates from around 1903. This active aid to navigation emits a white flash every 6 seconds.

2. Mary Island Light *Mary Island*

A white reinforced-concrete structure erected on the northeastern coast of Mary Island in 1937 to replace an older lighthouse, this consists of an integrated fog-signal building and 61-foot, square tower. Automated in 1969, its 250-mm optic produces a white flash every 6 seconds (range 7 miles, focal plane 76 feet).

3. Guard Islands Light *Guard Island*

This active lighthouse was erected at the entrance to the Tongass Narrows, near Ketchikan, in 1924. A rectangular, concrete oil house, with a 30-foot, white, square concrete tower, its beacon (automated 1969) is a Vega VRB-25, which flashes white every 10 seconds (focal plane 74 feet, range 20 miles).

4. Cape Decision Light *Kuiu Island*

This light has maintained its vantage point overlooking Shaken Bay since it was first lit in 1932. An Art Deco-style structure, its one-story, concrete keeper's quarters are integrated with the 76-foot, square light tower. Automated in 1974, its solar-powered Vega VRB-25 (installed 1996) flashes white every 5 seconds (focal plane 96 feet, range 21 miles). Before this, its light was generated by a third-order Fresnel lens (retired when a DCB-24 optic took over in 1974), which can now be admired in nearby Petersburg's Clausen Museum. Today owned by the Cape Decision Lighthouse Society, this light station is open to the public.

5. Five Finger Islands Light
Frederick Sound

This lighthouse was established in 1902, making it one of the oldest U.S.-built Alaskan light stations (*see* Spotter's Note). The white, concrete structure sits atop a pier and dates from 1935 (the first lighthouse here succumbed to fire in 1933). Its Art Deco architectural style is common among the lights of Alaska, and its 68-foot, square tower rises from the center of the one-and-a-half-story keeper's residence that supports it. Its solar-powered Vega VRB-25 optic that flashes white every 10 seconds (range 21 miles, focal plane 81 feet) began operating in 1997. Automated in 1984, the station is a weather-forecasting center as well as an active aid to navigation and is closed to the public.

6. Point Retreat Light   *Admiralty Island*

This concrete lighthouse overlooking the entrance to the Lynn Canal, comprising a 25-foot, square light tower and fog-signal building, was completed in 1924. Now with an extra 8-foot concrete block bearing a double-ended aerobeacon (flashing white every 6 seconds, focal plane 63 feet), it still serves as an active aid to navigation. The light station was automated in 1973, rendering the wooden, Cape Cod-style keeper's quarters uninhabited. These remain, however, as do an oil house, a water tank, a dock and boathouse, a fuel-storage platform, and a helipad.

ABOVE: *Cape Decision Light.*

> **SPOTTER'S NOTE**
> The Cape Decision Light, above, was the last major light station to be established in this state. The first to be built in Alaska after its acquisition from Russia in 1867 were those at (Southeast) Five Finger Island and Sentinel Island, both of which began operating on March 1, 1902.

BELOW: *Five Finger Islands Light.*

ABOVE: *Sentinel Island Light.*
BELOW: *Eldred Rock Light.*

7. Sentinel Island Light *Sentinel Island*

The second structure at this location was built in 1935; its solar-powered Vega VRB-25 aerobeacon flashes white every 10 seconds (focal plane 86 feet), and its integrated fog-signal building and 51-foot, square light tower are in the Art Deco style. The first Sentinel Island Light (1902) survived until 1971, when it was destroyed by arson. Visitors can tour the light station by appointment.

8. Eldred Rock Light *Sullivan Island*

This Lynn Canal light station has served continuously since it was first lit in 1906. Constructed from wood on masonry foundations, the 56-foot octagonal tower rises above a white-painted, red-roofed, octagonal, fog-signal building and keeper's accommodation. Today a 250-mm optic flashes white every 6 seconds (focal plane 91 feet). Several other structures also form part of the complex.

9. Cape Spencer Light
Glacier Bay National Park

A concrete, Art Deco-style light station (established 1925), this is a white, square tower above a rectangular, flat-roofed structure (once a combined fog-signal building and keeper's quarters). Automated in 1974, its solar-powered Vega VRB-25 flashes white every 10 seconds (focal plane 105 feet). The radiobeacon was the first to go into operation at an Alaskan light station.

LEFT: *Cape St. Elias Light.*
BELOW: *Cape Hinchinbrook Light.*

10. Cape St. Elias Light *Kayak Island*

Constructed in 1916 from concrete on rock foundations, this 55-foot, white, square tower is attached to a rectangular fog-signal building. Automated in 1984, the keeper's residence remains on site. The current optic that flashes white every 10 seconds (range 20 miles, focal plane 85 feet) is a solar-powered Vega VRB-25 (1998). Now under renovation, it is open to the public, and visitors can stay overnight in the restored boathouse, which sleeps up to ten people, by arrangement.

11. Cape Hinchinbrook Light
Hinchinbrook Island

The second lighthouse here was built in 1934 with earthquake-resistant reinforced concrete. Its 67-foot, square tower rises from the corner of a one-story, rectangular structure, and its clean, white lines are typical of the Modernist style. Automated in 1974, it now holds a solar-powered Vega VRB-25 whose light flashes white every 15 seconds (focal plane 235 feet, range 22 miles). There is also a radiobeacon.

12. Cape Sarichef Light *Unimak Island*

Now a skeleton tower (1979) bearing a diamond-shaped "NR" daymark (*see* page 253) and an automated, 375-mm optic that flashes white (focal plane 170 feet), this functional structure represents over a century of service notched up by a total of three lighthouses. Little visible evidence of the previous structures remains.

SPOTTER'S NOTE
Lighthouse spotters visiting Cordova Harbor can see an 18-foot, white-painted octagonal light tower on a barge next to a bed-and-breakfast inn overlooking Prince William Sound's Orca Inlet. This is the Odiak Pharos, a privately built (1970s) active aid to navigation at 1315 Whitshed Road, with a fixed white light (focal plane 26 feet). Its owner's proud claim is that the Odiak Pharos is the most northerly U.S. lighthouse.

HAWAII

When the United States acquired Hawaii in 1898, the islands had nineteen lighthouses, as well as a number of daymarks, lighted buoys, and private navigational aids. Of these lights, just one, Oahu's Diamond Head Light, had a Fresnel lens. Most were relatively crude structures, often in poor condition, with signals generated by oil lamps. The Lighthouse Board assumed responsibility for Hawaii's navigational aids in 1904 and began a gradual program of upgrading or replacing the existing lights and adding beacons in new locations. A series of similar square-pyramidal concrete light towers, painted white, began to appear along Hawaiian shores, most being constructed within the period 1915–30. An equipment room is set into the base of each, and a square, open gallery at the top provides access to the beacon. While these lights vary in height, type of optic, and signal characteristic, they are all of virtually identical appearance. Many survive today, and these are detailed below, keyed to the map, and identified simply with their location and date. Lighthouse spotters should note that the Hawaiian lighthouses included here are not open to the public unless the text specifies to the contrary.

HAWAII ISLAND

1. Kauhola Point Light *North Kohala*
Also known as the Kohala Mill Light, this cylindrical, white-painted, reinforced-concrete tower of 1933 is 86 feet tall and guides mariners past a reef-strewn headland at the north of Hawaii Island. This tower is similar to Barbers Point Light, Oahu (*see* page 256). It is the third light at this site. The lantern has been removed, and its exposed optic, which flashes white light every 15 seconds, has a focal-plane height of 116 feet above sea level. Visitors can find this lighthouse at the end of a dirt road off HI 270.

2. Kukuihaele Light *Kukuihaele* (1937)

3. Pauka'a Point Light *Hilo* (1929)

4. Coconut Point Light *Hilo Harbor*
   (1915)

> **SPOTTER'S NOTE**
> The 20-foot-high light pole at Laupahoehoe Point, on Hawaii's northeast coast, bears an optic that flashes white light at a focal-plane height of 39 feet above sea level. It is the fourth navigational aid at the site. The second light here, a white, square-pyramidal concrete tower 32 feet high, was built in 1915, but its foundations were fatally undermined by the tsunami of 1946, and the lighthouse collapsed the following year. A 36-foot-tall, wooden skeletal tower took over its duties in 1947, and today's light pole replaced this in 1975.

5. Cape Kumukahi Light

Cape Kumukahi

This light station has the distinction of being situated at the easternmost point of both the island and state of Hawaii. A white-painted, pyramidal, steel skeleton tower that rises above concrete foundations to a height of 125 feet, its DCB-24 flashes white every 15 seconds at a focal-plane height of 156 feet above sea level. The light was built in 1934 and automated in 1960 after a volcanic eruption destroyed the keeper's quarters and associated buildings, which all succumbed to the subsequent lava flow. Today, the light tower also hosts an air-sampling facility on behalf of the National Oceanic and Atmospheric Administration's Mauna Loa Observatory. Lighthouse spotters can enjoy a close-up view of the light tower if they drive to the end of secondary road 132.

> **SPOTTER'S NOTE**
> On nautical charts, daymarks are indicated by two- or three-letter abbreviations. A diamond-shaped daymark that is divided into four diamonds—a white diamond on each side and a black diamond at the top and bottom—and enclosed by a reflective white border is identified by the abbreviation "NB." Used as a warning or location marker, the first letter indicates the shape, and the second, its color. Daymarks that have green or red sectors, rather than black ones, but are otherwise identical to an "NB," are respectively denoted by "NG" and "NR."

6. Ka Lae Light *Ka Lae*

It may not look particularly impressive, but the 32-foot-tall, white concrete post that stands here is notable for being both Hawaii's and the United States's southernmost beacon, which is why it is also known as the South Point Light. Its optic flashes white every 6 seconds with a focal-plane height of 60 feet. An "NB" daymark (*see* Spotter's Note) is also fixed to this active aid to navigation.

> **SPOTTER'S NOTE**
> The Pepeekeo Point Light was a white, pyramidal skeletal tower. It has since been superseded by a post-mounted optic. To the southwest of Hawaii Island, a 20-foot-tall, pyramidal concrete tower (1965) was once designated the Miloli'i Point Light, but this was replaced with a 20-foot metal post. The new optic flashes white every 4 seconds and displays an "NB" daymark.

7. Napo'opo'o Light

Cook Point (1908)

8. Kailua Point Light

Kailuastkona Harbor (1915)

9. Keahole Point Light

Keahole Point (1915)

10. Kawaihae Light

Kawaihae Harbor (1915)

11. Mahukona Light

Mahukona Harbor (1915)

MAUI ISLAND

12. Ka'uiki Head Light
Ka'uiki Head (1914)

13. Hanamanioa Point Light
Keoneoio (1918)
Note: there is also a 21-foot-tall post with an optic that flashes white every 4 seconds (focal plane 73 feet) at this site.

14. McGregor Point Light
Maalaea Harbor (1915)

15. Lahaina Light
Lahaina Harbor (1915)

MOLOKA'I ISLAND

ABOVE: *Moloka'i Light.*

16. Moloka'i Light *Kalaupapa Peninsula*

This 138-foot-tall, octagonal-shaped, white-painted concrete light tower is also known as the Kalaupapa Light. It has presided over the peninsula—now part of the Kalaupapa National Park—since 1909, the year that marked its completion and the first lighting of the second-order bivalve Fresnel lens that was originally installed in its lantern room. Since 1997, a DCB-24 has generated the white flashing signal at a focal-plane height of 213 feet above sea level. The light was automated in 1970, but the one-and-a-half-story keeper's accommodation, constructed of volcanic rock, can still be seen alongside the lighthouse, as can a storage building and a concrete second keeper's cottage dating from 1951. This site is not easily accessible, but visitors can tour the Moloka'i Light (which is the tallest on U.S. Pacific shores) by appointment.

17. Kaunakakai Range Lights
Kaunakakai Lighthouse Park

The 26-foot front range light at this site consists of a rectangular red daymark bisected by a vertical white stripe (daymarks of this type are designated "KRW" on nautical charts) supported by a skeleton tower mounted on the roof of a workroom. Its optic emits a fixed red light at a focal-plane height of 27 feet. The rear range light stands about 200 yards away. It, too, takes the form of a skeleton tower—in this case, a 38-foot stand-alone structure—that displays a "KRW" daymark and a fixed red light, this signal shining at a focal-plane height of 41 feet above sea level. The site is open to the public.

SPOTTER'S NOTE
At La'au Point stands a 20-foot-high "spindle" (as the U.S. Coast Guard's light list terms it), which bears a flashing white optic (focal plane 151 feet) and a black-and-white, diamond-shaped daymark. The first light at this site was a white-painted stone tower that was raised in 1881, whose 1906 successor was a 35-foot square-pyramidal wooden tower.

OAHU ISLAND

SPOTTER'S NOTE
From 1926 until its deactivation in around 1970, the 184-foot Aloha Tower on Honolulu's Fort Street housed beneath its crowning cupola a beacon that was officially designated the Honolulu Harbor Light.

18. Pyramid Rock Light
Kaneohe Bay

Those visiting the Mokapu Peninsula, on the northeastern coast of Oahu Island, will immediately see why Pyramid Rock was so named. The white light that occults every 4 seconds (focal plane 101 feet) stands on the roof of a 15-foot-high, square concrete workhouse that is strikingly decorated with black and white diagonal stripes.

19. Makapu'u Point Light *Waimanolo*

With a diameter of 8 feet, 2 inches and a height of around 12 feet, no other U.S. lighthouse can boast a lens as large as the one at this light station. The hyperradiant, or radial, optic was installed in the cast-iron lantern atop this white-painted, 46-foot-high, cylindrical brick tower in 1909. The massive lens focuses a white light that occults every 10 seconds at an unusually high focal plane of 420 feet, due to the tower's naturally elevated position. It has a range of 22 miles and a vital role to perform as a navigational aid for mariners bound for Honolulu from the west. The light was automated in 1974, and its former keeper's quarters no longer exist. Lighthouse enthusiasts who visit this site should note that the interior is closed to the public, and that they face a steep climb to view its exterior.

ABOVE: *Diamond Head.*

BELOW: *Barbers Point Light, before its lantern was removed.*

20. Diamond Head Light
Waikiki Beach

The 55-foot, white-painted, square concrete lighthouse that has stood on Diamond Head since 1918 is not the first aid to navigation at this site. Indeed, it incorporates the watch room that served as part of the first, 1899, light station. Its red-roofed lantern room still holds the third-order Fresnel lens with which it was originally equipped, and this optic beams out its occulting white light—which has a red sector highlighting nearby reefs—at a focal-plane height of 147 feet. The light was automated in 1924, but the wood-frame keeper's house, a one-story building dating from 1921, still stands and currently serves as accommodation for U.S. Coast Guard personnel. The site is closed to the public, but the light can be seen clearly from the beach.

21. Barbers Point Light *Barbers Point*

A beacon has eased the passage of mariners past this point since 1888. The current 71-foot-tall, white-painted, cylindrical concrete tower, whose light can be seen up to 28 miles out to sea, went into operation in 1933. Its original fourth-order Fresnel lens was replaced with an automated DCB-224 in 1964, which still flashes white atop the now lanternless, capped structure, at a focal-plane height of 85 feet. The lighthouse grounds, which the Honolulu Department of Parks and Recreation leases from the U.S. Coast Guard, are open to the public, but the tower is closed.

KAUAI ISLAND

22. Kilauea Point Light *Kailauea Point*

This is Hawaii's most northerly light, a vital making light for vessels sailing to Hawaii from the east. A 1913 cylindrical, white-painted concrete light tower with a red-roofed lantern, the 52-foot tower had a focal-plane height above sea level of 216 feet. It was deactivated in 1976, when its signal was replaced by a post-mounted flashing white signal that stands next to the original tower. The lighthouse, which sustained some damage during Hurricane Iniki in 1992, is occasionally open to the public: it stands within a national wildlife refuge that is open daily, and visitors can also see the one-story, stone keeper's dwelling, as well as two assistant keepers' houses, three garages, an oil-storage building, three cisterns, and a radiobeacon electronics building.

ABOVE: *Kilauea Point Light.*
BELOW: *Nawiliwili Harbor Light.*

23. Nawiliwili Harbor Light

  Ninini Point

The pale yellow, concrete, 80-foot cylindrical lighthouse that currently guides mariners negotiating the entrance to Nawiliwili Harbor has performed its life-saving duties since 1933. The tower once had a lantern containing a first-order, bivalve Fresnel lens, which had a focal-plane height above sea level of 118 feet and was automated in 1953. This has been removed, however, and since 1985 its light—which flashes its white signal every 15 seconds at a focal-plane height of 112 feet—has been provided by a DCB-24 optic. This lighthouse is occasionally opened to the public by U.S. Coast Guard Auxiliary personnel.

24. Kuki'i Point Light

  Nawiliwili Harbor (date unknown)

SPOTTER'S NOTE
There has been a beacon at Makahu'ena Point, near Po'ipu, on Kauai Island's southernmost tip, since at least 1908, when a mast bearing a light was erected. In 1922 this was replaced by a white-painted, square-pyramidal concrete tower measuring 20 feet in height. The Makahu'ena Point Light's current incarnation is reminiscent of the earlier beacon, however, being a 20-foot-high post on which are mounted a diamond-shaped, black-and-white-quartered daymark and a flashing white optic (focal plane 80 feet).

CANADA

NEWFOUNDLAND & LABRADOR

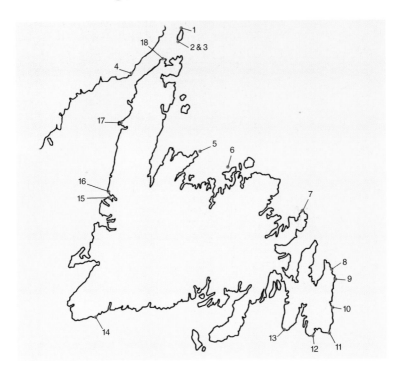

Newfoundland is the first landfall for vessels sailing from northern Europe. Her jagged coastline is so indented that, if it were flattened into an unbroken line, its length would be sufficient to encircle the globe. Consisting mostly of barren, wave-battered granite cliffs, whose coves and bays shelter icebergs and are blanketed with thick fog much of the time, these shores have accounted for more than their share of shipwrecks. Ships from the North Atlantic heading for the St. Lawrence River must either negotiate the narrow Strait of Belle Isle separating Newfoundland from mainland Labrador, which is only navigable for six months each year, or take a longer route around the southern coast of Newfoundland. Both options are beset with hazards, but from the early nineteenth century, lighthouses were erected to assist mariners on these fearsome waters.

Lighthouse spotters should note that all the lights listed below are white towers with red lanterns, unless otherwise noted. Inactive light-houses and small harbor lights are not included.

Opposite: *West Point Light, Prince Edward Island.*

BELOW: *Cape Bonavista Light.*
BELOW, RIGHT: *Twillingate (Long
Point) Light.*

1. **Belle Isle, North End Light** *St. Anthony*:
(1905) A 41-foot tower with flying buttresses.
2. **Belle Isle, South End Upper Light** *St.
Anthony*: (1858) A 62-foot conical tower. 3. **Belle
Isle, South End Lower Light** *St. Anthony*:
(1880) A 23-foot lantern on short tower, all red.
4. **Pointe Amour Light** *L'Anse Amour*: (1858) A
109-foot (second-tallest lighthouse in Canada) conical tower, white with a black band and red lantern.
5. **Gull Island (Cape St. John) Light** *Shoe
Cove*: (1884) A 45-foot conical tower, with vertical
red and white stripes. 6. **Twillingate (Long
Point) Light** *Twillingate*: (1876) A 47-foot,
square, red tower with octagonal white upper
part and white lantern. 7. **Cape Bonavista
Lighthouse** *Bonavista*: (1843, I) Painted with
red and white vertical stripes. 8. **Fort Amherst
Light** *St. Johns*: This was the first light station
in Newfoundland (1810), but the current 17-
foot lighthouse dates from 1951 (SP, museum).
9. **Cape Spear Light** *St. Johns*: (1955) A 35-foot
octagonal tower, with a white lantern. The old
lighthouse has been restored and is now the oldest
surviving lighthouse in Newfoundland (1836, I).
10. **Ferryland Head Light** *Ferryland*: (1871,

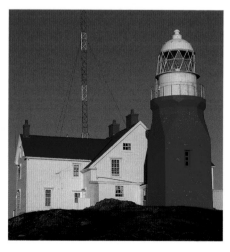

Att.) A 25-foot red, conical tower with white lantern. **11. Cape Race Light** *Trespassey*: (1907, C) This is the first landfall for most ships sailing to North America from northern Europe. The present lighthouse is 100 feet tall. **12. Cape Pine Light** *Trespassey*: (1851) A 47-foot conical tower with red and white bands and a white lantern. **13. Cape St. Mary's** *Branch*: (1860, OP) A white tower and lantern. **14. Rose Blanche Point** *Rose Blanche*: (1873, I) A stone keeper's dwelling with black lantern. **15. Woody Point Light** *Woody Point*: (1959, SP). **16. Lobster Cove Head** *Lobster Cove*: (1897) A conical tower with white lantern. **17. Point Riche Light** *Port au Choix*: (1892, OP). **18. Cape Norman Light** *Cook's Harbour*: (1980, OP).

ABOVE: *Fort Amherst Light.*

> **SPOTTER'S NOTE**
> The Tête de Galantry Light is one of six beacons on the French islands of Saint-Pierre and Miquelon, just off the southern coast of Newfoundland. The present lighthouse is a 60-foot triangular-cylindrical concrete tower built in 1978, with a focal-plane height of 154 feet, white with red trim.

BELOW: *(Old) Cape Spear Light.*

PRINCE EDWARD ISLAND

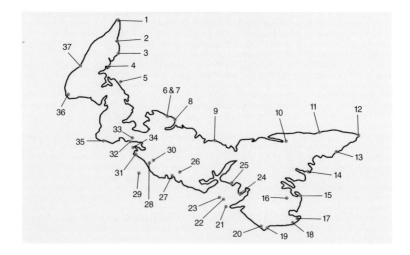

The picturesque shores of Prince Edward Island are lit by many active aids to navigation, including almost fifty light stations that consist of skeleton-tower lights and pairs of skeleton-tower range lights, which are excluded here. The lighthouses listed are built of wood and are white, with red trim and lanterns, unless otherwise noted; those built before 1873 are octagonal-pyramidal in shape, and the later towers are square-pyramidal (exceptions noted below). Those lights listed here as decommissioned have in some cases been replaced by modern signals, details of which are not included. See page 260 for abbreviations.

BELOW: *Cape Tryon Light (New).*

1-11. North Shore

1. **North Cape Light** *North Cape*: (1866, OP). 2. **Big Tignish Light** *Judes Point*: (1881, decommissioned). 3. **Miminegash Rear Range Light** *Cape Kildare*: (1886, decommissioned, private). 4. **Northport Rear Range Light** *Northport*: (1885, SP) Tapering structure painted white with a vertical red stripe and red corners on the lantern. 5. **Malpeque Outer Range Lights** *Malpeque*: (1922, SP, private) Both lights are painted white and have a red vertical stripe. 6. **Cape Tryon Light (Old)** *Park Corner*: (1905, I, deactivated, private) A cottage-style building. 7. **Cape Tryon Light (New)** *Cape Tryon*:

(1969, private) The light is threatened by cliff erosion. **8. North Rustico Harbour Light** *North Rustico*: (1899, I) A square-pyramidal tower, white with red trim, integrated with the keeper's residence, whose walls slope at the same angle as the tower. **9. Covehead Harbour Light** *Cape Stanhope*: (1976) Located in Prince Edward Island National Park. **10. St. Peters Harbour Light** *St. Peters*: (1865, SP). **11. Shipwreck Point Light** *Naufrage*: (1968, OP, private) One of two concrete lighthouses on the island.

12-17. East Coast

12. East Point Light *Souris*: (1867) Guided tours available. **13. Souris East Light** *Knight Point*: (1880) Can be seen from the waterfront at Knight Point. **14. Annandale Range Lights** *Annandale Harbour*: (c. 1925, SP, private) The rear range light is on Juniper Point; the front range light is on Banks Point and is a lanternless tower. **15. Panmure Head Light** *Panmure Island*: (1853) Stands near the end of the causeway to the island. **16. Georgetown Range Lights** *Lower Montague*: (front: 1969, C; rear: 1890, SP, private) The front range light is red with a central white band; the rear light is white with a central red band on one face only. **17. Murray Harbour Range Lights** *Murray Harbour*: (1879, SP) The front range light has a gray lantern and can be accessed via a hiking trail. The rear light has a vertical red stripe, located on private property.

ABOVE: *North Rustico Light.*
BELOW: *Covehead Harbour Light.*
BOTTOM: *Shipwreck Point Light.*

18-37. Charlottetown, South, and West

18. Cape Bear Light *Cape Bear*: (1881, museum). **19. Wood Islands Light** *Wood Islands*: (1876, I, museum) The keeper's dwelling is white with a red roof. **20. Wood Islands Harbor Range Lights** *Wood Islands*: (SP) Both have a vertical red stripe. **21. Point Prim Light** *Hillsborough Bay*: (1846) The island's oldest light-

Above: *East Point Light, Souris.*

house is a white conical tower made of brick and clad with shingles. **22. Blockhouse Point Light** *Rocky Point*: (1851, SP, Att.). **23. Warren Cove Range Lights** *Rocky Point*: Two white towers, each with a vertical red stripe. **24. Hazard Point Range Lights** *Charlottetown*: Two red towers, each with a vertical black stripe. **25. Brighton Beach Range Lights** *Charlottetown*: (1890) The front light is a square tower with a red daymark; the rear is a white tower with a red vertical stripe. **26. Palmers/Leards Range Lights** *Victoria*: (1960/1879) The rear lighthouse in the Palmers pair also houses the front signal for the Leards range. Its white tower has a red vertical stripe and daymark, each of which aligns with its corresponding range pair's daymarks. Leards Rear Range Light is a white tower with vertical red stripe (SP); Palmer's Range Front Light is a skeleton tower. **27. Wrights Range Lights** *Victoria*: (SP) Two white towers, each with a vertical red stripe. **28. Borden Range Lights** *Borden Point*: (1917, SP) Two white towers, each with a vertical red stripe. **29. St. Peters Island Light** *St. Peters Island*: (1981, SP) Has a red upper portion. **30. Borden Light** *Borden Point*: This white tower is located on the ferry pier. **31. Seacow Head Light** *Fernwood*: (1864). **32. Summerside Outer Range Lights** *Summerside*: (1991) Two white towers, each with a daymark with vertical red stripe.

BELOW: *Point Prim Light.*

33. Summerside Range Lights *MacCallum's Point*: (1898) The rear tower is white with a vertical red stripe; the original front structure is now privately owned, and the light is now mounted on a skeleton tower. **34. Indian Head Light** *Summerside*: (1930) An octagonal building with a tower rising from its center. **35. Cap-Egmont Light** *Cape Egmont*: (1884). **36. West Point Light** *O'Leary*: (1875, SP, museum) This tower has three black bands. It also serves as a guest house. **37. Howards Cove Light** *Howards Cove*: (1976, private) This compact structure is located on a hill above Seal Point Harbour.

NOVA SCOTIA

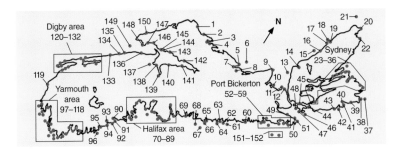

Nova Scotia boasts more lighthouses than any other Canadian province, including the oldest continuously operating lighthouse in North America, Sambro Island Light, and the much-photographed light at Peggy's Cove. Many are "pepper-shaker" lights (compact white, square-pyramidal towers). Unless otherwise noted, all lights are white, usually with red trim and lanterns. See page 260 for abbreviations.

1-12. Northumberland Strait to Aulds Cove

1. Coldspring Head Light *Northport*: (PS). **2. Pugwash (Fishing Point) Light** *Pugwash*: (1871, I, private). **3. Mullins Point Range Rear Light** *Wallace*: (1894, I, deactivated, private) White keeper's house and lantern tower. **4. Wallace Harbour Sector Light** *Wallace*: (1904, SP) White with horizontal red bands on one face. **5. Caribou Light** *Pictou*: (1971, Att.) Square tower and storage building. **6. Pictou Island South Light** *Pictou Island*: (PS). **7. Pictou Harbour range Lights** *Pictou*: (PS). **8. Trenton Range (Stonehouse Point) Light** *Trenton*: (PS). **9. Cape George Light** *St. George's Bay*: (1968, OP). **10. Pomquet Island Light** *Pomquet Island*: (PS). **11. Havre Boucher Range Lights** *Aulds Cove*: (PS). **12. North Canso Light** *Aulds Cove*: (1842, I, deactivated) Replaced with a white steel tower with two red bands.

13-48. Cape Breton Island

13. Henry Island Light *Port Hood*: (1902, OP) Alternate red and white faces. **14. Mabou Harbour Light** *Mabou*: (1908, PS, museum). **15. Margaree (Sea Wolf) Island Light** *Margaree Island*: (1958, OP). **16. Margaree Harbour Range Lights** *East Margaree*: (PS). **17. Chéticamp Harbour Front Range Light** *Chéticamp*: (1894, PS, deactivated). **18. Enragée Point Light** *Chéticamp*: (1957, OP). **19. Caveau**

SPOTTER'S NOTE

The striking octagonal-pyramidal 1904 Pictou Bar Light was painted with alternate white and red full-length vertical stripes. This popular landmark, located on a beach at the harbor, was destroyed in a fire in 2004.

ABOVE: *McNeil Beach Light.*
BELOW: *Cameron Island Light.*

SPOTTER'S NOTE
The former St. Paul Island
Light, a cylindrical steel
tower (1916, deactivated
1964) now stands on the
docks; there are plans to
restore it to its original
Dingwall site.

Point Range Lights *Chéticamp*: (PS). **20. Cape North Light** *Bay St. Lawrence*: (1980, SP, Att.) Red-and-white-banded tower and utility building. **21. St. Paul Island North Point Light** *St. Paul Island*: (1962, octagonal). **22. Neil's Harbour Light** *Neil's Harbor*: (1899) Doubles up as an ice-cream parlor. **23. Black Rock Point Light** *Bras D'Or*: (1978, C) White with a red band. Replaced a keeper's house with lantern (1868, I, private). **24. Man of War Light** *Englishtown*: (PS). **25. Munroe Point Light** *St. Ann's Bay*: (1906, deactivated) Available for vacation rentals. **26. Great Bras D'Or Range Front Light** *Bras D'Or*: (PS). **27. McNeil Beach Light** *Boularderie*: (PS, deactivated). **28. Ciboux Island Light** *Ciboux Island*: (1980, C) White with two red bands. **29. Point Aconi Light** *Bras D'Or*: (1989) Fiberglass; flares toward the top. **30. Low (Flat) Point Light** *Sydney*: (1938, OP) Has an old-style circular lantern. Located on one of the province's earliest light stations (est. 1832). **31. Sydney Range Lights** *Sydney*: (1905, OP) Front: white with a vertical red stripe; Rear: red upper portion. **32. Sydney Bar Light** *Sydney*: (PS). **33. Cameron Island Light** *Bras D'Or Lake*: (1903, PS). **34. Gregory Island Light** *Gregory Island*: (1950, C) White with two red bands. **35. Glace Bay Range Front Light** *Glace Bay*: (PS, deactivated). **36. Flint Island Light** *Flint Island*: (1962, OP). **37. Scatarie**

<small>ABOVE:</small> *Grandique Point Light.*

Light *Scatarie Island*: The largest pepper-shaker lighthouse in Nova Scotia. **38. Main-à-Dieu Light** *Scatarie Island*: (1979, C) White with two red bands. **39. Louisbourg Light** *Louisbourg*: (1923, OP) Stands on the site of Canada's first light station. **40. Gabarus Light** *Gabarus*: (1891) A hexagonal-pyramidal tower. **41. Rouse Point Light** *Gabarus*: (F). **42. Guyon Island Light** *Guyon Island*. **43. Fourchu Head Light** *Fourchu*: (C) White with two red bands. 44. **Jerome Point Light** *St. Peters*: (PS). **45. Grandique Point Light** *Isle Madame*: (I). **46. Green Island Light** *Green Island*: (1927, I, private) Replaced by a fiberglass tower (1986). **47. Marache Point Light** *Arichat*: (PS). **48. Jerseyman Island Light** *Jerseyman Island*: (PS).

49-103. South Coast

49. Queensport (Rock Island) Light *Queensport*: (1937, I). **50. Canso Range Lights** *Canso*: (PS). **51. Cranberry Island South Light** *Cranberry Island*: (F). **52. White Head Island Light** *Whitehaven*: (F). **53. Hog Island Light** *Hog Island*: (C) White with two red bands. **54. Charlos Harbour Range Rear Light** *Tor Bay*: (PS). **55. Berry Head Light** *Tor Bay*: (F). **56. Country Island Light** *Country Island*: (1965, OP) Replaced a keeper's house and light (1927, I). **57. Isaacs Harbour Light** *Isaacs Harbour*: (1929, I). **58. Fisherman's Harbour Light** *Port Bickerton*: (PS). **59. Port Bickerton Light** *Port Bickerton*: (1930, I, museum) A square tower is active at the site. **60. Liscomb Island Light** *Liscomb Island*: (1921, OP). **61. Beaver Island Light** *Beaver Island*: (1985, C). **62. Sheet Harbour Passage Range Lights** *Sheet Harbour*: (PS). **63. Sheet Rock Light** *Spry Bay*: (1988, C, offshore) White with two red bands. **64. Spry Bay Sector Light** *Spry Bay*: (1916, deactivated). **65. Ship Harbour Light** *Wolfes Island*: (Sk). **66. Owl's Head Light** *Jeddore Pond*: (1912, deactivated, private). **67. Egg Island Light** *Egg Island*: (Sk). **68. Jeddore Rock Light** *Jeddore Pond*: (Sk). **69. French Point Light** *Musquodoboit Harbour*: (1904) Stands on the grounds of a bed-and-breakfast inn. **70. Devil's Island Light** *Southeast Passage*: (1877, OP, active, lanternless).

71. Maugher ("Major") Beach Light *McNab's Island*: (1941, OP). **72. Halifax Harbour Inner Front Range Light** *George's Island*: (1919, OP) Has a vertical red stripe. **73. Chebucto Head Light** *Chebucto Head*: (1940, I, ruin) Burned down in 2004; a 1967 tower is active at the site. **74. Sambro Island Light** *Sambro Island*: (1758) Octagonal, shingle-clad stone tower, painted with red and white bands. The oldest lighthouse in North America. **75. Sambro Harbour Light** *Sambro*: (PS). **76. Pennant Harbour Light** *Sambro*: (1991) Fiberglass. **77. Terence Bay Light** *Sambro*: (PS). **78. Betty Island Light** *Betty Island*: (PS). **79. Peggy's Point (Cove) Light** *Peggy's Cove*: (1915, OP) Canada's most famous and most frequently visited light station. **80. Indian Harbour Light** *Peggy's Cove*: (PS). **81. Hubbard's Cove (Green Point) Light** *Hubbards*: (C) A mast tower, red with two white bands, on the site of a house and tower (1882, Att.). **82. Pearl Island Light** *Pearl Island*: A square tower. **83. East Ironbound Island Light** *East Ironbound Island*: (1871, I). **84. Quaker Island Light** *Chester Harbur*: (C) Red band at top. **85. Kaulbach Island Range Lights** *Kaulbach Island*: (PS). **86. Battery Point Breakwater Light** *Lunenberg*: (PS). **87. Cross Island Light** *Cross Island*: (1985) Steel tower on the site of a historic lighthouse (burned down 1960s). **88. West Ironbound Island Light** *West Ironbound Island*: (C)

BELOW: *Peggy's Point Light.*

89. Mosher Island Light *Lahave*: (1989) Fiberglass. **90. Port Medway Light** *Port Medway*: (1899, Sk, deactivated, museum). **91. Medway Head Light** *Port Medway*: (1927, I, deactivated, lantern removed, private) A 1983 light tower is active on the site. **92. Coffin Island Light** *Coffin Island*: (1914, OP). **93. Fort Point Light** *Liverpool*: (1855, I, deactivated, museum) Has a side-set lantern room; keeper's dwelling added 1878. **94. Western Head Light** *Liverpool*: (1962, OP). **95. Port Mouton Light** *Spectacle Island*: (PS). **96. Little Hope Island Light** *Port Joli*: (1906, C, no lantern) White, buttressed tower (collapsed). **97. Carter Island Light** *Lockeport*: (1982) White with two red bands. **98. Lockeport Light** *Lockeport*: (Att.) Square tower and keeper's house. **99. Cape Roseway Light** *Shelburne*: (1961, OP). **100. Sandy Point Light** *Shelburne*: (PS). **101. Cape Negro Island Light** *Cape Negro Island*: (1915, OP). **102. The Salvages Light** *Negro Harbour*: (1965, I). **103. Baccaro Point Light** *Baccaro Point*: (PS).

ABOVE: *Cape Forchu Light.*

104-152. West Coast and Bay of Fundy Lights

104. Seal Island Light *Seal Island*: (OP) Second-oldest in the province; marked with two red bands. **105. Cape Sable Light** *Clark's Harbour*: (1924, OP) Nova Scotia's tallest, at 101 feet. **106. West Head Light** *Clark's Harbour*: (1972, C, no lantern) Marked with two red bands. **107. Stoddart Island Light** *Shag Harbour*: (PS). **108. Outer Island (Bon Portage) Light** *Shag Harbour*: (F). **109. Woods Harbour Light** *Woods Harbour*: (1963) Short and square with octagonal lantern. **110. Pubnico Harbour Light** *Charlesville*: (1984, deactivated) Fiberglass, red. **111. Abbott's Harbour Light** *West Pubnico*: (PS, deactivated) Relocated in 2004 to the Acadian Historic Village. **112. Whitehead Island Light**: *Whitehead Island*: (F). **113. Tusket River Light** *Wedgeport*: (PS). **114. Pease Island Light** *Wedgeport*: Fiberglass. **115. Candlebox Island Light** *Candlebox Island*: (F). **116. Green Island (Chebogue Point) Light** *Green Island*: (F). **117. Cape Forchu Light** *Yarmouth*: (1962, museum) Hexagonal, flared at top, with red and white vertical stripes. **118. Bunker Island ("Bug") Light** *Yarmouth*: (F, offshore). **119. Cape St. Mary's Light** *Mavilette*: (F). **120. Church Point Light** *Corneauville*: (PS, deactivated). **121. Belliveau Cove Light** *Corneauville*: (PS, private navigational aid). **122. Gilbert's Cove Light** *Gilbert's Cove*: (1904, I, deactivated, museum). **123. Brier Island Light** *Brier Island*: (1944) Octagonal, flared at top, with red and white bands. **124. Grand Passage Light** *Brier Island*: (F). **125. Peter Island Light** *Westport*: (1909, OP). **126. Boar's Head (Tiverton) Light** *Petit Passage*: (PS). **127. Prim Point Light** *Digby*: (F). **128. Bear River Light** *Smiths Cove*: (PS).

129. Annapolis Light *Annapolis Royal*: (1889, PS, tourist center). **130. Schafner Point Light** *Port Royal*: (PS). **131. Victoria Beach Light** *Port Royal*: (PS). **132. Digby Gut Light** *Port Royal*: (F). **133. Hampton Light** *Bridgetown*: (PS). **134. Port George Light** *Port George*: (P, deactivated). **135. Margaretsville (Peter's Point) Light** *Margaretsville*: (1859, PS) Banded in black and white. **136. Black Rock Light** *Waterville*: (1967, C, no lantern) White with two red bands. **137. Borden Wharf Light** *Canning*: (1904, deactivated). **138. Horton Bluff Front Range Light** *Wolfville*: (F/Sk). **139. Mitchener Point Light** *Hantsport*: (C, deactivated) Red with two white bands. **140. Walton Harbour Light** *Walton*: (1872, deactivated, museum). **141. Burntcoat Head Light** *Noel*: (1913, I, replica). **142. Bass River (Saints' Rest) Light** *Economy*: (1907, deactivated, private). **143. Five Islands Light** *Five Islands*: (1914, PS, deactivated). **144. Parrsboro Light** *Parrsboro*: (F). **145. Cape Sharp Light** *Parrsboro*: (PS). **146. Port Greville Light** *Port Greville*: (1908, PS, deactivated, museum). **147. Spencer's Island Light** *Advocate Harbour*: (1904, PS, deactivated, museum). **148. Cape D'Or Light** *Cape D'Or*: F. (1965) Still active; one keeper's house is now a restaurant, and another is available for vacation rentals. **149. Ile Haute Light** *Ile Haute*: (Sk). **150. Apple River Light** *Apple River*: (1972) Square-pyramidal. **151. Sable Island West End Light** *Sable Island*: (Sk). **152. Sable Island East End Light** *Sable Island*: (1975) Square with red vertical stripes.

BELOW: *Brier Island Light.*

NEW BRUNSWICK

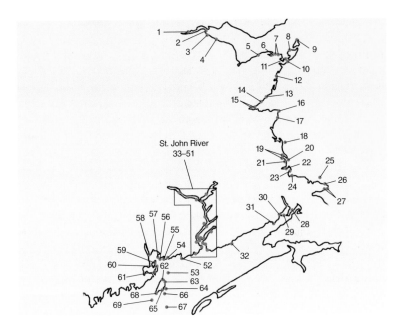

St. John River
33–51

New Brunswick's historic lighthouses are so popular with tourists that many towns have rebuilt discontinued lights, or built replicas, as tourist attractions, most of which are not included here. Unless otherwise noted, all lights are white, usually with red trim and lanterns. See page 260 for abbreviations.

1–25. North and Northwest Area

1. Campbellton Range Rear Light *Cambellton*: (OP) Attached to a youth hostel; has a red vertical stripe. **2. Inch Arran Point Light** *Dalhousie*: (1870, SP) Has a birdcage lantern. **3. Dalhousie Wharf Light** *Charlo*: (1879, SP, private) Replaced by a skeleton tower. **4. Belledune Point Light** *Seaside*: (SP, deactivated, private) Scheduled to be rebuilt and opened to visitors. **5. Grande-Anse Light** *Grande-Anse*: A replica lighthouse, painted with red, white, and blue bands, used as a tourist office. **6. Caraquet Light** *Caraquet*: (SP). **7. Caraquet Range Lights** *Bas-Caraquet*: (SP) The rear light was replaced by a skeleton tower and moved to Bas-Caraquet Municipal Park. **8. Black Point Light** *Lamèque Island*: (Sk) Painted with red and white bands. **9. Miscou Island Light** *Miscou Island*: (1856, OP). **10. Big Shippagan Light** *Lamèque Island*: (1872, OP). **11. Portage Island Rear Range Light** *Shippagan*: (SP, deactivated) Moved to the Shippagan Aquarium and Marine Center. **12. Grand Tracadie Light** *Tracadie*: (deactivated) An open wooden frame tower. A replica (SP) is attached to an office at Tracadie Marina, serving as a tourist information center. **13. Lower Neguac Wharf Rear Range Light** *Neguac*: (SP, deactivated) Has vertical red stripe. **14. Grand Dune Flats Front Range Light** *Burnt Church*: (I, private) The only light of this style in the province. **15. Grants Beach Range Lights** *Lower Newcastle*: (SP). **16. Point Escuminac Light** *Baie-Ste-Anne*: (1963) Hexagonal, flared at top. **17. Pointe Sapin Light** *Pointe Sapin*: (SP). **18. Richibucto Head Light** *Richibucto*: (SP). **19. Pointe à Jérome (Indian Point) Range Lights** *Bouctouche*: (SP) Has red vertical stripe/daymark. **20. Bouctouche Bar Light** *Bouctouche*: (SP). **21. Dixon Point Range Lights** *Bouctouche*: (SP, rear light deactivated). **22. Cocagne Point Range Lights** *Cocagne*: (SP/Sk). **23. Caissie Point Light** *Shediac*: (SP). **24. Pointe-du-Chêne Range Lights** *Shediac*: (SP). **25. Cape Jourimain Light** *Melrose*: (1880, OP, deactivated).

26–37. Cape Tormentine to St. John

26. Cape Tormentine Outer Wharf Range Lights *Cape Tormentine*: Front: square base, tapers at top; Rear: SP, deactivated. **27. Indian Point Range Lights** *Cape Tormentine*: SP, abandoned. **28. Pecks Point Light** *Pecks Point*: (SP, private). **29. Grindstone Island Light** *Grindstone Island*: (1908) Hexagonal, buttressed, and abandoned. **30. Anderston Hollow Light** *Riverside*: (SP). **31. Cape Enragé Light** *Cape Enragé*: (SP). **32. Quaco Head Light** *St. Martins*: (F) A replica of the 1883 light (I) is a tourist center. **33. Cape Spencer Light** *St. John*: (1983) Fiberglass. Red upper and white lower portion. **34. St. John Coast Guard Light** *St. John*: (OP). **35. Partridge Island Light** *Partridge Island*: (1961, OP) Alternate red and white faces. The province's oldest light station (est. 1791). **36. Courteney Bay Breakwater Light** *St. John*: (OP, lantern removed). **37. Old Digby Wharf Light** *St. John*: (SP, deactivated).

38–50. St. John River Lights

38. Swift Point (Green Head) Light *Randolph*: (SP). **39. Renforth Light** *Renforth*: (SP, private). **40. McColgan Point Light** *Kingston Peninsula*: (SP.) **41. Bayswater Light** *Kingston Peninsula*: (SP). **42. Sand Point Light** *Westfield*: (Sk) Red. **43. Belyeas Point** *Westfield*: (SP). **44. The Cedars** *Long Reach*: (SP, deactivated). **45. Oak Point Light** *Oak Point*: (SP). **46. Hampstead Light** *Hampstead*: (deactivated) Square. **47. Lower Musquash Island** *Musquash Island*: SP, abandoned. **48. Hendry Farm Light** *Lower Cambridge*: (SP, deactivated). **49. Gagetown Light** *Gagetown*: (Sk). **50. Wilmot Bluff Light** *Oromocto*: (SP).

BELOW: *The harbor at St. John.*

51–61. South Coast Lights

51. Musquash Head Light *Musquash*: (OP) Red band. **52. Point Lepreau Light** *Dipper Harbour*: (OP) Red and white bands. **53. Southwest Wolf Island Light** *Wolf Island*: Fiberglass. **54. Drews Head Light** *Pennfield Ridge*: Fiberglass. **55. Pea Point Light** *Pennfield Ridge*: (F). **56. Bliss Island Light** *Bliss Island*: (F). **57. Green's Point Light** *L'Etete Passage*: (OP, museum). **58. St. Andrews Light** *St. Andrews*: (OP, deactivated) Under restoration. **59. Leonardville Light** *Deer Island*: (SP). **60. Head Harbour (East Quoddy Head) Light** *Campobello Island*: (OP) Marked with a large red cross; New Brunswick's oldest lighthouse. **61. Mulholland Point Light** *Campobello Island*: (OP, deactivated).

62–69. Grand Manan Island

62. Long Eddy Point ("Whistle") Light *Long Eddy Point*: (F). **63. Swallowtail Light** *North Head*: (OP) A bed-and-breakfast inn. **64. Great Duck Island Light** *Great Duck Island*: (F). **65. Grand Harbour Light** *Grand Harbour*: (SP, abandoned). **66. Long Point Light** *Whitehead Island*: (F). **67. Gannet Rock Light** *Gannet Rock*: (OP, Att.). **68. Southwest Head Light** *Southwest Head*: (F). **69. Machias Seal Island Light** *Machias Seal Island*: (OP).

ABOVE: *East Quoddy Head Light.*

> **SPOTTER'S NOTE**
> East Quoddy Head Light, one of Canada's most distinctive lighthouses, is accessible by a road bridge from Lubec, Maine. Campobello Island's other lighthouse stands near the summer home of Franklin D. and Eleanor Roosevelt.

> **SPOTTER'S NOTE**
> Machias Seal Island is claimed by both the United States and Canada, While it lies closer to the Maine coast than to Grand Manan Island, Canadian sovereignty is claimed by the full-time presence of the Canadian Coast Guard staff at the light station.

BELOW: *Swallowtail Light.*

QUEBEC

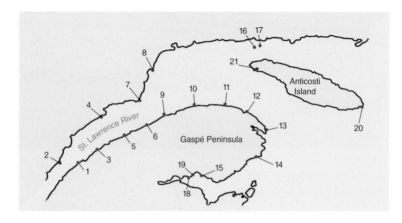

Each lighthouse listed here is white with a red lantern unless otherwise specified. Most inactive lights are omitted from this list. See page 260 for abbreviations.

ABOVE: *Pot-à-l'Eau-de-Vie Light.*
BELOW: *Matane Light.*

1. Pot-à-l'Eau-de-Vie Light *Rivière-du-Loup*: (1862, I) White with red roof; now an inn. The signal is generated from a nearby tower (Sk). **2. Dog's Head Cape Light** *Saint-Siméon*: (1909) Octagonal. **3. L'Île Verte Light** *Rivière-du-Loup*: (1809) The third-oldest lighthouse in Canada, its conical tower is open to visitors, who can stay in the former keeper's quarters. **4. Cap-de-Bon-Désir Light** *Les Escoumins*: Octagonal. **5. Pointe-au-Père Light** *Rimouski*: (1909, deactivated, museum) Has flying buttresses. **6. Matane Light** *Matane*: (1907, C, deactivated) Tourist information center. **7. Pointe-des-Monts Light** *Pointe-des-Monts*: (1830, C, no lantern) White with two red bands; now a bed-and-breakfast inn. **8. Île aux Oeufs Light** *Rivière-Pentecôte*: (1955, OP, deactivated) White lantern. **9. Cap-Chat Light** *Cap-Chat*: (1909) Square. **10. La Martre (River Martin) Light** *La Martre*: (1906, museum) Red hexagonal-pyramidal tower; the only active beacon in Quebec not yet auto-

mated. **11. Cap Madeleine Light** *Grande Vallée*: (1907, C) Guided tours available in summer. **12. Pointe-à-la-Renommée Light** *L'Anse à-Valleau*: (1907, C, deactivated) Red. **13. Cap-des-Rosiers (Cape Rozier) Light** *Cap-des-Rosiers*: (1858) This 112-foot conical tower is Canada's tallest. Guided tours available. **14. Cap-d'Espoir** *Grande Rivière*: (1939, OP) Overnight accommodation available in the former keeper's house. **15. Pointe Duthie Light** *New Richmond*: (1903, SP, deactivated) White lantern. **16. L'Île aux Perroquets** *Mingan Archipelago*: (c. 1915) Octagonal. **17. La Petite Île au Marteau** *Mingan Archipelago*: (1915, OP, deactivated). **18. Cap-de-Rabast** *Pointe Carleton*: (1919, OP) Also known as Pointe du Nord Light. **19. Carleton Point Light** *Pointe Carleton*: (OP). **20. Cap-de-la-Table (Table Head) Light** *Fox Bay*: (1919, OP). **21. Southwest Point (La Pointe du Sud-Ouest) Light** *Port Menier*: (1831) White conical tower with red banded markings; now optic mounted on a skeleton tower (1970).

ABOVE: *L'Île aux Perroquets.*
BELOW: *Cap-de-la-Table Light.*
BOTTOM: *Southwest Point Light.*

THE GREAT LAKES

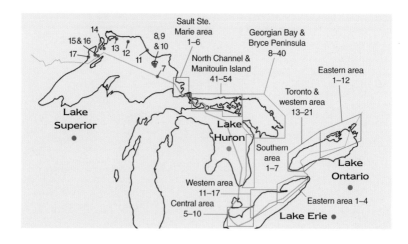

The lighthouses on the shores of the Great Lakes are listed in sequence, following the coastline from the eastern end of Lake Ontario to the western end of Lake Superior. From the middle of Lake Erie and westward, most lights are only operated seasonally, because the waters are iced in during the winter. Most of these lights are white with a red lantern, inaccessible (except by boat), and closed to the public; see page 260 for abbreviations.

LAKE ONTARIO

Below: *Main Duck Island.*

1-12. Eastern Area Lights *Ontario*
1. Prescott Breakwater Light *Prescott*: Octagonal. **2. Prescott Visitors' Centre Light** *Prescott*: Private navigational aid. **3. Windmill Point Light** *Prescott*: (1873, deactivated, museum) Originally a windmill; open to public. **4. Nine Mile Point** *Simcoe Island*: (1833, C) Grounds open to public. **5. Main Duck Island** *Kingston*: (1914, OP). **6. New False Duck Island** *Milford*: (1965) Flared hexagonal tower; red and white bands. **7. Old False Duck Island** *Milford*: (1828, decommisssioned, museum) Stone tower. **8. Prince Edward Point (Point**

LEFT: *New False Duck Island Light; its predecessor is part of Milford's Mariners Park Marine Museum.*

SPOTTER'S NOTE

Pigeon Island (southwest of Wolfe's Island, near Kingston) is home to a lighted red steel cylinder, supported by a white skeletal frame. This navigational aid stands among the ruins of an earlier lighthouse and keeper's dwelling.

Traverse) Light *South Bay*: (1881, SP, deactivated, lantern removed) Replaced by a skeletal tower. **9. Point Petre Light** *Cherry Valley*: (1967, C) Banded in red and white. **10. Salmon Point (Wicked Point) Light** *Cherry Valley*: (1871, SP, deactivated) Accommodation available. **11. Presqu'ile Point** *Brighton*: (lantern removed) White stone tower. **12. Cobourg East Pierhead Light** *Cobourg*: (1924, lantern removed) White, square tapered tower with red trim.

13-21. **Toronto and Western Area Lights** *Ontario*

13. Toronto Harbour Aquatic Park Light *Tommy Thompson Park, Toronto*: (1974) Steel tower; upper portion red, lower, white; grounds are open to public. **14. Gibraltar Point Light** *Hanlan's Point, Toronto Harbour*: (1808, deactivated) The oldest-surviving lighthouse on the Great Lakes; hexagonal-pyramidal stone tower with a red lantern; tourist attraction (grounds open) and private navigational aid. **15. Queen's Wharf Light** *Toronto*: (1861, deactivated) Octagonal stone tower, painted brown; in a city park near Exhibition Place. **16. Oakville Light** *Oakville*: (1889, deactivated, private) Hexagonal-pyramidal tower. **17. Burlington Main Light** *Burlington*: (1858, deactivated) Stone Imperial tower; grounds open. **18. Burlington Canal Front Range Light** *Burlington*: White square, tapered concrete tower. **19. Port Weller Outer Light** *Port Weller*: (1931) White Art Deco tower. **20. Port Dalhousie Range Lights** *Port Dalhousie*: (1879) Front: white with green lantern and trim; Rear: (deactivated) white with green trim; open to public. **21. Niagara-on-the-Lake Range Lights** *Niagara-on-the-Lake*: (1903, SP).

LAKE ERIE

Ontario

1. Point Abino *Port Colborne*: (1917, deactivated) Unusual Greek Revival–style building (square white tower atop square building); tours available in summer. **2. Port Colborne Outer Light** *Port Colborne*: (1928, I) Square tower atop square workroom. **3. Port Colborne Inner Light** *Port Colborne*: (1903) Square tower. **4. Port Maitland** *Dunnville*: (1898, SP) White. **5. Port Dover West Pier** *Port Dover*: (SP) White. **6. Long Point Light** *Long Point*: (1916, SP). **7. Long Point West End (Old Cut) Light** *Port Rowan*: (Att., deactivated, private) Wooden tower and keeper's quarters. **8. Port Burwell Light** *Port Burwell*: (1840, deactivated, museum) One of the oldest surviving wooden lighthouses in Canada; visitors may climb the tower. **9. Port Burwell Approach Light** *Port Burwell*: (1914, Sk, deactivated). **10. Port Stanley Breakwater Light** *Port Stanley*: (1908, SP) White.

BELOW: *Long Point Light.*

11. Rondeau East Pierhead Light *Erieau*: (Sk). **12. Rondeau West Breakwater Range Lights** *Erieau*: (Front: SP, white; Rear: Sk) Grounds accessible. **13. Southeast Shoal Light** *Pelee Point*: (1927, I) White with red vertical stripes on supporting structure and red trim on building. **14. Pelee Passage Light** *Point Pelee*: (1975, C) White with green lantern on green caisson. **15. Leamington Light** *Leamington*: (deactivated, private) White tower. **16. Kingsville Light** *Kingsville*: (1889, deactivated) White tower; grounds may be visited. **17. Colchester Reef Light** *Colchester*: (1954, Sk) White.

LAKE HURON

1-7. Southern Area Lights *Ontario*

1. Goderich (Main) Light *Goderich*: (1847) First Canadian light station on Lake Huron; square tower; grounds open. **2. Point Clark Light** *Kincardine*: (1859, museum) Imperial Tower; visitors may climb tower. **3. Kincardine (Rear Range) Light** *Kincardine*: (1881, I, museum) White, octagonal tower (red lantern, trim, and vertical stripe). **4. Southampton Harbour Rear Range (McNab Point) Light** *Southampton*: (1877, SP, deactivated). **5. Chantry Island Light** *Southampton*: (1859) Imperial Tower; grounds open. **6. Saugeen River Rear Range Light** *Southampton*:

(1903, SP) White with red trim and red vertical stripe; grounds open. **7. Saugeen River Front Range Light** *Southampton*: (1903, SP) White with red trim and red vertical stripe; grounds open.

8-40. Georgian Bay and Bruce Peninsula Lights *Ontario*

8. Stokes Bay Rear Range Light *Stokes Bay*: (1904, SP, Sk) White with enclosed upper portion. **9. Stokes Bay Front Range Light** *Stokes Bay*: (1990s, C) White with red upper and lower portions; replaced the adjacent white tower (1904, SP). **10. Tobermory (Big Tub) Light** *Big Tub Harbor, Tobermory*: (1885) Hexagonal-pyramidal; grounds open; vacation rental. **11. Cove Island Light** *near Tobermory*: (1858) Imperial Tower. **12. Flowerpot Island Light** *Flowerpot Island*: (1987) Steel tower. **13. Cabot Head Light** *Cabot Head Point*: (1896, rebuilt 1995, Att., museum) Replaced by steel tower. **14. Lion's Head Light** *Lion's Head Harbour*: (1983, SP) Grounds open. **15. Cape Croker Light** *Colpoy's Bay*: (1902) Octagonal tower. **16. Griffith Island Light** *Owen Sound, near Wiarton*: (1858) Imperial Tower. **17. Nottawasaga Island Light** *Collingwood*: (1858) Imperial Tower, *see* Spotter's Note. **18. Christian Island Light** *Christian Island, near Cedar Point*: (1859) White conical tower; grounds open. **19. Hope Island Light** *Midland*: (1884, SP, Att., deactivated). **20. Midland Point Rear Range Light** *Midland*: (c. 1913, SP, deactivated, private) On the grounds of a bed-and-breakfast inn. **21. Midland Point Front Range Light** *Midland*: (c. 1913, SP, deactivated, private). **22. Victoria Harbour Rear Range Light** *Victoria Harbour*: (1910, SP, deactivated, private). **23. Brebeuf Island Front Range Light** *near Honey Harbour*: (1878, SP, private). **24. Beausoleil Island Light** *near Honey Harbour*: (1915, SP, Sk) Also known as Brebeuf Island Range Rear Light; grounds open. **25. Western Islands Light** *Double Top Island*: (1895) Octagonal. **26. Jones Island Light** *Parry Sound*: (1894, SP, I). **27. Snug Harbour Light** *Snug Harbour*: (1894, SP, I). **28. Red Rocks Light** *Parry Sound, near Snug Harbour*: (1911) Elliptical concrete tower. **29. Pointe au Baril Range Rear Light** *Macklin Island, near Pointe au Baril*: (1908, SP, Sk) White with enclosed upper portion. **30. Pointe au Baril Range Front Light** *Pointe au Baril*: (1889, SP, Att.) Occasional tours in summer. **31. Byng Inlet Rear Range Light** *Byng Inlet, near Britt*: (1936, SP/Sk) White with enclosed upper portion (red on one face). **32. Byng Inlet Front Range Light** *Byng Inlet, near Britt*: (1936, SP) White with red vertical stripe. **33. Gereaux Island Light** *Byng Inlet*: (1880, SP) White with black lantern. **34–35. French River Inner Range Lights** *French River*: (both 1875; rear SP). **36–38. Bustard Rock Light**

ABOVE: *Griffith Island Light.*

ABOVE: *Bustard Rock Light (Bustards Range Lights).*

(Bustards Range Lights) *Bustard Island, French River:* (all SP; main and inner, 1875; outer, 1893; inner and outer deactivated). **39. Killarney East Light** *Killarney:* (1909, SP) Grounds open. **40. Killarney Northwest (Partridge Island) Light** *Partridge Island:* (1909, SP).

41-54. North Channel and Manitoulin Island Lights   *Ontario*

41. Lonely Island Light *near Manitowaning:* (1907) Octagonal tower. **42. South Baymouth Rear Range Light** *Manitoulin Island:* (1898, SP) White with vertical red stripe. **43. South Baymouth Front Range Light** *Manitoulin Island:* (1898, SP) White with vertical red stripe; can be viewed from road. **44. Manitowaning Light** *Manitowaning Harbor, Manitoulin Island:* (1885, SP). **45. Strawberry Island Light** *Manitoulin Island:* (1881, SP, Att., private). **46. Kagawong Light** *Mudge Bay, Manitoulin Island:* (1894, SP). **47. Gore Bay (Janet Head) Light** *Manitoulin Island:* (1879, SP, Att., private) Adjacent campground. **48. Great Duck Island Light** *Blue Hill Bay:* (1890, C) White with black lantern. **49. Mississagi Strait Light** *Manitoulin Island, Georgian Bay:* (1873, SP/F, museum) Also a restaurant, with adjacent campground. **50. McKay Island (Bruce Mines) Light** *St. Joseph Channel, near Bruce Mines:* (1907, I, deactivated) Keeper's dwelling and lantern; replaced by a skeleton tower; overnight accommodation available. **51. West Sister Rock Light** *North Channel, near St. Joseph:* (1885) Hexagonal-pyramidal tower. **52. Wilson Channel Rear Range Light** *St. Joseph Channel, near Sault Ste. Marie:* (1905, SP) White with orange vertical stripe. **53. Wilson Channel Front Range Light** *St. Joseph Channel, near Sault Ste. Marie:* (1905, SP) White with orange vertical stripe. **54. Shoal Island Light** *St. Joseph Island:* (1890, I) White lantern and red-roofed keeper's dwelling.

BELOW: *West Sister Rock Light.*

LAKE SUPERIOR

Ontario

1. Pointe aux Pins Front Range Light *Sault Ste. Marie*: Square tower with red vertical stripe; grounds open. **2. Pointe aux Pins Rear Range Light** *Sault Ste. Marie*: (1903, deactivated) Square. **3. Gros Cap Reef Light** *Sault Ste. Marie*: (1953, F). **4. Ile Parisienne Light** *Sault Ste. Marie*: (1912) Hexagonal. **5. Coppermine Point (Old) Light** *Hibbard Bay*: (1910, SP, deactivated, private) Grounds open. **6. Corbeil Point Light** *Batchawana Bay*: (1931, I, deactivated, private). **7. Caribou Island Light** *Wawa*: (1912) Hexagonal with flying buttresses; grounds open. **8. Michipicoten Island (Quebec Harbour) Light** *Quebec Harbour*: (1872, deactivated) Square. **9. Quebec Harbour Front Range Light** *Quebec Harbour*: (1918, deactivated) Square. **10. Davieaux Island Light** *Quebec Harbour*: (1918) Octagonal. **11. Otter Island Light** *Marathon*: (1903) Octagonal. **12. Slate Islands Light** *Terrace Bay*: (1902) Octagonal; grounds open. **13. Battle Island Light** *Rossport*: (1911) Occasional tours. **14. Shaganash Island Light** *Thunder Bay*: (1910, SP); grounds open. **15. Porphyry Point Light** *Thunder Bay*: (1960, Sk) White slatwork. **16. Trowbridge Island Light** *Thunder Bay*: (1910) Octagonal; grounds open. **17. Thunder Bay Main Light** *Thunder Bay*: (1937, I).

BELOW: *Trowbridge Island Light is located on a Lake Superior island near Thunder Bay.*

BRITISH COLUMBIA

44 41
43 39
40 38
42

37
35 34
36

33
32 31
30
1 29
2 25
45
Kootenay
Lake
28
Vancouver Island 27 23 19
20
3 21
26
4 24 22
5 18 17
6 16 15
7 12 14
8 13
9 11
10

The British Columbia coast is deeply indented and studded with rocks and ledges and, unusually, still maintains a number of staffed lighthouses. These lights are mostly very remote, only viewable by boat, and closed to the public. Many of the lights in the Vancouver, Victoria, and Southern Gulf Islands areas can be viewed from ferries or private boats, and those of the Inside Passage, from ferries and cruise ships. Where no description is given, the lighthouse is a skeletal tower. Unless otherwise noted, all lights are painted white, with red lanterns. See page 260 for abbreviations.

1–9. Vancouver Island

1. **Cape Scott Light**. 2. **Quatsino Light**: (C, no lantern). 3. **Nootka Light**. 4. **Estevan Point Light**: (1910) Octagonal; open to public. 5. **Lennard Island Light**. 6. **Amphitrite Point Light**: (1915, I). 7. **Cape Beale Light**. 8. **Pachena Point Light**: (1908, OP) Open to public. 9. **Carmanah Point Light**: (1920, OP) Open to public.

10–14. Victoria Area

10. Sheringham Point Light: (1912) Hexagonal. **11. Race Rocks Light**: (1860) Imperial Tower with black and white bands and red lantern. **12. Fisgard Light**: (1860, Att.) The oldest lighthouse in British Columbia; open to public. **13. Trial Islands Light**: (C). **14. Discovery Island**: (C) Open to public.

15–18. Southern Gulf Islands

15. Saturna Island. 16. Portlock Point Light: (SP). **17. Active Pass Light**: (1969, C). **18. Porlier Pass Range Rear Light**: (SP).

ABOVE: *Pachena Point Light.*
BELOW: *Sisters Islets Light*

19–21. Vancouver Area

19. Point Atkinson Light: (1912) Octagonal. **20. Prospect Point**: (I, no lantern) Tapered tower and workroom; white with red band. **21. Brockton Point**: (1915) Square tower; white with red band and red-roofed lantern.

22–26. Northern Strait of Georgia

22. Entrance Island Light: (C). **23. Merry Island Light**: (1966, F) White with a red maple leaf painted on each face. **24. Ballenas Islands Light**: (1900) Octagonal. **25. Sisters Islets Light**: (1967, C). **26. Chrome Island Light**: Concrete tower.

27–45. Inside Passage and Northern Lights

27. Cape Mudge Light: (1898) Octagonal; open to public. **28. Chatham Point Light**: (1959, C, no lantern) White with a green band. **29. Pulteney Point Light**: (F) On Malcolm Island; open to public. **30. Scarlett Point Light**: (C) Conical; publicly accessible on Balaklava Island. **31. Pine Island Light**: (1967) Narrow tower with skeletal supports; open to public. **32. Egg Island Light**. **33. Addenbrooke Island Light**. **34. Dryad Point Light**: (1919) Square; open to public. **35. Ivory Island Light**. **36. McInnes Island Light**: (1921, Att.) Open to public. **37. Boat Bluff Light**. **38. Lawyer Islands Light**. **39. Holland Rock Light**. **40. Lucy Islands Light**: Octagonal. **41. Green Island Light**: (OP) Open to public. **42. Bonilla Island Light**: (1960) Fiberglass; open to public. **43. Triple Islands Light**: (1920, Att.) Octagonal tower. **44. Langara Point Light**: (1913) Hexagonal; open to public. **45. Pilot Bay Light**: (1904, SP) South of Kootenay Bay; open to public.

Saving Lighthouses, One Donation at a Time

As you travel around the country spotting lighthouses, you will doubtless want to support the lighthouse preservation movement. The American Lighthouse Foundation is a national nonprofit group headquartered in Wells, Maine. From brick-and-mortar efforts to save the structures themselves to creating probably the largest archive of lighthouse history and photographs in the United States, educating the public at large on the importance and relevance of lighthouse history, acting as a national advocacy group for all lighthouse initiatives, and establishing the Museum of Lighthouse History in Wells, Maine, the American Lighthouse Foundation is leading the way.

The American Lighthouse Foundation operates solely on the donations and generosity of the general public. This is increasingly difficult as our cause competes with many other deserving charitable organizations.

Future generations will not judge us by what we have saved but rather by what we have allowed to be destroyed or lost. Time is literally running out to save some of our lighthouses. Many lights have already been lost, and, as people associated with our lighthouse heritage die, their memories and stories will also be lost forever. Immediate efforts are necessary to document these stories for future generations.

Lighthouses and their history provide an incalculable cultural and educational link to our past. Only through your generosity to the American Lighthouse Foundation will that link help determine our future.

American Lighthouse Foundation
P.O. Box 889, 2190 Post Rd—U.S.Rt.1
Wells, Maine 04090, Ph # 207-646-0245
www.LighthouseFoundation.org

American
Lighthouse
Foundation

Lighthouse Digest Magazine

As a lighthouse spotter you will soon realize that every light has a different story to tell. If their stories intrigue you and you want to learn more, may we suggest that you subscribe to *Lighthouse Digest* magazine? You'll read not only about lighthouses but the legends that surround them and the memories of the people who tended them; you will also see many previously unpublished photographs.

Each packed issue contains news stories about lighthouse people, current restoration projects, new lighthouse gifts, collectibles, and books. "Kids on the Beam" will delight children, and other regular features include crossword puzzles, monthly columns on collecting nautical antiques and women of the lights, and information on *Harbour Lights* replicas. For your own planning, the magazine also includes a calendar of lighthouse-related events and activities, tours, cruises, festivals, and meetings.

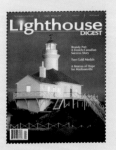

Published eleven times each year, *Lighthouse Digest* is an invaluable educational resource that makes for fun reading for the entire family.

A one-year subscription for $28.00 can be ordered from Lighthouse Digest, P.O. Box 68, Wells, Maine 04090 or by calling toll free at 1-866-643-4227. Subscriptions can also be ordered online at www.LighthouseDigest.com.

INDEX OF LIGHT STATIONS

ACKNOWLEDGMENTS

The publisher would like to thank the following people for their assistance in the creation of this book: Clare Haworth-Maden, Karen Fitzpatrick, Lone Nerup Sorensen, Lindsie Court, Phoebe Tak-Yin Wong; and also the institutions responsible for the following invaluable websites: www.unc.edu/~rowlett/lighthouse, www.lhdigest.com, www.lighthousefriends.com.

All photographs in this book are © Rudi Holnsteiner unless otherwise listed here. Grateful acknowledgment is made to the following individuals and institutions for permission to reproduce illustrations and photographs:

© 2005 JupiterImages Corporation: 19 (2nd t), 62, 99, 151 (r), 184 (t), 200, 219 (b), 230, 256 (t), 257 (both), 268; Courtesy of Lighthouse Digest Archives, Wells, Maine: 96 (b); Author's collection: 111 (t), 116 (t), 117 (all), 126 (b), 128; Courtesy of Canadian Coast Guard: 14, 20 (b), 275 (c & b), 276, 277, 278–81 (all), 283 (both); © Michael Connelly: 113; Library of Congress, Historic American Buildings Survey/Historic American Engineering Record Collections: 18 (b), 61, 91 (b), 93 (b), 100, 108 (b), 109 (b), 110 (b), 122 (c & b), 124 (l), 125

(c & b), 137, 152 (b), 153 (t & r), 161(c), 172 (t, c & bl), 179, 180, 184 (both b), 189 (b), 199 (t), 219 (t), 223 (t), 224 (c & b), 254; Library of Congress, Prints & Photographs Division: 10 (r), 12, 15, 143 (b), 194 (t), 256 (b); © Linda Muth—LJM Designs: 104 (also 18); © Glenn O. Myers: 11 (r); Courtesy of Parks Canada/M. Lachance: 75 (t); Courtesy of Save Our South Channel Lights/Photograph by Chuck Brockman: 39 (b); Courtesy of La Société Duvetnor Ltée: 174 (t); © John Sylvester: 5 (b), 258, 260–61 (all), 262-264 (all), 266–67 (all), 269, 270, 272–73 (all); Courtesy of U.S. Coast Guard: 9,17 (2nd t), 19 (b), 38, 46, 49, 50-51 (all), 71, 86, 87, 92, 97, 98, 101, 102, 103 (both), 107, 112, 127, 149 (t), 158, 174 (t & b), 210, 218, 220–222 (all), 223 (c & b), 225, 227, 228, 240 (both), 242 (t), 246 (both), 247, 248, 249 (both), 250–51 (all); Courtesy of Ville de Matane: 274 (b); Maps by Phoebe Tak-Yin Wong: 22, 94, 176, 216, 259, 262, 265, 271, 274, 276, 282; © Charles J. Ziga: 88 (b), 91 (tr, also 19), 93 (t), 95, 96 (t), 105, 106, 108 (t), 111 (b), 116 (b), 118, 119 (also 17), 120, 121 (both), 122 (t), 146 (t), 152 (t), 224 (t), 226, 229, 231, 243 (both), 245.